ECONOMIC BENEFITS OF ETHNOLINGUISTIC DIVERSITY

Economic Benefits of Ethnolinguistic Diversity

Implications for International Political Economy

Agnieszka Aleksy-Szucsich

Cambria Press
Amherst, New York

Requests for permission should be directed to:
permissions@cambriapress.com, or mailed to:
Cambria Press
20 Northpointe Parkway, Suite 188
Amherst, NY 14228

Library of Congress Cataloging-in-Publication Data

Aleksy-Szucsich, Agnieszka.
Economic benefits of ethnolinguistic diversity : implications for international political economy / a monograph by Agnieszka Aleksy-Szucsich.
p. cm.
Includes bibliographical references and index.
ISBN 978-1-60497-534-5 (alk. paper)
1. Economics—Sociological aspects. 2. Language and culture—Economic aspects. 3. Pluralism (Social sciences)—Economic aspects. I. Title.

HM548.A44 2008
306.44089—dc22

2008016518

To my beloved husband, Jakob

Table of Contents

List of Figures

List of Tables

Foreword

Coming at no better time, this book is perfectly placed to help unravel some of the great ongoing puzzles and debates in international political economy, economic development, and international relations. At contention is the role of political-cultural diversity as an agent of change within society.

Is political-cultural (ethno-linguistic) diversity a problem for society because of its possible negative impact on electoral consensus and social harmony? This is the contention, in particular, of those scholars in political science today who see ethno-linguistic fractionalization as generating points of conflict and polarization, thus undermining the foundations of democracy, especially in the large state where heterogeneity is thought to be greatest. Or, is political-cultural diversity instead a source of rich inspiration and output, both within the framework of democracy and within the framework of the economic market-place? According to this view, diversity opens up avenues for discourse, creates the potential for greater specialization, destroys local monopolies, and catalyses new idea.

Not just through abstract argument, but in terms of careful empirical analysis using multivariate statistical technique, Agnieszka Aleksy attempts to provide answer to these questions. I will examine the theoretical basis of argument underlying her empirical analysis. I will then turn to the specifics of her findings and look at the policy implications for advanced-industrial and developing polities in the 21st century.

One of the debates the book addresses is whether the strong presence of ethno-linguistic variables tends to hinder economic growth. Probably a majority of contemporary development economists holds this view. They perceive political-cultural diversity as a negative variable that poses roadblocks to the development process by draining resources away from more productive output. On that view, although all economic development is destabilizing, too much instability imperils growth. The findings in this book shed new light on the claim concerning the feasibility of growth in heterogeneous cultural communities, perhaps helping to shift the debate in another direction.

Another debate of contemporary theoretical and policy concern involves explanation for what causes states to fail. The findings in the book are helpful in understanding the place of democratic pluralism as an antidote to secession and to state break-up. Under democratic pluralism—a principle that enables diverse communities to live in equality and relative harmony inside a unified polity—centralization and decentralization of authority are in balance.

A further debate the empirical results in this book will help settle is that involving innovation and entrepreneurship in the market-place. At the level of the nation-state could there be a link between political-cultural diversity within society and the propensity of that society to invent, to create, and even to establish new institutions, structures, and ventures in both the public and private sectors? Could political-cultural diversity provide the well-spring for creative genius within society and the concomitant social energy necessary for entrepreneurial endeavor? Findings in this book help identify the conditions under which political-cultural diversity is likely to generate new idea within the market-place, and conversely, the conditions under which diversity is not likely to lead to success.

An assumption here is that a social and economic firebreak exists between the problems and issues faced by the developing country and the problems and issues faced by the advanced-industrial country. Hence in examining the impact of political-cultural diversity on a society, this Third World-First World dichotomy must be controlled for. The analysis in this book is limited to the OECD countries.

A second assumption is that political-cultural diversity is likely to possess positive benefits to society only under specific policy circumstances. It is the 'right policy context' in which political-cultural diversity operates that will determine whether positive benefits are delivered to political institutions and to the commercial market-place. This book makes explicit the scope and nature of this policy context.

What is meant by "right political context'? Suppose that in a complex system like a polity or a market, an independent variable has a dual impact–one positive, one negative. Suppose as well that the variable is a function of time, circumstance, the part of the system impacted, and the age of the system. Although both the positive and negative effects may be operative simultaneously, the positive effect might be stronger in one situation, the negative effect stronger in another. In other words, the impact of the independent variable on this system is conditional.

Like a traffic light on a street corner, this conditional independent variable operates all of the time. The light monitors traffic continuously; but sometimes, depending on traffic flow, time of day, and other factors programmed into the light, the light flashes red or the light flashes green. So with the impact of political-cultural diversity on a polity or a market, the net result of the dual effects of diversity may be positive or negative. A red light comes on for development when low per capita income, missing property rights, corruption, and lack of adequate political representation, on the one hand, and an absence of the 'right policy context' on the other, subvert the benefits of political-cultural diversity. A green light comes on in the developed polity when the right policy context composed of education, labor mobility, and research and development spending, are capable of generating innovation, creativity, and openness in political institutions and the market-place.

What are the societal conditions that determine which effect of political-cultural diversity will most shape outcomes? Implied here is the argument that although the positive and negative effects of political-cultural diversity are operative simultaneously all of the time, the positive effects are dominant in the advanced-industrial country with high per capita incomes and comparatively sophisticated governing institutions. The negative effects tend to be dominant in the developing country beset with problems of governance, weak regulatory institutions and property rights, and pronounced local rather than federal political identities. It is not that the benefits of political-cultural diversity are absent from the government and market-place of the developing country. It is that neither the institutional nor the policy context is present to enable the government of the developing polity to extract these benefits. Meanwhile, in a setting where the fundamental issues of governance have often not yet been settled in favor of state unity and coherence, the negative effects of political-cultural diversity become dominant.

Whether this hypothesis regarding the dual-faceted impact of political-cultural diversity on market-place and polity is valid, is still a subject for discussion. However, this book provides strong, though partial, support for the hypothesis. Since the emphasis here is totally on the advanced-industrial country, the extensions of argument to the developing setting, while plausible, can only be speculative. Yet the affirmative findings for the advanced-industrial market and polity receive quite clear and reliable empirical support. If replicated in other studies, the findings of this book are important and possess high policy significance. That political-cultural diversity leads to a greater propensity for innovation, openness, creativity and entrepreneurship, in the right policy context, and once a certain level of per capita income and political modernization have been achieved appears incontrovertible.

This is a result with implications that extend into sociology and management science.

Political-Cultural (Ethno-linguistic) Diversity and the 'Right Policy Context'

Let us look more closely at the argument and findings. Political-cultural diversity facilitates creativity, openness to change, and entrepreneurship, but this positive impact on society only occurs in the presence of the 'right policy context'. The right policy context is an intervening variable itself composed of democratic pluralism, a growth and innovation focused strategy, and a mixing of diverse individuals inside a society that enjoys a common language. In short, according to Agnieszka Aleksy, only when the correct combination of societal variables and policies is present will the benefits of political-cultural diversity be forthcoming. In the right policy context, political-cultural diversity is a marvelous attribute contributing to economic and social betterment.

Extensive statistical analysis underlies the empirical test of these complex relationships. Even without this test the theoretical argument would be inspiring and welcome. But when the variables are carefully indexed, aggregated into principal components through factor analysis, and then tested via least squares analysis (multiple regression), the conclusions are more reliably asserted.

The book explores in theoretical terms the underpinnings of each variable. For example, the origin of individual creativity is linked to the proposition that the more diverse the group, the more likely ideas among individuals will differ in an original way. Openness stems from a willingness to try new ideas and to break with old habits of thought that otherwise lead to failure in the market-place and in political administration. Entrepreneurship is far more likely among immigrants and minorities than among the older and more general population especially under the influence of education. Each of these variables is intensively researched in terms of the existing social scientific literature.

Throughout, Agnieszka Aleksy is careful to delineate concepts, variables, levels of analysis, and causation. For example, the book systematically distinguishes between the findings that account for behavior of consumer and citizen in the organizational literature and the findings that are explored here at the level of the state. Similarly, the book examines the psychological literature regarding individual motivation, and the sociological literature on the motivation of the collective, distinguishing between the effects. Finally, the book justifies the existence of the intervening variable, the right policy context, and tests it for reliability and direction of causation.

In short, the absence of citizenship laws that are inclusive, limits on high-skilled immigration, and negative citizen attitudes toward diversity drain political-cultural diversity of its benefits. Lack of a good business climate and lack of sufficient spending on research and development undermine the advantages of a diverse labor base. Failure to encourage labor mobility and the mixing of a diverse population, and the absence of democratic pluralism and a common language subvert the otherwise positive aspects of political cultural diversity for creativity and entrepreneurship.

IMPLICATIONS FOR POLICY

Three policy implications follow from the findings of this book. First, the great heterogeneous, democratic societies of the 21st century are likely to be the workshops of creativity and entrepreneurship worldwide. Far from stagnating, or collapsing because of fragmentation, these great storehouses of political-cultural diversity are likely to be the generators of new commercial enterprise and technological idea for decades to come.

Second, immigration, a long way from threatening the identity of the nation-state, is likely instead to be one of the greatest sources of innovation, commercial impulse, and new idea that the world has yet seen. Movement of labor may be, by the end of the 21st century, a more important source of increasing per capita income than the movement of capital.

Third, no country needs to be left out. By heeding the message of the right policy context, by encouraging diverse elements within a polity to express themselves, by providing education and research funding to its scientists, engineers, and inventors, and by heeding the political message of democratic pluralism regarding toleration and integration, every country in the world possesses the capacity to enjoy the societal benefits elicited by the presence of political-cultural diversity.

Charles F. Doran
Andrew W. Mellon Professor of International Relations
School of Advanced International Studies
Johns Hopkins University
Washington, DC

Preface

Before I became interested in the topic of ethnolinguistic diversity, I had been traveling quite a bit between the United States and the countries of the Balkans, such as Bosnia-Herzegovina, Kosovo, and Serbia. It felt like the two ends of the magnetic field of ethnic diversity: on one side, a country where ethnolinguistic diversity is employed with success as a resource of creativity and positive change; on the other side, a region full of rich and colorful cultural differences, where this difference is a trigger for bloody conflict, ethnic hatred, and economic decline. Those trips raised in me the question whether the impact of ethnic diversity on the economic performance of countries is, overall, positive or negative. And, furthermore, what is decisive about whether a country experiences the positive or negative effects of ethnic diversity?

Those questions appear to gain in importance because the world we live in is becoming increasingly diverse. Cultural diversity stems from the existence of ethnic minorities and it continuously increases due to the high levels of immigration experienced by most of the advanced economies. The existence of different cultures next to each other can lead to tensions and social conflicts. A recent study by Robert D. Putnam (2007) showed that immigration and ethnic diversity tend to reduce social solidarity and social capital. At the same time, this tension induced by diversity can become a crucial source of increased creativity and innovativeness, which can spur the economic development of countries. Scholars of this field argue that the interaction between people from different cultural backgrounds in a peaceful environment can stimulate creativity and openness to change in the society, and thus significantly benefit the economy. Therefore, it is becoming increasingly important to know how to manage diversity in order to bring out its positive potential and to avoid its possible detrimental effects. This is vital for all the countries that are ethnolinguistically diverse, either due to the existence of indigenous minorities or the more recent waves of immigration, as well as both for the advanced and the developing ones.

A prevailing opinion in the field of international political economy predicates that ethnolinguistic diversity has a negative effect on the economic performance of countries. Some of the scholars, however, argued against it and stated that under certain circumstances, the negative impact of diversity is mitigated or even reversed. According to these scholars, diversity can have a positive impact on the economy. The aim of this book is to assess whether diversity can indeed lead to higher levels of innovativeness for countries and what the circumstances are that allow for turning ethnolinguistic diversity into positive economic outcomes.

The study begins by identifying the conditions under which ethnic diversity can bring positive economic outcomes. It bases its quest of the moderating variables on the organizational science where scholars have conducted extensive research concerning the impact of diversity on the performance of firms. Then, the research from organizational science is transposed to the level of countries. Subsequently, a statistical model is designed to assess the impact of ethnolinguistic diversity on the economic outcomes, defined in terms of innovativeness. The underlying hypothesis of the study states that in the presence of the right context, ethnolinguistic diversity leads to higher levels of innovativeness, and it thus constitutes an economic benefit for countries.

The hypothesis is examined on the sample of 30 Organisation for Economic Co-operation and Development (OECD) countries. The statistical analysis, which includes factor analyses and simple cross-country regressions, generally provides support for the hypothesis. The innovation-focused strategy and democratic pluralism emerge as the main moderators of the positive relationship between diversity and innovativeness. Some support is also given for the growth-focused strategy as a moderator of that relationship. The results of the regressions demonstrate that the positive relationship between ethnolinguistic diversity and innovativeness is indeed a function of the right context.

The results reveal the double-edged sword nature of ethnic diversity. When accompanied by the right context, diversity leads to higher levels of innovativeness for countries. However, when the right context is not present, diversity brings negative results. This implies that once a country is diverse, the right context for diversity is a necessity. In such a situation, the right management of diversity benefits the country twofold. It allows the country to avoid the possible negative effects of diversity. It also enables the country to achieve the positive true potential of diversity in terms of higher creativity, openness to change, and innovativeness.

The results indicate that ethnolinguistic heterogeneity within a society adds to its capability for creativity and, therefore, to its innovativeness. Among the advanced industrial economies in particular, with all other circumstances being equal, this conclusion holds implications for the value of political unity. Secession is likely to fragment these economies, thus undermining some of the capacity of a multiethnic society to provide the full benefits of innovation.

Acknowledgments

There are many people who helped me on this project that I would like to thank. I owe enormous thanks to Prof. Charles F. Doran, my first advisor, who enabled me to continue my studies at the Johns Hopkins University Paul H. Nitze School of Advanced International Studies (SAIS) in Washington, DC. I am grateful for his amazing advice, support, and guidance throughout the whole process and for simply being the best mentor one can imagine. I owe extraordinary thanks to Prof. Gordon Bodnar, my second advisor, for his highly inspiring insights, invaluable advice on all of the complex topics, and much needed encouragement during our long and intense discussions. I would like to thank the members on my committee who supplied me with very important suggestions and insights: Prof. Susan Aud, Prof. Tamara Woroby, and Prof. Henry Nau. I owe many thanks to Prof. Francis Fukuyama for offering me his time and invaluable advice on the topic despite his very busy schedule. I also owe special thanks to Prof. Zbigniew Brzezinski for his precious time and recommendations.

During the course of working on this project I approached many professors at the Johns Hopkins University SAIS and I am very grateful for their highly valuable suggestions and insights: Prof. William Zartman, Prof. Bruce Parrot, Prof. David Calleo, Prof. Ernesto Hernandez-Cata, Prof. Jaime Marquez, Prof. Karen Macours, Prof. John Harrington, and the late Prof. Enzo Grilli. I have also received very strong support from the professors of the Warsaw University whom I would like to thank: Prof. Edward Haliżak, Prof. Marek Tabor, and Prof. Leszek Kasprzyk. Furthermore, I would like to thank very much the Paul H. Nitze School of Advanced International Studies (SAIS) at the Johns Hopkins University and the people working there for providing a great environment to work on that project, as well as Dean John Baker for helping to find ways to assure the necessary financial support.

My exceptional friends from Washington, DC, and Warsaw, Poland, encouraged me with their ongoing interest in my work and helpful discussions for which I am very grateful for. In addition, I would like to thank my friends Caterina Meloni and Thea Jokhadze for their help in the process of this project. I would also like to thank Ambassador Henry and Hertha Owen for their interest in my work and active support.

Finally, I would like to thank my family for their wonderful support. I owe special thanks to my father Józef Aleksy, the best strategic advisor in Central and Eastern Europe, for his advice on various topics from the beginning to the end of this project. I owe great thanks to my mother, Bożena, for her love and care, especially during the difficult periods of writing this book. I would like to thank my two grandmothers for helping me learn to keep a healthy distance to my work. I would also like to thank my brother, Arek, and his wife, Monika, for finding entertaining things to do together in order to unwind. I would like to thank my family from Okmiany for their interest in my work and emotional support, my family from Środa Śląska for providing a different perspective, and my family from Austria for their overall support.

And last but foremost, I would like to thank my husband Jakob Szucsich, who was very actively involved in this project from its outset to the end. He encouraged me to select this topic and then spent many days and nights discussing with me all the intricate aspects of it, reading and rereading my manuscript many times in order to help me with its content. The final shape of this book owes a lot to his brilliant and innovative insights. I would also like to thank him for his patience during the thorny times of writing this book, as well as for his optimism and encouragement throughout the whole process, which gave me the necessary strength and the buzz to accomplish this project.

Economic Benefits of Ethnolinguistic Diversity

Chapter 1

Introduction

Underlying Idea

Prevailing opinion in the field of international political economy holds that ethnolinguistic diversity has a negative impact on the economic performance of countries. Some scholars argue against this interpretation, however, asserting instead that under certain circumstances the negative impact of diversity is mitigated or even reversed. According to these scholars, ethnic diversity can have a positive impact on the economy. I examine this proposition within the context of the OECD countries to see to what extent this argument can be supported by the data.

The problem to be tackled is part of a broader discussion concerning the impact of ethnolinguistic diversity on economic outcomes.[1] There has been a vivid discussion in the field of political economy concerning the effects of ethnolinguistic diversity on the economic performance of countries. Most of the studies in the field of political economy have pointed to the negative effects of diversity and have shown that ethnic diversity reduces the rate of economic growth (Alesina & Spolaore, 2003; Alesina,

Spolaore, & Wacziarg, 2003b; Easterly & Levine, 1997; La Porta, Lopez de Silanes, Shleifer, & Vishny, 1999). The negative effects were mainly explained in terms of the hypothesized effects of diversity upon political choices. Other studies, however, have shown that ethnic diversity is not "guilty as charged" (Collier, 2001, p. 2) and that the argument of ethnic diversity being dysfunctional is not well-founded. The scholars noticed that there are certain circumstances, such as the existence of democratic institutions and higher income levels, under which the negative impact of diversity is mitigated or even reversed (Alesina & La Ferrara, 2004; Collier, 2001; Easterly, 2001). Moreover, some studies, which were conducted on the level of cities, have proven that ethnic diversity might have productivity-enhancing effects (Florida, 2002a, 2002b; Ottaviano & Peri, 2004).

Therefore, some of the studies conducted in the field of political economy imply that there are certain moderating variables that influence the relationship between diversity and economic performance. Those variables determine whether ethnic diversity would have a positive or negative impact on economic performance. I departed from that point and decided to conduct a thorough search for the moderators of the positive relationship between ethnolinguistic diversity and economic outcomes.

However, for the purpose of this study, the economic outcomes are not defined in terms of economic growth, as it has been done in the previous studies, but in terms of the level of innovation. I point to innovation as a channel through which ethnolinguistic diversity might lead to higher economic performance. The fundamental idea of the study is that ethnolinguistic diversity might increase the levels of creativity, openness to change, and entrepreneurship, and it might thus increase the overall level of innovation for countries.[2]

Theoretically, the increases in creativity associated with ethnolinguistic diversity come from the interaction between diverse individuals, which stimulates the generation of novel ideas. The increases in the openness to change come from the exposure to different cultures, which broadens the horizons of the people and makes the people more accustomed to difference and, therefore, more open to both new trends and change. Finally, the increases in entrepreneurship are associated with two phenomena. First, diverse societies tend to be more open to change; therefore, they provide more individuals with entrepreneurial potential, as well as a more receptive audience for entrepreneurial actions. Second, diverse societies have a higher percentage of minorities and immigrants, and those groups have a higher propensity to be entrepreneurial.

Since it is the creativity, openness to change, entrepreneurship, and innovation that could be the channels through which ethnolinguistic diversity impacts economic performance, it is sensible to analyze the direct impact of diversity on the innovativeness of countries. It is especially sensible because, until now, none of the studies in the field of the political economy have done this. Therefore, I would like to make a first preliminary assessment of the impact of diversity on the innovativeness of countries with a special focus on the conditioning variables of the right context. I assess whether ethnolinguistic diversity, when accompanied by the right context, can indeed lead to higher creativity, openness to change, entrepreneurship, and innovativeness of countries.

There are three main reasons for which the research is important. First, it is important because it tries to assess whether the ethnolinguistic diversity can actually constitute an economic benefit for countries, rather than be a detriment. Currently, the perception of ethnolinguistic diversity in the field of political economy is rather negative, and ethnolinguistic diversity is mainly perceived as dysfunctional for the economic performance of countries. Therefore, it is crucial to assess to what extent the data supports the alternative view, which perceives diversity in a positive light.

The second reason why the research is important is because it underlines the significance of the right context, and it aims at identifying the conditions which are necessary for ethnolinguistic diversity to bring positive results. The underlying assumption of the study is that the positive relationship between ethnolinguistic diversity and innovativeness is conditioned by the existence of the right context variables. If the right context is not present, ethnolinguistic diversity would actually lead to negative results. Therefore, it is essential to identify what constitutes the right context for ethnolinguistic diversity.

The third reason why the research is important is because it attempts to tackle the issue concerning the channels through which ethnolinguistic diversity impacts the economic performance of countries. This study points to innovation as the channel through which diversity positively affects the economy. The innovative potential of diversity has been already acknowledged by many other scholars. However, this study makes the first attempt to quantitatively assess the impact of ethnolinguistic diversity on the level of innovativeness of countries. By examining the impact of diversity on innovativeness, the study assesses whether innovation is indeed the channel through which ethnolinguistic diversity impacts the economic performance of countries.

RESEARCH APPROACH

The study bases its quest for the right context variables on the research conducted within organizational science. The scholars of that science conducted very extensive theoretical and empirical research concerning the impact of ethnolinguistic diversity on the performance of firms, groups, and organizations. First, the research is used to identify the context that is necessary for the ethnolinguistic diversity to fulfill its positive potential and to increase the levels of innovativeness of countries. Then, the findings from the research on the level of firms is applied to the level of countries.

As a follow-up empirical study, I conduct a quantitative analysis of the relationship between diversity and innovativeness, moderated by the existence of the right context. I pose the hypothesis that the countries that are ethnolinguistically more heterogeneous will have higher levels of innovativeness than the countries that are less heterogeneous; however, only if they have the right context in place. The hypothesis is tested using a simple cross-country regression analysis. The regressions evaluate the influence of ethnolinguistic diversity on innovativeness, and, most importantly, they assess the impact of the right context on the relationship between diversity and innovativeness. Before running the regressions, however, I conduct a factor analysis to identify the independent, dependent, and the intervening variables that are used in the regressions.

I design a two-step regression model to test the hypothesis and apply the model to each of the dependent, independent, and intervening variables. The first regression tests the significance of the relationship between diversity and innovativeness without the right context in place. It establishes whether there is a relationship between diversity and innovativeness. The second regression is the actual test of the hypothesis. It tests the significance of the relationship between diversity and innovativeness as a function of the right context.

The 30 OECD countries are used as a sample for the analysis. The decision to use only the OECD countries is deliberate and is dictated by the theoretical assumptions of the research and by the availability of data. I am aware of the fact that such a small sample size for a cross-country regression weakens the validity of the results and constitutes a main limitation of the research. However, the goal of the study is not to provide a robust proof but to make a preliminary check whether the hypothesis is plausible. For that goal, the limited sample is acceptable. Since there has not yet been an attempt to test such a hypothesis, this study makes a first step in that direction. It has to be left to future research to assess whether the hypothesis holds true when the sample size is enlarged and more countries are included.

Structure of Research

The research consists of five parts followed by the conclusions. The first part introduces the main problem that is tackled by the research. It describes the underlying idea, the importance, the approach, and the structure of the research.

The second part includes a brief literature review of the topic. The third part contains the theoretical foundations of the research. The first subsection of the third part describes the idea of innovation. The second subsection of the third part describes the links between diversity and the different elements of innovation which are creativity, openness to change, and entrepreneurship. It is based on the research developed in the organizational sciences.

The third subsection of the third part describes the conditioning nature and the importance of the right context, and then it identifies the various elements of the right context on the level of firms. Subsequently, the right context elements are transposed to the level of countries. This subsection contains a final list of the right context elements as they have been identified through the theoretical part of the research.

The fourth and last subsection of the third part describes the operationalization of the empirical analysis. The fourth subsection includes the description of the hypothesis, the description of the dependent, independent, and intervening variables, as well as the description of the empirical model that I have developed to test the hypothesis.

The fourth part of the research deals with the empirical analyses. First, it explains the measurement of the variables. Second, it describes the conduct of the factor analysis, and it presents the results of the analyses and subsequent creation of the single scales for the variables. Finally, it describes the conduct and the results of the regression analysis that test the hypothesis. In the fifth part, I discuss the results of the factor analysis and the regression analysis, and I describe the general implications of the research. This part is followed by the conclusions, which consist of a short summary of the topic, with special focus on the results obtained, the description of their contribution to research, and the suggestions for further research.

Endnotes

1. The literature on the topic interchangeably uses the terms *ethnolinguistic diversity, ethnic diversity, ethnocultural diversity, racial diversity* and *cultural diversity* when it refers to the diversity associated with different subnational identities based on the kin group, linguistic group, ethnic group, racial group, or religious group. I will also use these terms interchangeably.
2. I based the understanding of innovation on the theory of Joseph Schumpeter (1934, 1939).

Chapter 2

Background

Significant Prior Research

Differing Perceptions of Ethnic Diversity

Recently, there has been an increased discussion in the field of political economy concerning the impact of ethnic diversity on the economic performance of a country. There is disagreement among the scholars concerning the perception of ethnic diversity and its impact on economic performance. Some of them perceive ethnic diversity as a cost to the economy, while others perceive it as a benefit. The discussion between the two sides can be well depicted by presenting the views of Alberto Alesina and Charles F. Doran, since they specifically have been writing extensively about the issue most recently. A thorough review of the literature on the issue can be found in Alesina and La Ferrara (2004), as well as Collier (2001).

Many political economy writers (Alesina & Spolaore, 2003; Alesina et al., 2003b; Easterly & Levine, 1997; La Porta et al., 1999) perceived ethnic diversity as a cost to the society. The most recent work concerning this topic has been written by Alesina and Enrico Spolaore in *The Size of Nations* (2003). In that book, the authors argued that ethnic diversity constitutes both political and economic costs for the country because it increases the heterogeneity in preferences for public goods. Ethnic diversity leads to the increase in diverse preferences, cultures, and languages within a population. That, in turn, leads to disagreements over the basic characteristics of a government such as redistributive schemes, public goods, or foreign trade.

The disagreement over public goods and policies in heterogeneous societies leads to higher costs associated with the functioning of the society. Since belonging to a country implies agreeing to a set of policies, ethnic heterogeneity implies that very diverse individuals have to come to an agreement on those matters. The costs associated with that process are called by Alesina and Spolaore (2003) "the costs of heterogeneity" (p. 17). They wrote, "[I]f a great many diverse individuals share the same public goods and policies, they face increasing costs of heterogeneity of preferences, since they have to agree with each other and share common policies" (p. 17).

Alesina and Spolaore (2003) argued that due to the costs associated with heterogeneity, it is more beneficial for countries to be homogeneous. The members of more homogeneous countries find it easier to reach agreement over the policies of a jurisdiction, and thus the costs associated with heterogeneity of preferences over the policies of a jurisdiction are minimized. The authors contended that "homogeneous polities function more harmoniously" (p. 6).

According to Alesina and Spolaore (2003), the reason why the societies have not always formed small and homogeneous states lies in the fact that there are certain benefits associated with a bigger population size. The authors argued that "the sizes of national states (or countries) are due to trade-offs between the benefits of size and the costs of heterogeneity of preferences" (p. 3). The reason why we have historically seen a tendency to form big countries is that the benefits of size in the previous times were outweighing the costs of heterogeneity.

In the current times, however, the situation has changed, and we have been observing a trend toward a formation of smaller and more homogeneous countries. The first reason behind the change is the alternation of the trade-offs between the benefits of size and the costs of heterogeneity. The liberalization of trade and the reduction of warfare diminish the benefits stemming from a bigger size. The second reason behind the trend toward the formation of smaller and more homogeneous states is the increase in democratization. Democratization made it possible for people to voice their opinion and to make demands for the creation of separate states for their ethnic groups.

According to Alesina and Spolaore (2003), the trend toward the formation of smaller and more homogeneous states will continue in the future. The increases in democratization will lead to the breakup of large political jurisdictions into smaller ones. Decentralization can substitute for the secessions—but only up to a point. Especially in developing countries, the fiscal decentralization has not been successful, and it has created more problems than it has solved. Therefore, according to the authors, next to decentralization we will see an increased trend toward separatism and secession.

The breaking up of the multiethnic states into smaller and more homogeneous units is not perceived by Alesina and Spolaore (2003) as something negative. On the contrary, they said that "a more peaceful world can be organized in smaller and more numerous states" (p. 218). They presented a vision of the future where the world would be composed of small countries that would coexist peacefully in an economically integrated world. The small countries would depend on the supranational institutions to enforce free trade and the functioning of the markets. Therefore, the insistence on keeping heterogeneous states together in an increasingly integrated world is misplaced and unnecessary. "Excessive insistence on keeping heterogeneous countries together implied sizable costs in religious, ethnic, racial, and cultural animosities among peoples as recent events in the Balkan states amply testify" (p. 223).

Thus, the perception of ethnic diversity as a cost has led the scholars who share this view to perceive the secessionist movements and the breaking up of large multiethnic states into smaller and more homogeneous units as something desirable. That belief is not shared by the scholars who, on the contrary, perceive ethnic diversity as a benefit to the society.

Doran, in his book *Why Canadian Unity Matters and Why Americans Care* (2001), argued that ethnic diversity can constitute a political and economic benefit for a country. For that reason, as well as for the reasons of the benefits associated with a bigger size, it is advantageous for the multiethnic countries to remain united and heterogeneous.

According to Doran (2001), ethnic diversity lies at the heart of stability, productivity, and economic dynamism of a society. The interaction between people of different cultural origins breeds creativity, as well as broadens knowledge and perspectives. That, in turn, increases the openness to new ideas, to change, and to dialogue:

> [C]ultural and political benefits flow from contact and intercommunication with individuals of different communal orientation as well. Cultural interaction among children and young adults broadens knowledge and perspective. Creativity flourishes. Self-awareness grows. The total output of productivity in many fields of endeavor is likely to be greater than in a more homogenous community. (p. 246)

Cultural diversity, according to Doran (2001), translates both into political and economic benefits. The political benefits include the strengthened capacity for honest government. The economic benefits include a greater opportunity for specialization, more innovation, and higher productivity:

> Greater opportunity for specialization occurs in the larger community possessing a wider variety of culturally specific skills and aptitudes. Politically, the openness to new ideas, to change, and to dialogue strengthens the capacity for honest government. Local monopolies that quell innovation and change are less likely in a society composed of multiple ethnic and cultural communities than in those dominated by a few families of similar cultural outlook such as in some countries in the third world. (p. 247)

Doran adhered to the writings of James Madison in the *Federalist Papers, No. X* (1788/1987) to explain the logic behind the argument that diverse societies have a higher possibility of internal competition and less likelihood of having big monopolies. Madison wrote that a large size is advantageous for the country because a bigger territory is most likely to be more diverse, and thus less prone to factionalism. He stated that the larger the territory, the larger the variety of parties and interests in the society and, therefore, the smaller the chance of any one party being able to outnumber and oppress the rest. Doran argued that Madison's argument, put in the language of economics, means that the probability of local monopolies is smaller and balanced competition is greater in the larger polity.

Doran recognized, however, that the virtues of ethnic heterogeneity can be only realized if the cultural diversity is managed in the right way. The heterogeneous societies need to be governed by a system that is able to harmonize and integrate the diverse people under a single polity. According to him, the social system that allows the management of ethnic diversity in a single polity is *democratic pluralism*.

Democratic pluralism is defined by Doran (2001) as "a condition of society in which diverse ethnic, racial, religious, or social groupings 'maintain their autonomous participation in their traditional culture within the confines of a single civilization' or state" (p. 5). He described democratic pluralism in the following way:

> Democratic pluralism seeks to harmonize and to integrate politically. Although assimilation may be a goal in some states at some time (whereas other polities may reject it as counter to the ethos of the society) democratic pluralism is a political and legal guarantee that assimilation is not required. In democratic pluralism, regionally specific cultural-linguistic communities retain their 'traditional culture' while participating fully in the processes and institutions of the state. Above all, democratic pluralism ensures cohesiveness and political accord within the state. In a mature democracy, democratic pluralism is completely liberal. (p. 5)

The principles of democratic pluralism ensure that the diverse communities can live in harmony with each other inside of a single state.

More than that, democratic pluralism allows the members of diverse groups not only to live next to each other in peace, but also to thrive spiritually, economically, linguistically, and intellectually.

Doran claimed that the merits of democratic pluralism can be assessed only in a specific, propitious context. Judging the validity of democratic pluralism as a norm can be done, for the most part, only in advanced countries, because only those countries create a context that allows for the observation of the principles of democratic pluralism. The problems of development may overshadow what can be expected of pluralism. Furthermore, the lack of experience with democracy (and thus the lack of democratic culture) can also outshine the qualities of democratic pluralism. Finally, a pervasive and intense violence can also create a situation in which the merits of democratic pluralism cannot be assessed, because the observance of pluralistic principles in such a situation is highly unlikely.

The greatest risk for democratic pluralism, according to Doran, is the notion of divisive nationalism expressed as secessionist movements. He argued after Eric J. Hobsbawm (1990) that, unlike the earlier nationalism, which was essentially unifying in nature, the nationalist movements of the late 20th century are negative and rather divisive.

The philosophy of separation negates the principles of democratic pluralism because it professes the "incompatibility" of diverse cultural values and preferences. In liberal democracy, where the human rights of individuals and groups are guaranteed, separatist movements occur for the single purpose of refusing to associate politically and communicate intensely in a single democracy with citizens of differing ethnolinguistic affiliation. Such refusal to live next to someone culturally or ethnically different is equivalent to the desire to discriminate (Doran, 2001), and it stands against the principles of democratic pluralism and toleration.

Doran (2001) disagrees in principle with the argument put forward by Alesina and Spolaore (2003), which regards secessions and the creation of smaller homogeneous countries as desirable. While the preference for homogeneity might be regarded by some as natural and inevitable, at the same time it may be regarded as quite unnatural in the context of increasing multiculturalism in the 21st century. In mature liberal democracies, tensions created by the existence of diverse cultures under single polity should not be resolved by secessions but should rather be managed and eliminated though the democratic institutions and processes:

> Cultural-linguistic fractionalization must be recognized as an effort to homogenize or 'purify' along lines of language and culture. Such fractionalization cannot be considered in step with the effort to promote greater openness, toleration, and diversity. In fact, preference for a more homogeneous, closed society is *out* of step with the direction of change in most other multicultural communities. (Doran, 2001, p. 20)

According to Doran (2001), the adherence to democratic pluralism instead of secessions is very important, especially in the current times when populations within states become increasingly mixed. The increased immigration, emigration, and differential growth rates across populations of differing cultural backgrounds contribute to the mixing of populations, a trend that is especially vivid within the advanced countries. With the increased mixing of societies, democratic pluralism becomes an essential attribute of future world politics because it provides countries with the effective instruments to manage the tensions arousing in culturally and ethnically diverse societies.

Doran also drew attention to the impact of secessions, especially those occurring in the advanced democratic states, on the international community. Secessionist movements and the creation of smaller and more homogeneous states are most likely to bring a great stress to the international community because they put in doubt the principles of liberal democracy, as well as the possibility of cooperation between diverse cultures. The inability to resolve problems associated with diversity within stable democracies puts in doubt the ideals of liberal democracy.

Moreover, the secessionist movements—especially inside of mature democracies and the creation of homogeneous states—puts in doubt the ability to cooperate with people of different cultural backgrounds, not only within a state but also in the international arena. If diverse people cannot cooperate inside a mature democratic state, it is doubtful that they will be able to cooperate as independent actors.

Doran (2001) concluded with the message that "in the twenty-first century, breakup of the nation-state is not the answer to society's shortcomings" (p. 249). The tensions arising from the ethnic and cultural diversity of society should be managed not by secessions but rather by the institutions developed within democratic pluralism.

Empirical Studies on the State Level

There have been several cross-country studies conducted in the field of political economy that analyze the direct relationship between ethnic diversity and economic performance. Initially, the discussion has focused mainly on the costs of ethnic diversity. The work of William Easterly and Ross Levine (1997), which became a benchmark in the field, depicted a gloomy picture of ethnic diversity. In their study, ethnic diversity was linked with a lower rate of economic growth. The cross-country regression analysis indicated that going from complete homogeneity to complete heterogeneity is associated with a 2.3% fall in economic growth.

According to Easterly and Levine (1997), the negative impact of ethnic diversity can be explained by the fact that ethnically fragmented economies may find it difficult to agree on public goods and good policies. The results of their analysis lend support to the theories in political economy that suggest interest group polarization leads to competitive rent seeking by the different groups and reduces the consensus on public goods such as infrastructure, education, and good policies, which in the long run creates growth tragedies.

Africa is depicted in the study as a primary example of the negative impact of ethnic diversity on economic growth. According to Easterly and Levine (1997), Africa's high ethnic fragmentation explains a significant part of Africa's poor policies and slow growth. They stated that while the evidence from their study regarding the direct link between ethnic diversity and growth is more ambiguous, the evidence regarding the indirect link between ethnic diversity and growth, through the choice of poor public policies, is strong and significant. The data indicates that high levels of ethnic diversity in Africa are strongly linked to poor policies, low provision of infrastructure, and low levels of education, which in turn are strongly linked with slow, long-term growth. The authors concluded that while the results hardly support a monocausal view of Africa's difficulties, they do suggest that ethnic divisions have played a significant role in Africa's growth tragedy.

The study of Easterly and Levine (1997) has become a point of reference in the field. However, there have been several studies that criticized and questioned the findings of Easterly and Levine. Jean-Louis Arcand, Patrick Guillaumont, Sylviane Guillaumont Jeanneney (2000) called Easterly and Levine's results into question due to the problems of missing data. They argued that there is a potential problem of selection bias for the African countries because the data does not include the countries in Africa that have experienced the slowest growth rates. The authors noticed that the African countries constitute 27 out of 172 observations, and the data is missing precisely for those countries in Africa that have been experiencing the slowest growth. According to the authors, this is an important omission that can lead to a selection bias, which puts in question the results obtained by Easterly and Levine.

The conclusions of Easterly and Levine (1997) were also challenged by Paul Collier (2001). His empirical study showed that ethnic diversity is not "guilty as charged." In his study, "ethnic diversity neither increases the risk of civil war, nor reduces economic growth" (p. 2). Based on his cross-country regression analysis, multiethnic societies can be fully socially and economically viable.

Collier (2001) designed his study based on a question of whether the effects of ethnic diversity are moderated by the type of diversity, by the type of the political regime, or by the sector of the economy. He distinguished between two types of ethnic diversity: *dominance*, in which one group constitutes a majority; and *fractionalization*, in which there are many small groups. Furthermore, he distinguished between two types of political regimes: *democracy* and *dictatorship*. Finally, his analysis differentiated between two sectors of the economy: *public* and *private*. Collier laid out a theoretical argument that purported that ethnic diversity—while in general not associated with lower economic growth or the risk of civil conflict—might be damaging when it takes the form of dominance, when the country is a dictatorship, and when the sector under consideration is the public sector.

The results of the empirical analysis provided support for his theoretical argument. The study showed that fractionalization is normally unproblematic in democratic regimes; however, it can be destructive in dictatorial regimes. Moreover, it showed that ethnic diversity has no adverse effects on growth in fully democratic societies, but it reduces growth up to 3% in dictatorships.

According to Collier (2001), the reason why ethnic diversity has negative impacts on growth in dictatorships is because, in such regimes, it is more likely that even a remarkably small ethnic group can seize and maintain power to their own advantage. In such situations, the group chooses the redistribution to itself at the expense of the growth of the whole economy. In democracies, such a situation is not possible, except in circumstances of ethnic dominance when the size of the group is around 50%, which gives the group enough majority to control the national policy of the country.

In cases of ethnic dominance and regardless of the political system, ethnic diversity will have a negative impact on the growth of the economy. The results of Collier's study (2001) showed that countries characterized by dominance are, in principle, likely to have worse economic performance, although empirically the effect is weak.

According to Collier (2001), the reason why ethnic fractionalization has no adverse impact on economic growth in democracies is related to the fact that the negative impact of ethnic diversity on a public sector is offset by its positive effects on the private sector. The possible reason for the differential effects of ethnic diversity is that in the public sector, the benefit for the group is to capture rents, whereas in the private sector it is to enhance productivity. Therefore, ethnic diversity is likely to decrease the productivity of public capital, but it is also likely to increase the productivity of private capital.

The results of Collier's study (2001) showed that the ethnically heterogeneous countries have a higher productivity of private capital than the homogeneous countries. At the same time, however, they have a lower productivity of public capital. The productivity of public capital is 10% lower in the ethnically diverse society than in the ethnically homogeneous society. Simultaneously, the productivity of private capital is 5% higher in the ethnically diverse society than in the more homogeneous society. Collier argued that the two effects offset each other because the private capital stock is usually larger than the public capital stock; at the end, subsequently, ethnic diversity has no adverse effects on growth.

As far as the risk of conflict, Collier's study (2001) showed that fractionalization actually makes societies safer, while dominance increases the risk of a violent conflict. His explanation was based on the assumption that the causes of civil wars are economic in nature, rather than on identity preferences. This assumption is derived from an earlier study conducted by Paul Collier and Anke Hoeffler (1998, 2000), which provides empirical evidence that the risk of civil conflict is greatly influenced by the dependence on primary commodities. When two societies are compared with otherwise mean characteristics, the risk of conflict in the society with no primary commodity export is less than one percent, while it is 23% in a society where such exports constitute one fourth of the gross domestic product (GDP).

Collier brought forward the example of Ethiopia to illustrate how economic interests, rather than ethnic identities, shape the behavior of different ethnic groups. In Ethiopia, the Eritrean secession gathered together nine different ethnolinguistic groups into a common political community, at the same time splitting the Tigrini ethnolinguistic group between Eritrea and Ethiopia.

Collier (2001) argued that the results of his study pointed to specific policy implications. He stated that "contrary to the apparent implication of Easterly and Levine and Alesina et al., ethnic diversity is not, in general, problematic for economic policy" (p. 19) and, therefore, the international community has a stronger interest than currently recognized in preserving large, multiethnic states like Russia, Indonesia, and Nigeria. Currently, the fallacious popular orthodoxy has encouraged "radical social and political engineering, involving population movements and intricate border redesign and secession" in order to create ethnically more homogeneous, and thus allegedly more viable, states. Collier contended that the results of his study entailed contrary policy implications: fractionalized societies are viable and secession should be discouraged.

The study of Collier (2001) shed a new light on the discussion of ethnic diversity and its economic impact. It demonstrated that, under certain circumstances, the negative impact of ethnic diversity is eliminated. Furthermore, it showed that ethnic diversity may even have a positive impact on the economic outcomes. This new voice in the discussion drew more attention to the potential benefits of ethnic diversity. Despite the prevailing orthodoxy that still perceives ethnic diversity as an overall cost to the society, scholars are now more willing to recognize the positive potential of ethnic diversity.

In a recent study, Alesina and Eliana La Ferrara (2004) presented a model in which ethnic diversity constitutes both a cost and a benefit to the economy. It was a different approach from the initial one presented by Alesina and Spolaore (2003), where ethnic diversity was equated only with costs to the society because of the differences in preferences for public goods and policies. In 2004, the authors presented a position that recognizes that ethnic diversity, under certain circumstances, can also have a positive impact on the economy through gains in productivity. "Heterogeneity has evident potential costs, but an ethnic mix also brings about variety in abilities, experiences and cultures, which may be productive and may lead to innovation and creativity" (Alesina & La Ferrara, p. 11).

Alesina and La Ferrara (2004) presented two recent studies conducted on the level of cities as a part of the support for the argument that diversity has productivity-enhancing effects. In the study conducted by Richard Florida (2002a, 2002b), the amenities and diversity of U.S. cities is presumed to attract higher human capital. Florida constructed imaginative measures of diversity that are not directly related to ethnicity but include the share of gay and lesbian households, diversity of night life, arts, and so forth. The findings of his study showed that places that are high on diversity indeed attract a higher level of human capital.

The other study that provided support for the positive relationship between diversity and productivity is that of Gianmarco I. P. Ottaviano and Giovanni Peri (2004). The study examined the effects of ethnic diversity on economic productivity in American cities and found that ethnic diversity has productivity-enhancing effects and positive "amenity effects," both on production and consumption. The results showed that the individuals living in more culturally diverse cities earn higher wages and pay higher rents than those living in more homogeneous cities.

Enriched by the new insights about the productivity gains associated with diversity, Alesina and La Ferrara (2004) presented a simple model that analyzed the economic effects of diversity. The model highlighted the trade-off between the benefits of variety and the costs of heterogeneity of preferences in a multiethnic society. The authors argued that, on one hand, the potential benefits of heterogeneity come from the variety of individual skills used in the production process, which increases the overall productivity. The costs, on the other hand, come from the inability to agree on common public goods and public policies.

Alesina and La Ferrara (2004) referred to the work of Edward P. Lazear (1999a, 1999b), who also discussed the trade-off between the productive benefits of diversity and the costs of diversity arising from the problems of communication between people. He argued that there is an optimal point of this trade-off, which indicates the optimal degree of heterogeneity. According to Lazear, the optimal point of the trade-off between the benefits and costs of diversity for the production depends on the nature of the production unit and its technology.

In the model proposed by Alesina and La Ferrara (2004), the trade-off between the benefits and costs of diversity depends on the level of per capita output. The authors argued that the benefits from more ethnic fragmentation increase with the level of per capita output. Therefore, the benefits in production from a variety of skills are more likely to be relevant in more advanced and complex societies.

According to Alesina and La Ferrara (2004), there is one more important factor, which is left out from the model, that may significantly influence the relationship between ethnic diversity and economic outcomes. The missing factor is the type of institutions. Alesina and La Ferrara argued after Collier (2001) that certain types of institutions may be more conducive to ethnic harmony than others and should thus be taken into account when evaluating the impact of ethnic diversity.

Alesina and La Ferrara (2004) conducted an empirical cross-country analysis to examine the impacts of the level of income and institutions on the relationship between ethnic diversity and economic performance. The results of their empirical examination showed that, overall, the observed impact of ethnic diversity on growth across countries is negative. However, the analysis demonstrated that the level of income and the existence of democratic institutions mitigate the negative impact of ethnic diversity. The punch line is that rich democracies are more capable of productively handling ethnic diversity. They wrote, “it seems important to take into account that, whatever the mechanisms relating ethnic diversity to economic growth, channeling diversity toward productive uses may require a particular set of ‘rules of the game’” (p. 11).

Alesina and La Ferrara (2004) presented some results of their studies on ethnic diversity and population growth in the U.S. counties, which are in line with their cross-country results. In the analysis of the U.S. counties, the fractionalization has a negative effect of population growth in initially poor counties and a less negative (or even positive) effect for initially richer counties. According to the authors, the results from the counties are very important in corroborating the cross-country evidence because they were obtained from a setting where institutional and political differences are smaller than in the case of cross-country analysis.

It is noteworthy that despite the change in the approach and the recognition of potential benefits associated with ethnic diversity by Alesina and La Ferrara (2004), the authors did not offer much different policy implications than the ones suggested in the previous study of Alesina and Spolaore (2003). One would expect that, in the wake of acknowledging the potential benefits of diversity, the authors would support the existence of multiethnic states. Counterintuitively, the authors still supported the creation of smaller and more homogeneous states. They argued that with free trade, countries can be small and homogeneous, which allows them to enjoy the benefits of homogeneity (as far as public goods provision is concerned) and the benefits of diversity in production coming from international trade. Alesina and Spolaore said that promoting racial homogeneity is "unappealing and probably incorrect," but still they argued that secessions should not be perceived as threatening. "To the extent that small countries can prosper in a world of free trade, then peaceful separatism of certain minorities should not be viewed as threatening, at least from an economic point of view" (p. 29).

The authors brought forward the study conducted on American localities by Edward L. Glaeser, José A. Scheinkman, and Andrei Shleifer (1995) as a support for their proposition that small and more homogeneous units are more viable in a situation of diverse environment. The study found that in the cities with large nonwhite communities, segregation is positively correlated with population growth. According to Alesina and La Ferrara (2004), those results suggested that growth is higher when racial interaction is lower. The explanation behind it is that segregation allows the group to avoid the costs of diversity and take advantage of the benefits of diversity at the same time. "A suggestive interpretation of these results that goes back to our model may be that racial fractionalization with segregation may allow for diversity in production and lower interaction in public good consumption and social activity" (p. 11).

As far as domestic policies are concerned, Alesina and La Ferrara (2004) argued that the issue at stake is to what extent the policies promote racial integration. They made a case that the type of democracy that is most likely to promote harmony among diverse people is the consociational democracy based on power sharing among different segments of the society, a concept developed by Arend Lijphart (1977). They argued, however, that due to certain requirements that are necessary for the system to function, the consociational democracy is difficult to implement and ultimately unstable in some developing countries.

Furthermore, they put into question the effectiveness of power sharing as a means of *generating* interethnic cooperation because the power sharing might rather be a *result* of a preexisting tradition of power sharing in the society, as it has been the case of Somaliland.

The authors concluded that the question of how different people can peacefully interact with each other still remains open.

Chapter 3

Theoretical Foundations of Research

Innovation

Schumpeter's Theory of Innovation

The understanding of innovation is derived from the writings of Joseph A. Schumpeter (1939), who has placed innovation at the core of his theory of economic development. According to Schumpeter, innovation is a central feature of the economic evolution of the capitalist system. The carrying out of innovations defines the economic development. It is the innovation that creates the basis of the dynamics of the capitalist system and brings about the changes in the economic process. "[N]othing can be more plain or even more trite common sense than the proposition that innovation, as conceived by us, is at the center of practically all the phenomena, difficulties, and problems of economic life in capitalist society" (Vol. I, p. 87).

Schumpeter (1939) argued that even though there are other internal factors of economic evolution, such as tastes and changes in growth, it is the innovation that has the most profound impact on the economic development. The impact of innovation is so immense in relation to the other factors that we can satisfy ourselves logically by visualizing societies in which internal change is merely caused by innovation. The capital investment and the expansion of wealth in the capitalist society derive mainly from the plowback of profits associated with innovation.

> [W]e immediately realize that innovation is the outstanding fact in the economic history of capitalist society or in what is purely economic in that history, and also that it is largely responsible for most of what we would at first sight attribute to other factors. (Vol. I, p. 86)

In *Business Cycles*, Schumpeter (1939) defined innovation as the setting up of a new production function. Since in the economic sense the production is nothing more than combining productive services, innovation can then be understood as combining factors in new ways—this is also referred to as carrying out new combinations: "in short, any 'doing things differently' in the realm of economic life—all these are instances of what we shall refer to by the term of innovation" (Vol. I, p. 84).

Schumpeter (1939) made a distinction between innovation and invention. The distinction is important for the modeling of his analysis, where the invention is considered an external factor and the innovation is considered an internal factor of the economic evolution. While invention is often a part of innovation, they are two separate phenomena—and invention is not synonymous with innovation. Invention is related to the discovery of new ideas that add to the existing store of knowledge but do not necessarily affect the current of life. They bring up the possibilities, but not the acts, of realization. They acquire relevance to the economic development only when they are turned into commercial and industrial reality. Thus, invention becomes innovation only when it is turned into commercial and industrial usage.

In Schumpeter's theory (1939), the agents who carry out innovations are referred to as entrepreneurs. The function of the entrepreneur is to introduce innovations into the firm. Schumpeter stressed, however, that the term should not be understood explicitly. He said that "nobody ever is an entrepreneur all the time, and nobody can ever be only an entrepreneur" (Vol. I, p. 103). An entrepreneur is a person who, at a given time, performs the entrepreneurial function of introducing the new combination.

Schumpeter underlined (1939) that what makes a person an entrepreneur is his or her leadership in introducing an innovation. Most of the time, it is the owners who perform the entrepreneurial function in the firm. However, at the end "it is the leadership rather than ownership that matters" (Vol. I, p. 103). Therefore, entrepreneurs can be found not only among owners, but also among the heads of firms, the managers, or some other salaried employees.

Three-Fold Understanding of Innovation

In this study, the understanding of innovation is based on the Schumpeterian theory of innovation and entrepreneurial profit. From the analysis of Schumpeter's theory (1939), carrying out the innovation requires the following elements: creativity, entrepreneurship, and openness to change. Therefore, I adapt a three-fold concept of innovation, which includes all three elements. Reference to innovation in the theoretical part is specific to this three-fold understanding of it.

The first element of the three-fold innovation, the creativity, is required throughout the whole process of carrying out an innovation. Innovation refers to "any 'doing things differently' in the realm of economic life" (Schumpeter, 1939, Vol. I, p. 84), and doing things differently requires creativity on the part of the people who engage in the process. Therefore, creativity is required to: (1) create an idea of how to use the invention for commercial or industrial purposes, and (2) create an idea of a new production function in terms of the following: creating a new product; creating new methods of production; and opening a new market, the conquest of a new supply of raw materials, and carrying out the new organization of the industry.

Creativity is also required for the act of invention, which very often is a prerequisite for the innovation. Schumpeter (1939) has not included invention into his concept of innovation because his analytical model of economic evolution required the separation of the external and internal factors. However, for the purpose of this analysis, such separation is not necessary; therefore, I include invention in the concept of innovation since it is very often an important prerequisite of innovation.

The second element of the three-fold innovation, the entrepreneurship, is required for the sole act of carrying out the innovation. It is required for taking the action and turning the existing possibilities into economic reality. It is "doing the thing" (Schumpeter, 1934, p. 88) that lies at the heart of the entrepreneurial function. New possibilities are continuously being offered by the surrounding world, but if there is no action to turn them into commercial usage, they become dead. Many people may see and contemplate the possibilities, but they do not have the entrepreneurial spirit to act upon them. It takes a person who has the initiative, the vision, the openness to change, the leadership, and the drive to take the action and turn ideas into reality. Thus, the carrying out of the innovation is not possible without an entrepreneur who does the new thing that others are just thinking about.

The third element of the three-fold innovation, the openness to change, is required to allow for the change (which is innovation) to take place and to be successful. In order for innovation to be successful, it has to fall on a receptive ground. The societies, which are open to change, are more receptive to the new things that come with the innovation. The openness of the society increases the possibility of entrepreneurial profit from innovation and encourages the entrepreneur to take the initiative of carrying out an innovation. If the society is not open to change, then the initiative of the entrepreneur is resisted and therefore discouraged or wasted. In economic matters, the resistance may manifest itself, first of all, through opposition in the groups threatened by the innovation, then in the difficulty in finding the necessary cooperation, and finally in the difficulty in winning over the customers (Schumpeter, 1934). Therefore, in order for the innovation to take place and to be successful, the society has to be open to change.

Diversity-Innovation Link

Innovation is considered to be a crucial factor in economic development, which in turn makes it a crucial factor in building the competitive advantage for countries. If the competitive advantage of countries is determined by their ability to conduct innovations, then societies—which have a higher capacity to innovate—should have a competitive advantage over those societies where this capacity is lower.

I argue that an important factor that influences the aptitude for innovation within a society is the level of ethnic diversity present in that society. More specifically, the aptitude depends on how diverse the society is and how the society manages its diversity. I claim that ethnically diverse societies should be more innovative than homogeneous societies because ethnic diversity, if put in the right context, induces greater creativity, entrepreneurship, and openness to change, which in turn leads to a higher level of innovation.

I refer to the research conducted in organizational science in order to provide evidence for the existence of links between ethnic diversity and each of the elements of innovation: creativity, openness to change, and entrepreneurship. Organizational science is a field where the scholars have conducted an extensive research concerning the impact of diversity on the creativity and performance of firms.

Diversity-Creativity Link

Since the publication of the managerial report *Workforce 2000* (Johnston & Parker) in 1987, which stressed the increasing diversity of the labor force in the United States, the topic of diversity has received prominent attention in the field of organizational theory (Janssens & Steyaert, 2003). The report argued that the U.S. workforce is becoming increasingly diverse and that the trend is going to continue in the future. It predicted that traditional minority groups, such as women and people of color, will become increasingly present in the workforce in the coming decades and will form a bigger part of the labor force than the existing majority of white men. The publication triggered a discussion among the scholars in the field of organizational science, mostly in the

United States, concerning the impact of increasing workforce diversity on organizational outcomes. A new line of research, focused on analyzing the effects of diversity, has been developed as a result of the debate.

The study of diversity has referred to different categories of diversity (Milliken & Martins, 1996), one of them being ethnic diversity (also referred to as racial or cultural diversity). Two major approaches have emerged concerning the effects of ethnic diversity on the organizational outcomes. One emphasized the negative effects of diversity, and the other focused on the positive outcomes of ethnic diversity. The explanation of the negative impact of ethnic diversity was related mainly to the *affective effects* (Milliken & Martins), which refer to involvement, satisfaction, identification, role conflict, role ambiguity, perception of discrimination, and social integration. The theoretical basis for this argument has been provided by the *social identity theory* (Taifel, 1982). This theory suggested that greater diversity causes work group members to employ divisive social categorizations based on their differences, which in turn reduces the cohesiveness and increases the possibility of a dysfunctional conflict within the group impeding the organizational performance.

The explanation of the positive impact of ethnic diversity has been related to the *cognitive effects*, which refer to creative thinking, flexibility, novelty, synthesis, analysis, reorganization, redefinition, and complexity. The proponents of the positive effects of diversity argued that greater diversity among the group members leads to greater variety of ideas and perspectives; therefore, this leads to greater creativity and flexibility of thinking. I draw on the theoretical basis and the empirical findings provided by the research related to the positive effects of ethnic diversity to explain the diversity-creativity link.

Value in Diversity Hypothesis and Supportive Theories

The approach in organizational science that stresses the positive impact of ethnic diversity uses the *value in diversity* hypothesis to explain the positive effects of ethnic diversity on the group performance. The hypothesis states that "ethnic diversity, at least if properly managed, produces tangible, positive effects on organizational outcomes" (McLeod, Lobel, & Cox, 1996, p. 249). The positive effects of ethnic diversity are derived from *cognitive* effects of greater creativity and flexibility (Cox & Blake, 1991; Jackson, 1992).

Based on the examination of the origins of creativity in ethnically diverse groups, as presented by the *value in diversity* hypothesis, I distinguish two channels of creativity that stem from diversity. The first channel is attributed simply to the production of a broader range of ideas by diverse but separate individuals, which in turn provides a wider spectrum of alternatives from which to choose when solving a problem. The second channel is attributed to the generation of new quality ideas resulting from the interaction between diverse individuals. It is the second channel, however, that is crucial for explaining the origins of higher creativity in diverse groups.[1]

The first channel of creativity has a relatively straightforward logic behind it. The diverse ethnic background endows members of the group with a richer base of perspectives, knowledge, experiences, and skills. Therefore, when the diverse group is faced with a problem, it will come up with a bigger variety of ideas and solutions to the problem than a more homogeneous group. The more diverse the group, the higher the possibility that the ideas of the individuals will be different from each other; therefore, there is a higher probability that among this wide range of ideas there will be an idea that provides the most appealing solution to the problem. In more homogeneous groups, there is a bigger possibility that the ideas of the members will be more similar to each other, if not the same; consequently, the possibility of arriving with a novel solution to the problem is much lower.

The first channel of creativity has an important insight into the origins of creativity in diverse groups. However, it appears that it is the second channel that provides the most essential explanation of why diverse groups are more creative. The second channel captures the whole dynamic of cognitive processes of idea generation in a diverse group. It puts emphasis on the interaction between diverse individuals and the ways in which the exposure to different perspectives, approaches, and experiences changes the individual's creative thoughts and creates a new quality idea.

The wider spectrum of perspectives present in a diverse group gives the individuals an opportunity to see the problem in a new light. The psychologists of creativity (e.g., Guilford, 1950; Mednick, 1962; Kanter 1968; Lubart & Sternberg, 1993; Lipshitz & Waingortin, 1995; Kurtzberg & Amabile, 2001; Georgsdottir and Getz, 2004) argued that seeing a problem in a new way is important for finding a creative solution.

The shifting of the perspective allows for the redefinition of the problem. That, in turn, facilitates creative insights and permits novel solutions that were not thinkable with the old definition of the problem. The importance of redefining the problem for finding creative solutions is very well explained by the following example provided by Raanan Lipshitz & Mario Waingortin (1995, as cited in Georgsdottir and Getz, 2004):

> A hotel manager was receiving frequent complaints about the hotel's lifts being too slow. Before replacing the elevators with a faster model (a very expensive option) he decided to get a psychologist's point of view on the problem. The psychologist saw the problem not originating in the speed of the lifts, but rather in the boredom caused by the wait. He then suggested installing large mirrors in front of the lifts, so that people could pass the time and entertain themselves looking in the mirrors. The manager opted for this (much cheaper) solution, and had no more complaints about lifts being too slow. Thus, taking a different perspective on the problem led to an innovative, low-cost solution. (p. 167)

Furthermore, the second channel of creativity puts emphasis on the collective creativity and the evolution of ideas within a group process. Terri R. Kurtzberg and Teresa M. Amabile (2001) underlined that diversity does not only provide the benefits stemming from a bigger number of diverse ideas present in a heterogeneous group. More importantly, diversity provides the benefits coming from "the potential changes in the generation of creative ideas that can occur when the inputs and interactions of other people are introduced" (p. 285). As the idea progresses from one mind to another, it is shaped into new forms. The interaction between the group members and the exposition to the variety of perspectives stimulate further idea generation by the group members, which results in higher quality ideas.

The interaction between diverse individuals changes the individual's creative thought also by increasing the probability of more associations. The ability to produce more associations has been defined by cognitive psychologists as an essential element of creative thinking.

Joy Paul Guilford (1950), the founder of creativity research in psychology, argued that the associations from one topic to another allow for the generation of divergent thoughts. The scholars of creativity research observed that the human mind is inclined to think consistently along predictable lines and tends to be influenced by the surface features of problems (Gick & Holyoak, 1987; Novick, 1988). What distinguishes the creative mind is the ability of associative thinking, in which thoughts can leap from category to category rather than simply follow preexisting paths of cognition. The crucial skill in associative thinking is the ability to notice similar features in seemingly unrelated elements (Lubart & Sternberg, 1993; Mednick, 1962). The cognitive psychologists who focus on the team-level creativity (Kurtzberg & Amabile, 2001) argued that a direct interaction among diverse individuals highly contributes to associative thinking and, thus, to creativity.

The sole cognitive act of idea generation resulting from the interaction between people in a group has been tagged by Rosabeth M. Kanter (1968) as *kaleidoscope thinking*. The generation of ideas under the notion of kaleidoscope thinking is based on "twisting reality into new patterns and rearranging the pieces to create a new reality" (p. 11). In another study, Kanter (1983) also observed that the most innovative companies deliberately established heterogeneous teams to "create a 'marketplace of ideas,' recognizing that a multiplicity of points of view need to be brought to bear on a problem" (p. 167). Furthermore, she stated that "[i]t is not the 'caution of committees' that is sought—reducing risk by spreading responsibility—but the better idea that comes from a clash and an integration of perspectives" (p. 167).

The whole process of interaction between the group members, which gives rise to the creation of new ideas, has been referred to by the scholars of the psychology of creativity as *creative synergy* (Kurtzberg & Amabile, 2001). It is a process in which ideas are formed, shared, adapted, and inspired simultaneously by more than one person. The advocates of creative synergy argued that "the input of other people's ideas, knowledge structures, and perspectives at particular stages of the thought process might have important effects on how creative ideas are formed, perhaps by increasing the probability of lateral associations" (p. 289).

The proponents of creative synergy underlined that the group creativity "has something to offer over and above the simple combination of individually generated ideas" (Kurtzberg & Amabile, 2001, p. 289). They argued that "synergy is the behavior of whole systems that cannot be predicted by the behavior of any parts taken separately" (Fuller, 1981, as cited in Kurtzberg & Amabile, 2001, p. 289). The ideas created in the process of group interaction are the result of both an ongoing sharing of ideas and the twisting of ideas over and over again to develop a completely new idea, which is different from the ones initially developed by the individual minds. In that case, the interaction adds an extra value and generates a new product.

The isolated effect of the exposition to the variety of perspectives on idea generation in a group is well captured by the research of *minority dissent*. It focuses on the impact of minority views on the majority's process of thinking. The studies conducted within that realm of research have provided evidence that the minority dissent is beneficial and productive for the organization because it enhances creativity and divergent thought in majority members (De Dreu & Beersma, 2001; Nemeth & Staw, 1989; Van Dyne & Saavedra, 1996). The minority dissent occurs when a minority publicly opposes and challenges the beliefs, attitudes, ideas, procedures, and policies assumed by the majority of the group (McLeod, Baron, Marti, & Yoon, 1997). The enhancement of creativity under minority dissent stems from the consideration of the issue from multiple perspectives which is forced on the majority by the minority dissent.

The mechanism that leads to enhanced creativity and divergent thought under minority dissent is explained by the scholars along the following lines. When the minority dissent occurs, the majority starts wondering why the minority thinks the way it does (Nemeth, 1986). However, the reason why the majority tries to understand the minority position is not to justify, or to verify it, but to reject it (Moscovici, 1980). The rejection of the minority idea is perceived as essential for the majority to maintain its position. Nevertheless, at the same time, the majority tries to resolve the tension produced by minority dissent in a way that preserves harmony and intergroup relations (Crano & Chen, 1998). The tension produced by the minority dissent and the desire of the majority to resolve the tension in an accommodative way leads to the increased creativity and the production of divergent thinking on the side of the majority. The majority members have to look at the problem from different perspectives, one of which has been suggested by the minority (Nemeth).

Empirical Support for Diversity-Creativity Link in Organizational Science

There were several studies conducted within organizational theory that provided empirical support for the value in diversity hypothesis.[2] Taylor Cox, Sharon A. Lobel, and Poppy Lauretta McLeod (1991) found that the ethnically diverse groups made more cooperative choices in the two-party prisoner's dilemma game than the all-Anglo groups. Later, McLeod and Lobel (1992) found that the ethnically heterogeneous groups produced higher quality ideas during a brainstorming session than the more homogeneous groups.

In another study, Kamalesh Kumar, Larry K. Michaelsen, and Warren E. Watson (1993) found that with time, the nationally/ethnically heterogeneous groups scored higher on the range of perspectives and alternatives generated than the homogeneous groups. They analyzed the interaction and performance of the heterogeneous and homogeneous groups for 17 weeks. Initially, the homogeneous groups scored higher on both process and performance effectiveness. Over time, however, both types of groups showed improvement on process and performance, and differences between the groups have diminished. At the end of the study period, there were no differences between the two groups in regard to process and overall performance, but the heterogeneous groups scored higher on two task measures: range of perspectives and alternatives generated. Overall, heterogeneous groups made much more rapid process improvements than the homogeneous groups.

Another study by McLeod, Lobel, and Cox (1996), conducted as a controlled experimental brainstorming session, reported that the ethnically diverse groups generated ideas that were of a higher quality and more feasible than the ideas generated by ethnically homogeneous groups. The study focused on the performance of groups on a creativity task, requiring knowledge of different cultures. The ideas produced by the heterogeneous groups were judged as "significantly more feasible, and more effective" (p. 257) than the ideas produced by the homogeneous groups. Thus, the results of the study were consistent with the previous research, suggesting that ethnically diverse work teams have potential performance advantages over homogeneous teams, at least with respect to creativity.

Other than the laboratory studies described previously, there were also field studies that supported the value in diversity hypothesis. Orlando C. Richard (2000) found that the business strategy of the firm moderates the relationship between racial diversity and firm performance. The results of his study showed that cultural/racial diversity has a positive impact on a firm's performance if the firm pursues a growth strategy. His study demonstrated that "in association with growth, cultural/racial diversity enhances productivity, and this relationship intensifies as strategic growth increases" (p. 171). At the same time, the results showed that cultural/racial diversity has a negative effect on a firm's performance if the firm has no growth strategy or it has a downsizing strategy. In sum, the study showed that the same resource, which is cultural/racial diversity, can offer a competitive advantage to some firms and can be a performance detriment to other firms, depending on the context.

The contextual factors, as well as their mediating effects on the relationship between cultural/racial diversity, were further analyzed in a subsequent study by Orlando Richard, Amy McMillan, Ken Chadwick, and Sean Dwyer (2003). This time, the researchers designed a study to explore the moderating role of firm innovation on the relationship between racial diversity and a firm's performance. The study, founded on the *contingency/resource-based* theory, proved again the importance of the context in which racial diversity is placed. It demonstrated that racial diversity, as a knowledge-based resource, needs to be set in an appropriate context to fully realize its potential benefits. The study identified an *innovation strategy* as one such contextual variable. Specifically, the researchers found that racial diversity enhanced performance for banks pursuing an innovation strategy, whereas for banks low in innovation, racial diversity diminished their performance. The authors concluded, "Simply put, racial diversity is beneficial to innovators" (p. 114).

Diversity–Openness to Change Link

Ethnic diversity can lead to a higher openness to change in a society. The interaction with people of different cultural origins, and thus the exposure to different cultures, can increase their openness to change (Doran, 2001). People who are immersed in a diverse environment, which values diversity, become more accustomed to differences and to new ideas, and that broadens their horizons and makes them less afraid of differences and more open to new things. Moreover, ethnically diverse societies include a bigger number of bilingual or bicultural individuals, who—as argued by the scholars (Lambert, 1977)—tend to have a higher tolerance for ambiguity and a higher level of divergent thinking, which is associated with higher openness to change.

The openness to change is important for the economy at least in three ways. First, a society that is characterized by a higher openness to change can provide a higher pool of individuals who are open to change to carry out the innovations. As argued by Schumpeter (1934), openness to change is one of the essential characteristics of the entrepreneur. Doing something new implies objective difficulties that stem from the fact of entering an unknown ground, which is always more difficult than walking on an old, well-known path. Doing something new also implies difficulties that originate from the psyche of the human being from the insight of the human mind, which by nature feels reluctant toward new things. The human mind prefers to stay attached to the old habits of thinking that are familiar and tested by experience. The entrepreneur has to be particularly open to change to be able to successfully combat the objective difficulties, as well as the psychological difficulties, associated with change.

A second way in which openness of the society contributes to the economy is related to the higher receptivity of open-minded society. A society that is open to change can provide an audience that is more receptive to new ideas, and thus more receptive to innovation. Other than providing a bigger pool of potential entrepreneurs, a diverse society also provides an audience that is more amenable to change. Such an audience is very important for the successful carrying out of the innovations. If the audience is open to new things, then it is easier for the entrepreneurs to find the necessary cooperation and to win over customers for their endeavors. If a society is resistant to change, then the entrepreneurial attempt to introduce novelty will be met with opposition or even condemnation. The refusal to accept innovation will put in vain the entrepreneurial effort and discourage entrepreneurs from introducing new things to the society. Therefore, a society that is open to change is essential for the innovation to take place.

A third way in which ethnic diversity can be beneficial for the economy is through increasing the adaptability of a given country to global markets. The diverse workforce of a country better reflects the environment of the companies acting internationally than a homogeneous workforce. Therefore, a diverse workforce allows for the companies to be more adaptive to the changing international environment and to be more competitive on the global market.

The process of globalization entails that in order to remain competitive on the global scale, countries have to address not only the consumer needs of their own societies but also the needs of the consumers on the global markets. To understand consumer markets throughout the world and to compete in them, countries need to possess the insight into the characteristics of consumers who come from many different cultures. Countries with a more ethnically diverse workforce are in a better position to address those needs. Thus, ethnic diversity can be very beneficial in terms of global competitiveness. It can increase the chances of carrying out innovations that would be well received on the global markets.

Diversity–Openness to Change Research in Organizational Science

Within the organizational science, the support for the diversity–openness to change argument is provided by the value in diversity hypothesis (introduced earlier). There are also several studies conducted in the field of cognitive and behavioral psychology that provide support for the argument. The studies relate to the concept of *divergent thinking, minority dissent*, and *groupthink*.

The proponents of the value in diversity hypothesis argued that ethnic diversity can add value to an organization not only through increased creativity and innovation but also through increased organizational flexibility that is induced by diversity. They pointed to two main sources of this phenomenon: one stems from the changes in cognitive processes of the members of the diverse groups, and the other stems from the changes in the organizational structure stimulated by the adjustment related to diversity (Cox, 2001).

The scholars (e.g., Cox, 2001) advocating the value of diversity stated, "[O]ne way that diversity can make organizations more flexible is through changes in the patterns of employees' cognitive structures" (p. 8). In that case, the greater flexibility stems from the exposure to different perspectives, approaches, and experiences that are provided by ethnic diversity. The exposure leads to the increase in divergent thinking in the individuals, which is related to higher flexibility of thought.

An indirect support for this argument was found in the research of bilingual individuals. The researchers found that bilingual individuals have a substantially higher level of cognitive flexibility than monolinguals (Lambert, 1977). The exposure to two cultures and two languages enhances the cognitive complexity of bilingual individuals and increases their ability of divergent thinking. A similar mechanism works in situations when people are exposed to different cultures even to a lesser extent, for example, at work or in everyday life.

The positive changes in cognitive processes inside of ethnically diverse organizations are contributed not only to the exposure to different perspectives but also to the fact that ethnically diverse organizations include a significantly bigger number of bilinguals, who are proven to be more cognitively flexible. The inclusion of a bigger number of bilingual individuals increases the organization's competitive advantage in terms of flexibility and divergent thinking potential of its members, and thus in terms of adaptability to change.

The logic behind the process, which leads to the increase of divergent thinking as a result of the exposure to different ideas, is well explained by the previously described minority dissent concept. The scholars of minority dissent provided evidence that the minority dissent enhances both creativity and divergent thought in majority members (De Dreu & Beersma, 2001; Nemeth & Staw, 1989; Van Dyne & Saavedra, 1996). The rationale behind the mechanism that leads to divergent thinking in minority dissent situations is similar to the one related to creativity. Simply, the exposure to different views allows the members to perceive the problem from different perspectives and that stimulates the recognition of multiple alternatives, which is related to divergent thinking. The occurrence of different perspectives within a group reduces the possibility of a single-minded process or a *tunnel vision*, which is often distinctive of groups that are not exposed to diverse viewpoints (Sauser, 1988).

The problem of single-minded thinking in groups is very well depicted by the groupthink concept developed within the psychology of groups. The groupthink concept relates to the absence of critical thinking in groups caused by the excessive preoccupation with maintaining group cohesiveness. Irving Janis (1982) defined groupthink in the following manner:

> I use the term 'groupthink' as a quick and easy way to refer to a mode of thinking that people engage in when they are deeply involved in a cohesive in-group, when the members' strivings for unanimity override their motivation to realistically appraise alternative courses of action…Groupthink refers to a deterioration of mental efficiency, reality testing, and moral judgment that results from in-group pressures. (p. 9)

The social pressures for groupthink typically develop in cohesive, homogeneous groups (Janis, 1982). When group cohesiveness is high, all the members are more likely to express solidarity, mutual liking, and positive feelings toward the processes within the group. The members of such a group "tend to evolve informal normal norms to preserve friendly intragroup relations and these become part of the hidden agenda at their meetings" (p. 7). The hidden agenda and the accompanying concurrence-seeking tendencies interfere with the critical thinking of the group. In order to keep cohesiveness and friendly intragroup relations, the group resorts to distorting member's observation and ignoring realistic challenges whenever those observations and challenges call into question the cohesiveness of the group.

Until the emergence of the groupthink research, most group psychologists were underlining the positive aspects of group cohesiveness. They emphasized the importance of group cohesiveness and the positive valuation of the group by the members. They argued that it has an important effect on members' motivation to continue to belong to the group and a positive effect on the group performance (Lewin, 1952).

The potentially detrimental effects of group cohesiveness were first emphasized by Wilfred R. Bion (1961), who explained how the efficiency of all working groups can be adversely affected by the preconscious myths and misconceptions of their mutually dependent members, that is, by shared basic assumptions that tend to preserve the group without regard for the work at hand. Further research of groupthink underlined the fact that cohesiveness not only has positive effects, but also can lead to gross errors in group decisions (Janis, 1982). The cohesive groups develop strong conformity pressures. The greater the group's cohesiveness, the more power it has to bring about conformity. For the reasons of defending the unity and the *esprit de corps* of the cohesive group, the members of the group take steps—often without being aware of it—to counteract the disruptive influence of inside critics which question the shared basic assumptions of the group. Therefore, they are more likely to reject a nonconformist than the members of a less cohesive group. The rejection of points of view other than the ones shared by the group does not allow for divergent thinking within the group; consequently, it hinders the creativity and flexibility of the group.

The proponents of value in diversity have stressed the fact that heterogeneous groups are much less cohesive than the homogeneous groups; therefore, they are much less likely to fall into the trap of the groupthink. The decrease in group cohesiveness related to higher heterogeneity is perceived by the scholars of social identity theory (e.g., Taifel, 1982) as having a negative impact on the group performance. However, the scholars of value in diversity argued that it might also have a positive impact because it allows the avoidance of the consequences of groupthink.

The heterogeneous groups consist of members with diverse perspectives and backgrounds, so it is much harder to impose on them a common set of basic assumptions that would be shared by everybody. Therefore, the diverse groups are much less constrained by the pressure to conform to the shared assumptions than the homogeneous groups. As a result, the heterogeneous groups are inclined to be much more open to change, while the homogeneous groups are much more willing to stay with the status quo.

In addition to the positive effects of diversity on openness related to the cognitive processes within a group, there is another way in which diversity can contribute to greater flexibility and openness. According to the proponents of the value in diversity hypothesis (e.g., Cox, 2001; Cox & Blake, 1991), diversity can increase the openness of an organization through the responses that an organization has to make to adjust to the diverse workforce. In that case, an increased flexibility is a kind of by-product.

Cox (2001) argued that the increase in workforce diversity induces the broadening of the policies and the reduction of standardization in the operating methods, which, in result, makes the organization more fluid, more agile, and adaptable. The increase in fluidity of the organization is important because it "should allow the organization to respond to environmental changes faster and at lower cost" (p. 8). Moreover, if the organization has been able to deal with the challenge of diversity, it is more likely to cope better when it is faced with other types of challenges that involve change. "Most important of all, if organizations are successful in overcoming resistance to change in the difficult area of accepting diversity, it should be well-positioned to handle resistance to other types of change" (Cox & Blake, 1991, p. 52).

In addition to the aforementioned, Cox and Blake (1991) proposed a *marketing argument*. This argument stated that the organizations that can successfully attract a diverse workforce will obtain value by matching the demographic characteristics of the market they serve. They will position themselves to sell to a broader and more diverse customer base and, subsequently, increase their organizational performance.

Diversity-Entrepreneurship Link

I argue that there is a positive link between ethnic diversity and entrepreneurship. It is related to two phenomena. First, ethnic diversity can lead to higher openness to change—and that, in turn, can promote entrepreneurship. The second phenomenon reflects the more direct link between ethnic diversity and entrepreneurship. It is related to the fact that diverse societies have a higher percentage of minorities and immigrants, and those groups have a higher propensity to be entrepreneurial.

Empirical Support for Higher Entrepreneurial Propensity Among Minorities and Immigrants

It has been observed that minorities and immigrants exert a higher propensity to be entrepreneurial than the native majority. The phenomenon was first observed and investigated in the United States, and then studies from other advanced economies have followed, reaffirming the observation. The studies concern either minorities in general, including immigrants and native-born minorities, or immigrants in particular.

As for the United States, it has been observed that in every decennial census from 1880 to 1990, immigrants were significantly more likely to be self-employed than natives ("Immigrant Entrepreneurs," 1997, p. 1). George Borjas (1986), an immigration economist, was one of the first to bring the issue to broader attention. Using the data from the 1970 and 1980 U.S. censuses, he conducted an extensive study of self-employment rates among immigrants and found that the self-employment rates of most immigrant groups exceeded those of native-born Americans. For example, among white male labor force participants, the probability of self-employment was 16.5% for foreign born and 11.7% for native born. Among Cuban labor force participants, the probability of self-employment was 15.6% for foreign born and 10.9% for native born. Among Asian labor force participants, the probability of self-employment was 12.6% for foreign born and 12.1% for native born. Among black labor force participants, the probability of self-employment was 5.3% for foreign born and 3.7% for native born. The relationship did not hold true for the Mexican and other Hispanic labor force participants where the probability of self-employment was 4.2% for foreign-born Mexicans and 5.6% for native-born Mexicans, and it was around 8% for both foreign- and native-born other Hispanic participants (Borjas).

The recent analysis of data in the United States confirms the phenomenon observed by Borjas. The *Minorities in Business 2001* report stated that the minority businesses are growing faster than the population in terms of both numbers of new firms and revenues. It reported that, in 2001 they owned about 15% percent of the total firms in the United States (U.S. Small Business Administration, 2002). The data concerning the number of firms, as well as the growth rates for 1982, 1987, 1992, and 1997, showed that the minority-owned firms outpaced nonminority-owned firms substantially in each of those periods. In the period of 1982–1987, the minority-owned firms grew at a rate of 55%, compared to the rate of 11% for the nonminority-owned firms. In 1987–1992, the minority-owned firms grew at a rate of 68%, compared to the rate of 22% for the nonminority-owned firms. And for the period of 1992–1997, the minority-owned firms grew at a rate of 30%, compared to the rate of 4% for the nonminority-owned firms (U.S. Small Business Administration).

Yet another study found strong support for the argument that ethnic minorities exert a higher propensity for entrepreneurship. The Panel Study of Entrepreneurial Dynamics (PSED) (Reynolds, Carter, Gartner, & Greene, 2002) found that black men and women are about 50% more likely to engage in start-up activities than white men and women, and the difference between the two is statistically significant. The prevalence rate for Hispanic men is about 20% higher than for white men, but the difference is not statistically significant. And Hispanic women are about equally likely to be involved in starting a business as white women.

Furthermore, the PSED study found that the education is a significant predictor of nascent entrepreneurs, especially for ethnic groups (Cater et al., 2002). Among black men and women and Hispanic men, those reporting any graduate training are two to three times more likely to be involved in a firm start-up. The impact of graduate education on nascent entrepreneurs among white men and women is very small. The data showed that approximately 26 of every 100 African American men and 20 of every 100 Hispanic men with graduate education experience report efforts to start a new business. This compares to 10 of every 100 white men with graduate experience. The PSED study also found that the effect of household income on entrepreneurial activity is similar to the effect of education. Those with higher incomes are more likely to be involved in starting a business.

The PSED study revealed that the entrepreneurial propensity among minorities is even higher and more widespread than previously disclosed by the data. Previously, the propensity to be entrepreneurial among minorities had been measured by the actual business start-ups. The problem with such measurement is that it measures the outcomes of entrepreneurial propensity and not the entrepreneurial propensity itself. Therefore, the entrepreneurial propensity of an individual who was involved in start-up activities but did not manage to form the company would not be accounted for by the start-up measure.

The PSED measure is based on a different approach. It uses the involvement in start-up activities as an indicator for the individual's entrepreneurial propensity. It shows that the real level of entrepreneurial propensity for many ethnic groups is actually much higher than the level that is indicated by the business start-ups. For example, the PSED study found that even though black people are 50% more likely to engage in start-ups than whites, they actually make up the smallest percentage of subjects whose business idea had gotten off the ground. Among the blacks originally polled, just 21% had actually started the business, compared to 34% of whites. As for the Hispanic population, only 31% of Hispanics originally surveyed had gotten their ideas translated into reality.

The authors of the PSED (Reynolds et al., 2002) study discussed some of the reasons for the discrepancy that exists within the black and Hispanic communities between the real level of entrepreneurial propensity and the actual business start-ups. They argued that an important part of the explanation of that discrepancy is related to obstacles that minority members may face when attempting to start a business. Such obstacles include difficulties with accessing the financing and the lack of access to a network of successful businesses. The members of minorities reported that the obstacles often made it impossible to start their businesses and stay afloat.

An important upshot of the study is the realization that the members of the black and Hispanic communities actually exert a high entrepreneurial propensity. Based on the data regarding start-ups, those groups did not appear to be very entrepreneurial. When the entrepreneurial propensity was measured by successful start-ups, only Asians, Cubans, and Indians showed higher entrepreneurial propensity than the native born. However, when the entrepreneurial propensity is measured by the actual engagement in start-up activities, irrespective of their outcomes, then the blacks and Hispanics also emerge as having a higher entrepreneurial propensity than the native-born. In that situation, it is even more plausible to argue that the members of minorities, regardless of where they come from, have a higher propensity to be entrepreneurial than the native-born majority.

Studies conducted in other Western countries have confirmed the assertion that minorities have a higher propensity to be entrepreneurial than the native population (Hammarstedt, 2001). In Sweden, studies showed that the non-Nordic European immigrants, as well as Asian immigrants, have a higher probability to be self-employed than the native population. In Australia, several studies noted that many minority groups have a higher propensity to be self-employed. They have made a significant contribution to the growth of the Australian economy through their involvement in small business enterprises (Strahan & Williams, 1988).

In the United Kingdom, reports showed that ethnic minorities are overproportionately represented in business start-ups. While the minorities comprise approximately 6.4% of the total population of Great Britain (Office for National Statistics, 1999), they are believed to be responsible for about 10% of business start-ups in the United Kingdom (Bank of England, 1999). Furthermore, the analysis of the latest self-employment data revealed that a lot of minority groups in the United Kingdom have a higher propensity to be self-employed than the whites. The U.K. Office of National Statistics reported that the self-employment rate for whites is around 12%, while it is 19% for Bangladeshis and Pakistanis, 18% for Chinese, and 15% for Indians. Scholarly analyses (Basu & Altinay, 2000) estimated the rate of self-employment for Turks and Turkish Cypriots in the United Kingdom to be around 20%.

The aforementioned figures indicate that the phenomenon of higher entrepreneurial propensity among minorities, which was first observed in the United States, is also present in other Western countries. The phenomenon has been less apparent in France and Germany (Radaev, 1994). Nevertheless, it has already been recognized by the scholars that the phenomenon of growing ethnic entrepreneurship has become virtually universal for Western countries.

Why Are Minorities and Immigrants More Entrepreneurial?

There is a big discussion concerning the determinants behind the phenomenon of ethnic minorities exerting a higher propensity to be entrepreneurial in comparison to the native population. There are different explanations offered by scholars that study the occurrence of ethnic entrepreneurship. However, most scholars agreed that a significant part of the explanation lies in the fact that the burdens of immigration are frequently assumed by groups of the population known to be more active, and migration in this sense becomes a kind of "filter" (Radaev, 1994).

Julian L. Simon (1989), an immigration economist who was one of the first to emphasize the positive sides of immigration, claimed that the immigrants are likely to be self-selected on the basis of economically positive characteristics. "It makes sense that those persons who believe that they have characteristics that will enable them to succeed in a new country will be the most likely persons to migrate" (p. 104).

The scholars argued that the members of the household who are "chosen" or who self-select themselves to emigrate abroad often have personal characteristics similar to those of entrepreneurs: "Like entrepreneurs, for example, they tend to be dynamic risk takers—especially in the early stages of a flow when information about the point of destination is incomplete and the likelihood of success uncertain" ("Immigrant Entrepreneurs," 1997, p. 1).

Another way of explaining the higher rates of entrepreneurship among minorities and immigrants compared to the native majority is provided by the *disadvantage theory*. The theory argues that the motives for ethnic entrepreneurship lie in the challenges imposed on the minorities by their less favored position in the society. The supporters of the disadvantage theory (Johnson, 2000; Light, 1972; Moore, 1983; Ram & Deakins, 1996; Ram & Jones, 1998) argued that disadvantages coming from poverty, difficulty speaking the language of the country, unemployment, or discrimination, as well as constrain in the labor market of opportunities for ethnic groups, causes those groups to favor self-employment.

Everett E. Hagen (1958, 1961) argued that the high entrepreneurial motivation among minorities is linked to their attempts in the economic sphere to compensate for their low social status. He stated that men in minority groups often feel discriminated against; they try to compensate for that in the best (and often the only) way open to them, which is by succeeding in business. Also, Schumpeter (1934) noticed this pattern and argued that the fascination with accumulating material wealth, which is one of the central motivations for entrepreneurial action, "is specially strong for people who have no other chance of achieving social distinction" (p. 93).

Hagen (1958, 1961) mentioned many historical examples of such behavior—the Dissenters in England, the Protestants in France, the Samurai in Japan, the Jews in many countries, and the Parsees in India.

Those minorities were prohibited from entering other types of activities in the host countries. Therefore, they resorted to trade, which was open to them as a way of acquiring economic wealth and social status. Those trading peoples of minority status are referred to as *middleman minorities* (Bonacich, 1973).

Another explanation for higher entrepreneurial propensity among immigrants and minorities points to the higher level of achievement motivation among those groups, which is stimulated by the "hunger" for wealth. Simon (1987) proposed a model in which the effort-exertion function is dependent upon wealth (and opportunity). According to him, the hunger for wealth, which is created by the lack of it, stimulates people for an increased amount of effort in comparison to the people who possess a satisfying amount of wealth. Therefore, since immigrants on average arrive with less material assets than the natives possess, they experience a lack of wealth. According to Simon (1987), that lack of wealth is a spur to their achievement.

The scholars in the field did not agree on one explanation for the increased initiative, vigor, and entrepreneurial propensity among immigrants and minorities. However, they said that the most important point is that such increased entrepreneurial propensity exists among those groups. As iterated by Simon (1989),

> How much of the vigor of immigrants is due to their being "hungry" rather than being settled and affluent, how much due to their being self-selected for vigor among the populations they come from, and how much due to the fructifying effects of living in the tension of two cultures is an open question;...what matters is that the vigor exists. (p. 107)

Identifying the Right Context

It has been demonstrated by the scholars of organizational science that the relationship between ethnic diversity and innovation, and thus performance, is indirect and depends on the context in which it is placed. These scholars have observed that there are several moderating variables, which affect the impact of ethnic diversity on a firm's performance. Those variables, referred to as moderating or conditioning variables, create the right context in which ethnic diversity can realize its benefits in terms of increased innovation, creativity, and flexibility.

The conditioning variables identified by the scholars of organizational science relate to the level of firms. My intention is to adopt those conditioning variables to the level of countries. First, it is essential to explain the importance of the right context for the relationship between ethnic diversity and innovation.

Importance of the Right Context

The existing theories in the field of organizational science indicate that ethnic diversity can have both positive and negative effects on the performance of firms (Williams & O'Reilly, 1998). Approaches to diversity based on the value in diversity hypothesis (Cox & Blake, 1991; Elsass & Graves, 1997; McLeod, Lobel, & Cox, 1996; Richard, 2000), as well as those using the resource-based theoretical framework (Richard, 2003),[3] suggest that ethnic diversity has a positive impact on the organization. At the same time, the theorists supporting the social identity theory argued that ethnic diversity has a negative effect on organizational behaviors and performance (Chatman, Polzer, Barsade, & Neale, 1998; Pelled, Eisenhardt, & Xin, 1999; Riordan & Shore, 1997; Thomas, 1999; Tsui, Egan, & O'Reilly, 1992). Both theories have earned significant empirical support.

The contrasting theories and contradictory empirical findings regarding the outcomes of ethnic diversity have urged scholars to explore the possibility that certain conditions may moderate these outcomes, and thus, the relationship between ethnic diversity and performance may be context specific. The scholars argued that it is most likely that there is not a simple, direct relationship between diversity and performance. Instead, the effect of ethnic diversity on firm performance is indirect and depends on the organizational context in which it is based.

Richard et al. (2000, 2003) used the *contingency approach* to describe the mechanism behind the indirect relationship between ethnic diversity and performance. The contingency approach states that the effect of one variable on another variable depends upon some third variable. The approach is used when it is most likely that there is no direct relationship between X and Y, but the relationship is contingent upon the existence, or the level, of a third variable W, and thus a more complex causal statement is required. The third variable, W, moderates the relationship between X and Y, and it can therefore be called either a moderator of the relationship or a conditioning variable of the relationship (Donaldson, 2001).

The indirect nature of the relationship between ethnic diversity and innovation might lead to confusion concerning the attributes of diversity. If one looks only at the direct relationship between diversity and innovation and does not find the positive relationship, or even finds a negative one, then one implies negative attributes to ethnic diversity. That is what has often happened in organizational science, as well as in political economy. Ethnic diversity has been charged by some scholars with strictly negative allegations.

What the proponents of value in diversity found out, however, is that the assumption about ethnic diversity being strictly negative in outcomes is incorrect. Scholars believe this is wrong because it is based on research that implies a direct relationship between ethnic diversity and performance, while the relationship is actually indirect. If diversity is placed in the right context, then it can add value and enhance the performance of the firm. However, if the right context is not present, then ethnic diversity can actually impair the performance of the firm.

Therefore, ethnic diversity displays the qualities of a *double-edged sword*. The positive properties of ethnic diversity include the following: increased creativity and innovation, increased problem solving capabilities, increased organizational flexibility, increased human talent, and benefits for marketing strategy. The negative qualities of ethnic diversity include the following: increased potential for conflict, decreased effectiveness of communication, and decreased levels of social attraction and commitment within the group (Cox, 1991). The context decides which attributes of ethnic diversity will be realized.

Therefore, putting the right context in place is essential for being able to seize the benefits of ethnic diversity. As stated by Cox (1991),

> Even though theory and research suggest that diversity can be a resource to enhance organizational performance, there is a crucial distinction between merely having diversity in the workforce and developing the organizational capacity to leverage diversity as a resource. The challenge of diversity is not simply to have it but to create conditions in which its potential to be a performance barrier is minimized and its potential to enhance performance is maximized. (pp. 15–16)

The double-edged qualities of ethnic diversity imply that once you have diversity, you simply have to have the right context in place. Otherwise, not only will you be unable to reap the benefits of it, but also you may experience the negative sides of ethnic diversity, for example, high levels of conflict and communication breakdowns. Having diversity is not enough to reap the benefits associated with it because the presence of a resource does not imply its use (Hartenian & Gudmundson, 2000). What is necessary is the right management of diversity.

Therefore, ethnic diversity is a type of resource that cannot be just left idle. It needs to be managed and leveraged. Furthermore, the scholars underlined that the management of diversity is not something that you can do once and then forget about it. On the contrary, it requires a constant and ongoing commitment that is genuine and serious.

Right Context on Group and Firm Level

Having asserted that the relationship between ethnic diversity and innovation is indirect and depends on the existence of the right context, the scholars of organizational science took upon themselves the endeavor of finding out what the right context is. Several studies were conducted in the last decade in order to identify the elements which are part of the right context. Different approaches were used, and the topic was examined from several perspectives ranging from structural to cognitive and psychological.

The research on identifying the right context is still under way, and it has not yet been fully solidified into one encompassing theory. However, the scholars have pointed out several variables that moderate the relationship between cultural/racial diversity and performance of groups, organizations, or firms. Until the present, the following variables either have been clearly indicated by the scholars of organizational science or can be deducted from their writings as being conducive to the translation of ethnic diversity into positive outcomes: (1) valuing diversity, (2) growth- and innovation-based strategy, and (3) interaction between diverse individuals.

Within the value in diversity approach, cognitive psychologists have identified some additional conditioning variables such as: (a) the integration and learning perspective, (b) the verification of personal self-views, and (c) the simultaneous verification of personal and social self-views.

Valuing Diversity

The scholars of organizational science underlined that the most important requirement, which lies at the heart of building the right context for ethnic diversity, is to *perceive diversity as a value*. Valuing diversity allows an organization to translate ethnic diversity into innovation, and thus increase performance.

The scholars argued that preparing organizations to have and to leverage diversity requires a fundamental change in thinking about assumptions and relationships concerning ethnic diversity. The organizations have to start perceiving ethnic diversity as a resource, which has a potential to add value and not just to disrupt performance. As argued by Cox (2001),

> Managing and leveraging diversity requires a process of deep organizational change...The process recognizes that real change in this area will require a systemic approach toward an ultimate goal of institutionalizing a new culture—one that welcomes diversity and allows all members to use their skills and abilities to achieve their full potential in pursuit of business and personal goals. (p. 30)

Integration and Learning Perspective on Diversity

The analysis conducted by Robin J. Ely and David A. Thomas (2001) provided proof for the argument that valuing diversity as a resource is essential for creating the environment in which cultural diversity can realize its potential benefits. The authors conducted a qualitative research in three culturally diverse organizations and analyzed the impact of different diversity perspectives on the functioning of those organizations.

Ely and Thomas (2001) defined the diversity perspective as the "group member's normative beliefs and expectations about cultural diversity and its role in their workgroup" (p. 234). They analyzed the impact of three different types of diversity perspectives: integration and learning, access and legitimacy, and discrimination and fairness.

The *integration and learning* perspective is essentially the valuing diversity approach. It is a perspective where diversity is treated as a resource for learning and adaptive change, where the insights, skills, and experiences employees have developed as members of different cultural identity groups are regarded as potentially valuable resources that the workgroup can use to rethink its primary tasks and redefine its markets, products, strategies, and business practices (Ely & Thomas, 2001).

The *access and legitimacy* perspective is based on the recognition of the marketing value of the culturally diverse workforce, where diversity is used for gaining access to and legitimacy with the culturally diverse markets. The groups with this approach to diversity do not include the cultural competencies of their diverse workforces into their main functions; they only use their diversity at the margins, to connect with a more diverse market (Ely & Thomas, 2001).

The *discrimination and fairness* perspective is an approach where cultural diversity is perceived as an end in itself. Unlike the other two approaches, the discrimination and fairness perspective does not connect having a culturally diverse workforce with the enhancement of organization's functioning. The reasons for having a culturally diverse workforce are dictated by the moral imperative to ensure both justice and a fair treatment of all members of the society. A diverse workforce serves as an evidence of just and nondiscriminatory treatment of employees. An organization with such an approach focuses its efforts on providing equal opportunities in hiring and promotion, suppressing prejudicial attitude, and eliminating discrimination, but it does not try to use diversity to its advantage in terms of functioning and performance (Ely & Thomas, 2001).

The results of the analysis conducted by Ely and Thomas (2001) showed that, out of all the three perspectives, only the integration and learning perspective gave the right foundation and guidance needed to realize sustained benefits from diversity. The members of diverse groups that embraced this perspective felt valued and respected. They reported feeling that their "whole person" was known, valued, and respected by others and that they could express "more of who they were" at work, including those things that differentiated them from others. As a result of the integration and learning perspective, the functioning of the organization was "enhanced by the cross-cultural exposure and learning, and by work processes designed to facilitate constructive intergroup conflict and exploration of diverse views" (pp. 254, 258, 261).

The other two perspectives did not provide the right foundation and guidance needed to achieve the sustained benefits from diversity. According to Ely and Thomas (2001), the crucial dimension along which the three diversity perspectives varied was whether and how cultural diversity was linked to the group's work and work processes. The authors described the impact of the two perspectives on the functioning of groups in their study in the following way:

> In the access-and-legitimacy perspective, cultural diversity is a potentially valuable resource, but only at the organization's margins and only to gain access to and legitimacy with a diverse market...this view of the role of racial diversity led to race-based staffing patterns that matched the racial make-up of the markets they served. This fostered perceptions of white-staffed functions as higher status than functions staffed by people of color; racially segregated career tracks and opportunities, which fostered concerns among staff of color about the degree to which they were valued and respected;...The resulting interracial/interfunctional tensions appeared to inhibit learning and people's ability to be maximally effective in their work.

> Finally, in the discrimination and fairness perspective...this view of the role of racial diversity restricted the discourse about race to one in which employees negotiated the meaning of all race-related differences on moral grounds. Questions and concerns about fairness led inevitably to strained race relations characterized by competing claims of innocence, with each group assuming a defensive posture in relation to the other. (pp. 265–266)

In the study of Ely and Thomas (2001), the intervening process, through which the integration and learning perspective enhanced group performance, was the creation of the feeling of being valued and respected among diverse people. That feeling enabled the diverse members of the group to openly voice their ideas, and thus contribute to the creativity and divergent thinking of the group.

There is a theory developed in the field of social psychology, called the *self-verification theory*, which explicitly focuses on that phenomenon and explains its dynamics on the level of individual cognitive processes. This theory is discussed next.

Verification of Personal Self-Views

The *self-verification theory* was developed in the course of searching for the social psychological moderators that would allow translating diversity into positive outcomes. The self-verification theory focuses on defining the context, which would create the feeling of being valued and respected among the members of diverse groups. That feeling would ensure the communication of distinctive ideas and unique perspectives by the diverse individuals. The proponents of this theory recognized (e.g., Swann, Polzer, Seyle, & Ko, 2004) that the creation of such a social psychological climate is essential in order to turn diversity into innovation: "There are sound reasons to believe that the social psychological climate that prevails in groups will be a powerful determinant of innovation—even more powerful, perhaps, than the abilities of individuals who make up the group" (Swann, Polzer, Seyle, & Ko, 2004, p. 23).

The self-verification theory aims at identifying the cognitive individual processes that would moderate the harmful effects of diversity caused by intergroup categorization processes. The theory was created as an alternative to the *self-categorization theory*, which has also provided an answer to the question of how to moderate the potential negative effects of diversity. The two approaches differ significantly.

The answer provided by the self-categorization theory points to the establishment of *superordinate goals* as moderators of the harmful effects of diversity. It contends that the members of diverse groups must shift their focus from the qualities that make them unique to the superordinate identity of the group in order to avoid harmful categorizations based on demographic differences (Chatman et al., 1998).

The self-verification theorists argue on the contrary. They contend that while evoking a collective categorization may minimize the use of category-based biases and stereotypes, it may also discourage individuals from behaving in ways that are distinct to their unique identities (Polzer, Milton, & Swann, 2002). From that perspective, the self-categorization theory falls short as a strategy for finding value in diversity because it is precisely these unique ways of thinking and acting that constitute the potential benefits of a diverse group. William B. Swann Jr. et al. (2004) explained the logic behind that argument in the following way:

> Indeed, taken to its logical extreme, self-categorization theory suggests that members of diverse groups should become so single-mindedly committed to the groups' agendas that distinctions among them become blurred. Such blurring of the differences that make a team diverse will necessarily thwart efforts to find value in diversity. From this vantage point, although emphasizing superordinate identities may serve to unify members of diverse groups initially, as a strategy for finding value in diversity, it is a tantamount to arguing that the best way to exploit a resource (in this case, the unique characteristics of diverse group members) is to minimize and disregard that resource! (p. 10)

Therefore, the self-verification theory offers a different solution to the one offered by the self-categorization theory, which implies suppressing diverse identities for the group identity. The self-verification theorists argue that there is abundant anecdotal evidence suggesting that diverse groups sometimes do emphasize their differences and still simultaneously become socially integrated (Polzer et al., 2002). How it happens, however, is still unclear. Hence, they want to "provide the answer to the following daunting question: *How can diverse groups interact effectively while remaining cognizant of their differences?*"

The self-verification theorists contend that, in order for ethnic diversity to be translated into innovation,[4] diverse people have to attain confirmation of their self-views. Only under such circumstances will the diverse people feel comfortable enough to actually voice their opinions, and thus contribute to creative thinking. The atmosphere of acceptance, understanding, and tolerance toward people from different groups is essential for ethnic diversity to bring positive results in terms of creativity (Polzer et al., 2002; Swann et al., 2004).

The self-verification scholars focused on the processes through which people seek and attain confirmation of their self-views. There is a growing body of research that supports the proposition that people want to be known for who they believe they are. It has been observed that when people enter into relationships with others who verify their self-views, they will feel more intimate and satisfied with the interaction and will be more inclined to want to continue the relationship (Polzer et al., 2002). Furthermore, the self-verification will enhance the feelings of connection to the group and foster creative task performance. Swann et al. (2004) summarized the results of their study concerning that discovery in the following way:

> Apparently, when group members had their unique attributes and perspectives verified, they felt recognized and understood. Such feelings emboldened them to offer creative ideas and insights they might otherwise have felt too inhibited to share. In addition, feeling known and understood by the group may have increased motivation to cooperate with one another by making members identify more with the group. (p. 16)

The self-verification theorists argue that the effect of greater diversity on group functioning is likely to depend on the level of *interpersonal congruence* in the group. Interpersonal congruence is defined as "the degree of similarity between a person's self-views and others' appraisals of that person" (Polzer et al., 2002, p. 297). High interpersonal congruence occurs when there is an agreement between people's self-views and the appraisals of their partners.

High interpersonal congruence fosters mutual understanding and appreciation for one another's perspectives, and thus buffers the group from the potentially disruptive effects of diversity coming from negative categorizations. In a situation of high interpersonal congruence, the members of diverse groups feel valued and respected. Therefore, they are more inclined to make higher investments and have a greater willingness to open up and take risks, which all are qualities that stimulate creativity and divergent thinking in groups.

Simultaneous Verification of Personal and Social Self-Views

Even though the self-verification theory provides an alternative approach to the one offered by the self-categorization theory, the self-verification theorists recognize the validity of some of the main assertions made by the self-categorization theorists (Swann et al., 2004). They agree with the claim made by Chatman et al. (1998) that the superordinate goal can reduce the destructive intergroup categorizations through replacing the negative categorizations with the collective categorizations. That, consequently, encourages group members to unite around their shared social self-views. The self-verification theorists argue that their intention is not to question the importance of the verification of social self-views for the well-functioning of diverse groups, but rather to complement the work of the self-categorization scholars with new insights.

The self-verification theorists argue that the problem with the self-categorization theory is that it "captures only a portion of the psychologically significant processes that unfold in groups" (Swann et al., 2004, p. 21). It correctly underlines the importance of the verification of social self-views but it neglects the importance of the verification of personal self-views. Moreover, the principle of *functional antagonism* propagated by the self-categorization scholars states that the verification of social self-views and personal self-views is mutually exclusive (Turner, 1985). According to the self-categorization theorists, people cannot enjoy verification of distinct personal and social self-views simultaneously—they have to make a trade-off between the two.

The scholars of the self-verification theory disagree with the assertion of functional antagonism and argue that people can "have it both ways." They argue that the verification of the personal and social self-views can occur independently and simultaneously. They believe that many social and personal self-views are quite compatible and may even complement one another. According to these scholars, a simultaneous verification of both personal and social self-views is actually necessary for the well functioning of diverse groups engaged in creative tasks (Swann et al., 2004).

Swann et al. (2004) noted that the configuration where both the personal and social self-views was verified was actually present in the organizations featuring an integration and learning perspective in the study of Ely and Thomas (2001). It was possible because the collective goals of the group were compatible with the personal self-views. What made the two goals compatible was the perception of diversity as a value to the group.

The collective goal of the group with the integration and learning perspective was to learn from diversity. Thus, diversity was perceived as a cherished and desirable characteristic of the group. The individuals who were diverse felt that they could verify their personal self-views related to their different cultures because their self-views were totally compatible with the superordinate goal of the group. As a result, the members of the group that followed the integration and learning perspective could verify their personal and social views simultaneously.

Swann et al. (2004) explained the psychological dynamics that unravel from the simultaneous verification of the personal and social self-views in the following way:

> Verification of their personal self-views will make them feel known and understood, and thus increase their attraction to other group members as well as their commitment to the group. Quite independently, verification of their social self-views will increase their allegiance to and interest in remaining in the group. (p. 20)

The scholars of the self-verification theory argue that the combination where both personal and social self-views are verified is optimal for diverse groups engaged in creative tasks. This combination allows for both the development of coherence in the group and commitment to its collective goals. At the same time, it permits the preservation of diversity of its members, and thus allows the group to take advantage of its diversity and utilize it as a resource for creativity and divergent thinking.

Growth- and Innovation-Focused Strategy

Another variable that conditions the positive relationship between diversity and creativity, as identified by the scholars of organizational science, is the growth- and innovation-focused strategy. Empirical studies conducted on the firm level demonstrated that cultural diversity brings positive outcomes in terms of performance for the firms that follow a growth- or innovation-focused business strategy (Richard, 2000; Richard et al., 2003). At the same time, cultural diversity brings negative outcomes to firms that follow either a downsizing strategy or a strategy that is low on innovation (Richard; Richard et al.).

The authors of these empirical studies concluded that ethnic diversity is a resource that can offer a competitive advantage to some firms, while it may be a performance detriment to others, depending on the business strategy of the firm. Richard et al. (2003) found that in association with a growth- or innovation-based strategy, racial diversity enhances productivity. Furthermore, the results of their studies showed that the positive relationship between diversity and productivity intensifies as strategic growth increases (Richard, 2000). For the firms, however, which pursue either a strategy low on innovation or a downsizing strategy, the relationship between diversity and productivity becomes negative. Given the results of their studies, the authors concluded that "[s]imply put, racial diversity is beneficial to innovators" (Richard et al., p. 114).

The first attempt to assess the moderating effect of business strategy on the relationship between cultural diversity[5] and firm performance has been undertaken by Richard (2000). In the first part of his study, he did not find any empirical support for a positive direct relationship between cultural diversity and firm performance. However, when the growth strategy was added to the context in the second part of the study, the relationship between cultural diversity and firm performance became positive. The results showed that racially diverse firms that pursue a growth strategy experience a higher return on equity than firms that have the same level of diversity but do not follow a growth strategy or follow a downsizing strategy.

Richard concluded that the results of his study demonstrated that the positive impact of racial diversity on firm performance depends on the context. In the absence of the right context, the relationship between cultural diversity and organizational outcomes is either insignificant or negative. Only when the moderating variable is added to the equation does the relationship between diversity and performance become significant and positive. According to Richard, the growth strategy is just one possible moderating variable, and there is a need to look for other moderators of the relationship between diversity and performance.

Subsequently, Richard et al. (2003) conducted another study that had a very similar design to the previous one but assessed a different type of business strategy as a moderating variable. The authors chose and analyzed the innovation-focused strategy as a moderator of the relationship between racial diversity[6] and firm performance. As in the previous study, Richard et al. used the resource-based view of the firm and the contingency approach as a foundation for their analysis.

The *resource-based* view offers the theoretical basis for predicting a positive relationship between diversity and organizational performance. It states that resources constitute a sustainable competitive advantage for a firm to the extent that they create value, remain hard to imitate, and appear rare (Barney, 1991; Lado, Boyd, & Wright, 1992). The scholars of diversity and strategic human resource management argued that, since the competitive advantage gained from technological and physical resources has become easier to emulate, it is the human resources that provide the crucial differentiating factor between firms. Therefore, they can aid firms in gaining an enduring competitive advantage. However, in order for human capital to constitute a source of sustainable competitive advantage, it must create value, stay difficult to imitate, and remain rare (Barney & Wright, 1998).

According to the proponents of the resource-based view, cultural diversity in human capital constitutes a source of enduring competitive advantage for firms because it does create value that is both imperfectly imitable and rare. The value of cultural diversity comes from enhanced creativity, problem solving, and flexibility, all of which are stimulated by the interaction of individuals with diverse cultural backgrounds. Moreover, cultural diversity can add value to the firm in terms of reaching a broader customer base and adjusting its human resources to mirror the culturally diverse market targeted by the firm.

As for the limitability element, cultural diversity is hard to imitate due to social complexities and synergies created when culturally diverse people work together and cooperate to achieve organizational goals (Harrison, Price, & Bell, 1998; Richard, 2000; Richard et al., 2003). Moreover, it is almost impossible to create the same set of human resources with similar attributes and characteristics (Wright & McMahan, 1992). In addition, the competitors may not even attempt to imitate the resource because they may simply not realize that the increased creativity and flexibility of the competing firms comes from the cultural diversity of their workforce (Richard et al.).

As for the rarity element, the scholars argued that cultural diversity is a rare asset because there are not yet many firms who realize its value. Many firms still perceive diversity as a cost that needs to be managed and not as an asset that should be fostered. Furthermore, the representation of minorities in the labor market remains relatively sparse, and companies must compete for the individuals with the skills, qualifications, and characteristics needed for the firm within the small minority populations (Richard et al., 2003).

Richard et al. (2003) argued that the resource-based view does not consistently take into account the social context within which resources are embedded; therefore, the economic foundation of their analysis has to be supplemented with the contingency theory. The *contingency theory* states that the features of the environment, strategy, and structure all interact together and influence the organization. Richard et al. used the contingency theory to examine how the innovation-focused strategy may interact with cultural diversity to exert a positive influence on firm performance.

The innovation-focused strategy is chosen as a contingency variable because it allows the firm to assume a position in which it can exploit and benefit from cultural diversity. A firm can take advantage of its resources only if it is in a position to exploit and benefit from them (Barney & Wright, 1998; Richard, 2000). Therefore, a strategic focus on innovation can allow the firm to assume such a position with respect to cultural diversity, which is a resource of innovation and creativity.

The authors put forward the following hypothesis, for which they find empirical support later in the course of their study: “Racial diversity and innovation strategy will have a positive interaction effect on firm performance, such that the more a firm pursues an innovation strategy, the more it will benefit from a racially diverse workforce” (Richard et al., 2003, p. 114).

Richard et al. (2003) argued that the positive interaction effect between racial diversity and innovation strategy on firm performance indicates that a racially diverse workforce in conjunction with high levels of innovation can provide a competitive advantage to firms. In their study, racial diversity was likely to enhance performance for banks pursuing an innovation strategy, while it was likely to decline performance for banks low in innovation.

Richard et al. (2003) pointed to several implications of their study. They underlined that increasing workforce diversity may not benefit the firm in a direct manner. In order for a firm to benefit from diversity, it has to have the right context in place. In case of diversity, the right context is the growth- and innovation-focused business strategy. In the case when there is no appropriate context, diversifying the workforce of the firm might have detrimental effects on the firm’s performance.

Therefore, it is essential for the firm that is either racially diverse or seeking to increase their workforce diversity to assess their organizational strategy. The firm has to ensure that their organizational strategy corresponds with the attributes of a racially diverse workforce. Only then will the firm be able to ensue competitive advantage from the cultural diversity that it posseses.[7]

Interaction Between Diverse Individuals

The theoretical concepts developed within the field of organizational science point to another conditioning variable that is necessary for the positive outcomes of diversity to crystallize, which is the interaction and communication between diverse individuals. The value in diversity hypothesis states that the creation of new quality ideas stems from the interaction between diverse individuals, because it exposes the individuals to the diverse ideas and experiences of other people.

The interaction between diverse individuals is also considered crucial for the notion of *kaleidoscope thinking*. The most important condition necessary for kaleidoscope thinking to take place is for there to be contact with people from a variety of perspectives. Finally, the interaction between diverse individuals lies also at the basis of the process of *creative synergy*. Creative synergy is only possible when there is an interaction between diverse individuals inside of a group.

As stressed by the scholars of creative synergy and kaleidoscope thinking, the interactions between people with diverse perspectives, experiences, and backgrounds "has something to offer over and above the simple combination of individually generated ideas" (Kurtzberg & Amabile, 2001, p. 289). In case of the ongoing sharing of ideas, and twisting them over and over again, the interaction of individuals adds an extra value and generates a new product. This new product is a novel idea produced as a result of the interpersonal interaction between diverse individuals. Thus, the interaction between diverse individuals is a necessary condition for the ethnic diversity to be translated into creativity, and thus higher productivity.

Right Context on Country Level

The conditioning variables on the level of groups, firms, and organizations that have been identified by organizational science as critical for translating ethnic diversity into positive outcomes can be summarized as the following: (1) *valuing diversity*—and within valuing diversity: (a) integration and learning perspective, (b) verification of personal self-views, and (c) simultaneous verification of personal and social self-views; (2) *growth- and innovation-focused strategy*; and (3) *interaction between diverse individuals*. Each one of them can be translated to the level of countries.

Valuing Diversity on the Country Level—Democratic Pluralism

Valuing diversity on the country level means that a country is run by rules and policies that cherish diversity among its citizens. Cherishing diversity means that a country is encouraging the cultivation of diverse ethnocultural identities and practices of its citizens. It signifies that a country promotes the attitude of tolerance toward diversity among its citizens. When translated to the state level, a system that provides the best basis for valuing diversity is democratic pluralism.

As argued by Doran (2001), democratic pluralism seeks to harmonize and politically integrate the different ethnic groups living within a single state. It is based on principles that support the cultivation of diverse ethnocultural identities and practices of its citizens within a single state. Through allowing the diverse groups to retain their traditional culture and through endorsing a harmonious coexistence between diverse communal groups, democratic pluralism promotes tolerance and appreciation for cultural diversity.

The principles of democratic pluralism ensure that diverse communities not only can live in harmony with each other inside of a single state, but also can thrive spiritually, economically, linguistically, and intellectually. Pluralism protects the culture and identity of respective communities. Since the preferences of the communities are secure, the communities are able to participate in the activities of the larger state. Democratic process, on the other hand, helps to mediate the differences in preferences, which usually exist between the different communities, when making a common policy (Doran, 2001). Thus, it is a united concept of both pluralism and democracy that makes the system work and makes democratic pluralism successful in managing diversity within a state.

There are three additional elements within the value in diversity approach that help to build the system of appreciation toward ethnic diversity and, therefore, support democratic pluralism: (1) integration and learning perspective, (2) verification of personal self-views, and (3) simultaneous verification of personal and social self-views. They can take several forms on the level of countries.

Integration and Learning Perspective on Diversity on the Country Level

The integration and learning perspective on diversity regards diversity as a resource for learning and adaptive change. The diverse skills, perspectives, and experiences of the individuals are perceived as potentially valuable resources, which can be utilized with benefits.

When translated to the state level, the integration and learning perspective is reflected in policies that aim at integrating the diverse people into the society, as well as in policies that demonstrate that a country treats diversity as a learning resource. The policies that aim at integrating the diverse people into the society consist of (a) inclusive citizenship laws, and (b) multicultural policies; while the policies that demonstrate that a country treats diversity as a learning resource include policies that (a) encourage high-skilled immigration, and (b) ensure labor market access and promote social mobility for minorities.

It is important to notice that in regard to policies that aim at integrating the diverse people into the society, they are considered positive and desirable only in relation to immigrants, but not in relation to national minorities. The national minorities usually want to resist integration. They usually demand some form of self-government, so they would be able to live and work in their own culture and not have to integrate to the mainstream society. The immigrants, on the other hand, usually demand that they would be integrated into the larger society. As summarized by Will Kymlicka (2001a), "National minorities have resisted integration and fought to maintain or rebuild their own societal culture while immigrants have accepted the expectation that they will integrate into the dominant societal culture" (p. 156).

Inclusive Citizenship Laws

The country can be considered as having inclusive citizenship laws if (a) the naturalization of immigrants is a relatively easy process, (b) the country promotes citizenship among foreign born through explicit campaigns that encourage naturalization, or (c) the country has schemes that allow naturalization not only for regular but also for irregular and temporary immigrants.

Kymlicka (2001b) especially stressed the importance of the latter point, which is the access to citizenship for irregular and temporary immigrants, also referred to as *metics*. This term has been propagated by Michael Walzer (1983). He defines "metics" as groups of long-term residents who are nonetheless excluded from the society. The term has been borrowed from the ancient times where it referred to long-term residents who were nevertheless excluded from the *polis*. Due to the legal, political, economic, social, and psychological exclusion, the metics tend to exist in the margins of the larger society.

Kymlicka (2001b) explained that the metics include *irregular immigrants* and *temporary immigrants*. The irregular immigrants include those who either entered the country illegally or overstayed their visa, who are, therefore, not legally domiciled—for example, like many North Africans in Italy. The temporary immigrants include those who entered either as refugees seeking temporary protection or as *guestworkers* (from German: *Gastarbeiter*)—for example, like many Turks in Germany (Kymlicka).

The most basic claim of the metics is to regularize their status as permanent residents, as well as to gain access to citizenship. Kymlicka (2001b) argued that the approach that denies citizenship to metics is both morally and empirically flawed; "it violates the very idea of liberal democracy to have groups of long-term residents who have no right to become citizens" (p. 41). As for empirical evidence, it has been demonstrated that once the metics have settled, founded a family, and started raising their children, nothing short of expulsion is likely to persuade metics to return to their country of origin.

According to Kymlicka (2001b), the best-known examples of countries that are very reluctant to integrate metics into the national community are

Germany, Austria, and Switzerland. The policy in those countries toward the metics has been either the denial of citizenship or the attempt to dispose of them through expulsion or voluntary return. The policy did not bring the desired results. In most cases, it did not manage to force the metics out of the country. The metics stayed, but they became marginalized. This, in turn, led to the increase in criminality, political alienation, and even religious fundamentalism among those immigrants.

Kymlicka (2001b) argued that countries unwilling to naturalize their foreigners, including the metics, should not allow the foreigners to enter their territory in the first place. It is a common theme, he said, that the governments—knowing that their economy requires large numbers of illegal immigrants—would turn a blind eye to the situation. The same hypocritical approach can be recorded among the citizens who decry illegal immigration but are more than happy to take advantage of the cheaper services offered by illegal immigrants.

Kymlicka (2001b) stressed how crucial it is for a country to have a coherent policy in regard to illegal immigration. On the one hand, if it does not want to grant citizenship rights to metics, it should completely ban any forms of temporary or illegal immigration. On the other hand, if it allows the temporary and irregular immigrants to come into the country, it should introduce schemes that would make it possible for them to gain the citizenship:

> Some democracies may strongly dislike the idea of naturalizing foreigners. If so, they must not allow foreigners to settle in the first place, by eliminating 'guestworker' programs and by preventing illegal immigration. Democracies have no obligation to admit would-be metics. But if a country allows a group of non-nationals to settle and become permanent residents, then liberal-democratic principles require that these metics be able to naturalize. (p. 42)

Multicultural Policies

Multicultural policies can be taken on by a country in either an explicit or an implicit manner. In an explicit manner, the multicultural policies are adopted as an official policy of a state (e.g., Canada or Australia). In an implicit manner, the multicultural policies are adopted not as an official approach, but rather as part of a broader range of policies concerning immigration (e.g., the U.S. and many Western European countries).

The multicultural policies provide a favorable environment for the integration of the immigrants, and they assist the settlement process of immigrant communities. They make it easier for the immigrants to integrate because they do not require the assimilation to the dominant culture, which is usually a long, painful, and strenuous process. They only require the integration into the institutional and linguistic structure of the country. The immigrants are allowed to retain their distinctive culture, and they still become part of the broader society.

Furthermore, since they can retain their distinctive culture, the diversity of individuals is not going to be obliterated as a result of integration. In a situation when the immigrants are not permitted to retain their distinct cultural identities, the result of the integration is assimilation, and assimilation annihilates diversity. Therefore, only countries which have the approach of integration, but not assimilation, toward minorities can be considered as having an integration and learning perspective on diversity.

Openness Toward High-Skilled Immigration

A country that has a relatively high ratio of high-skilled immigration to low-skilled immigration demonstrates that it has a learning perspective on diversity. A country that employs immigrants in the high-skilled sectors of the economy, where the contribution of new ideas adds a lot of value, reveals that it recognizes the potential benefits of diversity for new idea creation and learning.

It should be underlined that this does not mean that the low-skilled diverse individual does not carry the potential benefit of creativity related to his or her diversity—the individual does. The creativity coming from the interaction of diverse individuals is also present in the context of low-skilled labor activities. However, the benefits coming from creativity in the low-skilled areas of the economy are lower than in the high-skilled areas because the latter are more focused on new knowledge production.

The different approach toward high-skilled immigration can be observed among the countries of North America on the one hand, and Continental Europe on the other. As argued by G. Pascal Zachary (2000), a journalist who writes about diversity issues, the countries of Continental Europe absorb foreigners as an act of charity, rather than as an act of increasing the country's competitiveness. Germany is chosen to illustrate the attitudes prevailing in Continental Europe toward high-skilled immigration. According to Zachary, the words of a known German migration scholar, Rainier Munz, give a good feeling about the present approach of Germans toward immigration: "The country doesn't want talented immigrants…Immigration is seen as a burden. If we take people, it's for humanitarian reasons, not because we want them." The reason why Germans do not want talented people from abroad, according to Munz, is because they "like their cozy world the way it is, and they want to avoid competition" (Zachary, p. 129).

Zachary (2000) argued that while the countries of North America to a large extent set their immigration targets based on potential economic benefits, the countries of Continental Europe do the opposite. By setting the immigration targets based on charity, the countries of Continental Europe increase the economic burden to their economies because the low-skilled laborers are less prepared to integrate and live in the new countries.

There is a striking similarity between the approach described by Zachary as prevalent in the countries of Continental Europe and the one described by the scholars of organizational science, known as the discrimination and fairness perspective. The discrimination and fairness perspective does not connect having a culturally diverse workforce with the enhancement of an organization's functioning. In that perspective, the reason for having a culturally diverse workforce is dictated by the moral imperative to ensure justice and a fair treatment. The empirical studies conducted on the level of firms showed that the discrimination and fairness perspective did not provide the right foundation and guidance needed to achieve the sustained benefits from diversity in terms of increased innovation, creativity, and openness to change.

Labor Market Access and Social Mobility for Minorities

A country that has favorable conditions for labor market access and social mobility for ethnolinguistic minorities reveals that it values diversity and has a learning perspective on diversity. Favorable laws concerning labor market access for the immigrants indicate that a country wants to persuade immigrants to enter the labor market. That, in turn, reveals that it sees value in their work. If the social mobility of immigrants in a given country is relatively high, it also means that their work is valued and that they receive a due recognition for it.

Furthermore, the two elements are usually considered by the scholars of immigration as the indications of an integrative approach of a country toward its foreign-born residents. Therefore, a country that encourages labor market access and social mobility of its immigrants shows that it has an integration and learning approach toward diversity.

Verification of Personal Self-Views on the Country Level

When translated to the level of countries, the verification of personal self-views of diverse individuals is possible when the country gives recognition to cultural difference. In simple words, this is possible when the state gives its citizens the feeling that it is "OK" to be culturally different, when it gives a feeling that it is fine to pursue your particular cultural identity—even if it is different from the cultural identity of the dominant group.

Generally speaking, a system that gives recognition to cultural difference of its citizens is plural democracy. As argued by Doran (2001), democratic pluralism is "a condition of society in which diverse ethnic, racial, religious, or social groupings maintain their autonomous participation in their traditional culture within the confines of a single civilization or state" (p. 5).

More specifically, a country is recognizant of diversity if its institutions are designed to accommodate diversity with a high regard for difference. In relation to national minorities, this requirement is fulfilled in case of *multinational federalism*. In relation to immigrants, this requirement is fulfilled in case of *immigrant multiculturalism*. Furthermore, a country can be considered as being recognizant of diversity if the attitude of its citizens toward diversity is tolerant and positive.

Multinational Federalism

The way in which multinational federalism accommodates the cultural diversity of national minorities is by shifting part of the power to regional political units. Doran (2001) argued that "[t]he wise government is the government that devolves as many decisions as possible to the local level in which communities can best express their collective wills" (p. 11).

In multination federations, the federal political units often correspond with distinct ethnocultural groups who desire to retain their self-government and cultural distinctiveness (Kymlicka, 2001b). As argued by Kymlicka, in multinational federations the boundaries and powers of one or more subunits are defined with the intention of enabling a national minority to exercise self-government. In such federations, the shifting of the power to the regional level controlled by national minorities is a way of accommodating the claims for recognition of cultural distinctiveness of the national minorities.

The examples of countries that use federalism for the very reason of accommodating minority groups include Canada (for the Quebecois), Belgium (for the Flemish), Spain (for the Catalans, Basques, and Galicians), and Switzerland (for the French and Italian speakers). Other multination federations around the world include Nigeria, Malaysia, India, Ethiopia, and Russia (Kymlicka, 2001b).

There are other types of federations that were not designed explicitly for the purpose of accommodating ethnocultural difference, but which have adopted some forms of territorial autonomy to accommodate their historic minorities. Kymlicka referred to them as *administrative-territorial federations* (2001b). There are also countries, which are not federations, that have adopted certain forms of quasi-federal territorial autonomy to accommodate the claims of their national minorities. All those countries that adopted some forms of territorial autonomy for their historical minorities can be called the *multination federations*, a term coined by Philip Resnick (1994).

Kymlicka (2001b) stated that, currently, we can see a growing trend toward quasi-federal forms of territorial autonomy as a way of accommodating the claims of national minorities and indigenous peoples. Following Resnick, he also referred to those countries as the multination federations, despite the fact that not all of them are federations in the technical sense:

> They are not all federations in the technical sense, but they all embody a model of the state in which national minorities are federated to the state through some form of territorial autonomy, and in which internal boundaries have been drawn, and powers distributed in such a way as to ensure that each national group is able to maintain itself as a distinct and self-governing societal culture. (p. 30)

The countries indicated by the scholars (Kymlicka, 2001b) as examples of multination federation, in a sense that they have adopted some quasi-federal forms of territorial autonomy, include the following: the United Kingdom (in reference to Scotland and Wales), the United States (in reference to Puerto Rico and the American Indians), Italy (nonfederation, in reference to German speakers in South Tyrol), Finland (nonfederation, in reference to Swedes in the Åland Islands), the Scandinavian countries (in reference to the Sami community) and New Zealand (in reference to the Maori community).

Kymlicka (2001b) argued that the trend toward multination federalism, understood in the broader sense, is very widespread in the West. Among Western democracies with national minorities, only France and Greece have firmly rejected any notion of territorial autonomy for their historic minorities. Most national minorities in Western democracies currently have more autonomy than they had in the 1990s and 2000s. Furthermore, there are hardly any national minorities that have had their autonomy reduced over this period.

Immigrant Multiculturalism

The way in which plural democracies accommodate the claims for recognition of the immigrants is through the adoption of multicultural policies. The existence of multicultural policies ensures that the immigrants can become part of the society without giving up their traditions and cultures, and without having to assimilate to the dominant culture of the country.

The immigrant multiculturalism is based on the assumption that pressured, quick integration, as well as the lack of recognition to diverse identities of the immigrants, might lead to undesirable results such as a serious damage to people's self-respect and sense of agency (Kymlicka, 2001a; Taylor, 1994). Charles Taylor (1994) argued that a nonrecognition or misrecognition can inflict a serious harm on a human. It can be a form of oppression; it can push someone into an imposed and destructive identity, imprisoning someone in a false, distorted, and reduced mode of being. He argued that "misrecognition shows not just a lack of due respect. It can inflict a grievous wound, saddling its victims with a crippling self-hatred. Due recognition is not just a courtesy we owe people. It is a vital human need" (p. 126).

The adoption of multicultural policies, in either an explicit or implicit manner, is a way in which plural democracies can aid their recognition of cultural difference in relation to immigrants. Kymlicka (2001a) presented a wide range of policies, which are usually associated with immigrant multiculturalism:

- *affirmative action programs* (e.g., preferential treatment of visible minorities in access to education, training, or employment);
- *representation in the state legislative or advisory institutions* (e.g., guarantees of a certain number of seats in the legislative and advisory institutions to ethnic minorities);
- *curriculum reform in schools* (e.g., revision to the history and literature curriculum within public schools to give greater recognition to the historical and cultural contributions of ethnocultural minorities; bilingual education programs for the children of immigrants at the primary school level);
- *institutional adaptation* (e.g., regulatory guidelines about ethnic stereotypes in the media; revision of the work schedules or dress

codes as to accommodate the religious holidays and practices of immigrant groups; adopting workplace harassment codes prohibiting racist comments);

- *public education programs* (e.g., antiracism educational campaigns; cultural diversity training for the police, social workers or healthcare professionals);
- *cultural development programs* (funding of ethnic festivals and ethnic studies programs; providing mother-tongue literacy courses for adult immigrants). (pp. 159, 163)

Kymlicka (2001b) stated that the multicultural model of immigrant integration is already very widespread in the West. The first country to officially adopt the multicultural policies was Canada in 1971, but since then, multiculturalism has been adopted by many other countries, from Australia and New Zealand to Sweden, Britain, and the Netherlands. Most recently, Germany is also moving closer to the immigrant model of multiculturalism. According to Kymlicka, currently in Western Europe only France and Greece continue to resist any official recognition of immigrant multiculturalism, while Switzerland and Austria continue to resist any serious move to integrate metics. Otherwise, argued Kymlicka, reiterating the words of Nathan Glazer (1997), "we are all multiculturalists now" (p. 88).

Kymlicka (2001b) stressed that even though the United States does not have an official multiculturalism policy adopted at the federal level, the country has implicitly adopted a multiculturalist approach. John C. Harles (2004), among other scholars who share this opinion, argued that, taking the official multiculturalism apart, the substance of multicultural policy is not much different in the United States and Canada. Moreover, the United States, with its nonexplicit multicultural approach, has been as successful in integrating immigrants as those countries that have officially adopted multiculturalism, for example, Canada or Australia.[8]

Positive Attitudes of the Citizens Toward Diversity

When assessing the level of recognition for cultural difference in a given country, one should also consider the attitudes of its citizens toward diversity. In order for the immigrants to feel respected and valued, they have to receive recognition not only from the state but also from fellow citizens. If the attitude of the citizens toward the immigrants is negative, attempts from the government to give recognition and make the immigrants feel valued and respected will fail. In order for the immigrants to feel valued and respected, they have to reassert themselves as worthy in everyday interactions with the other citizens.

The image of the immigrants presented by the media and by the political and public campaigns has a very important role to play in shaping a positive attitude toward immigrants. According to a study conducted in California (Cain, Citrin, & Wong, 2000), the variations in citizen's opinions concerning immigrants were not best explained by what goes on in local contexts, as many would assume. Actually, the variations were best explained by the citizen's political orientations, as well as by what they learned from the respective proethnic and antiethnic campaigns. Based on the California example, it appears that the way in which political leaders and the mass media frame the issues is more critical to racial and ethnic attitudes than the local context (Cain et al.). Therefore, it is essential to have positive media and political campaigns concerning ethnic issues.

Simultaneous Verification of Personal and Social Self-Views on the Country Level

When translated to the state level, the configuration in which both personal and social self-views can be verified by the members of the society occurs when the state (a) defines itself as a nation composed of diverse individuals, and (b) asserts that it perceives this diversity as a value. In such a case, the state gives the citizen a feeling that the cultural difference does not exclude the person from the society and that the cultural difference is actually valued and encouraged by the state.

Such a situation is possible on the state level if the country has a broad definition of nationhood, one which is inclusive and tolerant toward all the diverse individuals living in the country.

Broad Definition of Nationhood

In his recent study, Robert D. Putnam (2007) argued that immigration policy should not be just about numbers and borders, but it should also focus on promoting a sense of shared citizenship. He stressed the importance of creating new, cross-cutting forms of social solidarity and more encompassing identities in order to avert social fragmentation of diverse nations. The social identities should be redrawn in order to become more inclusive, and the objective for diverse nations should be "to create a novel 'one' out of a diverse 'many'" (p. 165).

A similar view is shared by Kymlicka (2001a), who advocated for the creation of a broad definition of national community for diverse nations. According to him, a broad definition of national community is not restricted to those of particular race, ethnicity, or religion: "anyone can join the nation if they want to do so" (p. 40). In such a situation, being part of the nation requires only the adherence to the institutional and linguistic structure of the country. It does not require the cultural assimilation to the dominant group.

Countries that are inclusive toward diverse individuals exhibit a thin conception of national identity:

> In order to make it possible for people from different ethnocultural backgrounds to become full and equal members of the nation, and in order to allow for the widest possible range of individual diversity and dissent, the terms of admission are relatively thin—e.g., learning the language, participating in common public institutions, and perhaps expressing a commitment to the long-term survival of the nation, but do not require adopting a particular religion or conception of the good life. (Kymlicka, 2001a, p. 40)

Michael Ignatieff (1993) named the thin conception of nationhood a *civic nationalism*, in opposition to ethnic nationalism, which is based on a thick conception of nation. The distinction has been adopted by many scholars of political science. In this standard view, the civic nationalism is a form of nationhood, which is defined purely in terms of adherence to certain principles of democracy and justice. The civic nations are neutral with respect to ethnocultural identities of their citizens, and in those nations ethnic dissent does not constitute the criteria for membership. The ethnic nationalism, on the contrary, defines the national membership based on common ethnic dissent, language, and culture. The ethnic nations perceive the reproduction of a specific ethnonational culture and identity as one of their most important goals (Pfaff, 1993).

Walzer (1992a, 1992b) argued that the United States is the clearest example of a state that is neutral with regard to language, history, and calendar of the various ethnic and national groups existing within its borders. A strong indication of the United States' neutrality, in terms of ethnic identity, is the fact that the nation does not have a constitutionally recognized official language.[9] According to Walter, the United States is a good example of a country where state and ethnicity have been separated, and the state stands above all the various ethnic and national groups present in the society.

The examples of states where the idea of nationhood is perceived in a more narrow sense, and thus less inclusive to diverse individuals, are most of the countries of Continental Europe. As argued by Francis Fukuyama (2004a; 2004b), a lot of the European countries until most recently have had, or still have, a definition of nationality based on ethnicity. Fukuyama argued that such thick a definition of nationality is not open to newcomers. It constitutes a problem because it makes it very hard, or even impossible, for the immigrants to integrate, and that often leads to their marginalization in the society:

> [T]he problem in Europe is that they do not have a concept of citizenship, in most European countries, that would allow Muslim immigrants to really assimilate; the way people can come to the United States and hope to become Americans. That is a relatively easy process in the U.S. and one that has been done by a lot of immigrants in the United States; and that involves a couple of things. It involves defining citizenship in a universal, democratic way, but one that is fundamentally open to people. The Germans did not do this up until 2000; the German citizenship law said that you had to have a German mother, so that was really ethnically based. There is still much more ethnic consciousness, even though it is not the official policy. The Europeans have a much

more ethnic sense of who they are as a community. (Fukuyama, 2004b)

Growth- and Innovation-Focused Strategy on the Country Level

According to the scholars of organizational science (e.g., Richard et al., 2000; 2003), diversity is a resource that needs a special strategy in order for a firm to benefit from it. Their research showed that the firms were able to accrue a competitive advantage from a racially diverse workforce when their human resources were in line with the strategy of the firm. That happened when the strategy emphasized growth and innovation. This same logic applies to the level of countries. Therefore, if a country wants to take advantage of the diversity it possesses, it has to have the right strategy in place—a strategy focused on growth and innovation.

When translated to the state level, a growth- and innovation-based strategy is present when a country pursues a strategy that aims at strengthening the competitiveness and innovativeness of the economy. A good indication of the existence of a growth-focused strategy on a country level would be the existence of good business climate and flexible labor markets. The existence of an innovation-focused strategy on a country level would be indicated by relatively high levels of spending on innovation, more specifically by the levels of expenditure on research and development (R&D).

Interaction Between Diverse Individuals on the Country Level

Based on the theory of organizations, the interaction and communication between diverse individuals is necessary for ethnic diversity to be translated into creativity, and thus higher productivity. Only if the diverse individuals interact and communicate with each other, presenting their different views on the issues, can the benefits of diversity be realized.

When translated to the state level, the interaction and communication between diverse individuals is possible if they have contact with each other at various levels of social life, which I refer to as *mixing*. Furthermore, an element that makes the communication among diverse individuals possible is the existence of a common language. It does not have to be only one common language; it could be more than one. However, it is important that there is a common language in which all the members of the society can communicate.

Mixing

Contact between diverse individuals is possible when there is a mixing between different ethnocultural groups of the society, which occurs on the level of secondary group relationships, as well as on the level of primary group relationships. According to Milton M. Gordon (1964), primary group relationships are based on the intimate bonds present in the context of family and friendships. The secondary group relationships relate to the interactions in the context of jobs, institutions, and more formal interactions. I refer to the mixing on the two levels of social life as the secondary level mixing and the primary level mixing.

In the secondary level mixing, people of different ethnic backgrounds are placed into secondary contacts with each other. Such a situation is possible when there are no ethnic barriers in the operation and employment of public and private institutions, facilities, and services. Moreover, it is possible when there are no barriers to settlement based on ethnicity. Secondary level mixing is usually related to the full achievement of civil rights for all groups constituting the society.

The primary level mixing involves the formation of intimate relationships of love, caring, and friendship between people from different ethnocultural groups. Since the primary contacts across ethnic lines increase the warmth, personal friendships, and trust between ethnically diverse individuals, they also increase tolerance toward differences in those people who are engaged in these contacts. Stereotypes fall away and are exchanged with positive attitudes toward difference and change. Furthermore, since the attitudes were created by the primary contacts, they are lasting and deep. Thus, primary level mixing contributes greatly to the building of tolerance for diversity in the society.

Common Language

The country should encourage the cultivation of diverse languages and cultures; however, at the same time, the country should have at least one common language. There should be at least one language that is spoken by the entire population of the country. This common language would ensure that all the members of the society can fully participate in the functioning of the state. Therefore, the state should strongly encourage and sponsor language courses for all members of the society.

Right Context Identified

To summarize, the right context that allows countries to translate ethnic diversity into positive outcomes consists of the following elements:

1. **Value in diversity—democratic pluralism**
   a. Integration and learning approach policies
      - Inclusive citizenship laws
      - Multicultural policies
      - Openness toward high-skilled immigration
      - Labor market access and social mobility for minorities

   b. Verification of personal self-views
      - Multinational federalism
      - Immigrant multiculturalism
      - Positive attitudes of the citizens toward diversity

   c. Simultaneous verification of personal and social self-views
      - Broad definition of nationhood
2. **Growth- and innovation-focused strategy**
   - Good business climate
   - Flexible labor markets
   - High spending on research and development (R&D)
3. **Interaction between diverse individuals**
   - Mixing
   - Common language

Operationalization of Country Level Analysis

Hypothesis

The underlying idea of this analysis is that ethnolinguistic diversity can constitute a resource for a country that possesses it. The channel through which ethnolinguistic diversity can positively affect the economy is through the increases in creativity, entrepreneurship, and openness to change that it brings about. The value of ethnolinguistic diversity in human capital comes from enhanced creativity, problem solving, flexibility, and adaptability, all of which are stimulated by the interaction of diverse individuals.

Nonetheless, the positive impact of ethnolinguistic diversity on the economy depends on the context in which it is placed. Ethnolinguistic diversity can lead to higher creativity, but only if there is the right context in place. In the absence of the right context, diversity does not bring positive economic outcomes—and even more, it can be a detriment to the economy. Therefore, the existence of the right context is crucial.

Given the aforementioned, I put forward the following hypothesis: *The countries that are ethnolinguistically more heterogeneous would have higher levels of innovativeness (creativity, openness to change, and entrepreneurship) than the countries that are more ethnolinguistically homogeneous, but only if they have the right context in place.* In other words, the hypothesis claims that the relationship between ethnolinguistic diversity and innovativeness is not unconditional, but it is a significant function of the right context variable.

Dependent, Independent, and Intervening Variables

Dependent Variables

The dependent variable of this analysis is the innovativeness of the country, or more precisely, the innovativeness of its people. I call this dependent variable Innovation. Additionally, since the concept of innovativeness can be seen as three-dimensional, I would like to distinguish three other dependent variables, which are the subparts of innovation: creativity, openness to change, and entrepreneurship.

However, due to the lack of comprehensive and comparable data, I am not able to directly include the entrepreneurship variable into the analysis. Entrepreneurship is usually measured by business start-up (or birth) rates. As argued in OECD's *The Statistics Newsletter* (2005b), there are big methodological differences in national data sets concerning business start-ups, and those differences do not allow for a consistent international comparability of the data.

The newsletter mentions that the OECD is currently undertaking steps to create a comprehensive and comparable data set on business start-ups. At this time, however, such data has not yet been distributed. Therefore, the entrepreneurship variable cannot be directly included into the analysis at this point.

The analysis includes the entrepreneurship dimension in an indirect way through the creativity variable. The creativity variable is partially measured by the size of the services sector and the size of the knowledge-intensive market services. Both of those variables are related and dependent on the levels of entrepreneurship existing in the society, because entrepreneurship is needed for the creation of the firms in the services sector. Thus, the measure of creativity also includes the entrepreneurial dimensions of innovativeness.

In result, I utilize three dependent variables for this analysis: creativity, openness to change, and innovation. The creativity variable is intended to measure the creation of new knowledge (and to a limited extent, when it is related to entrepreneurship, also the commercialization of new knowledge[10]). The openness to change variable is intended to measure the diffusion of new knowledge. Finally, the innovation variable is supposed to incorporate all of the aforementioned dimensions of innovativeness, so it comprises both the creativity and the openness to change variables put together.

I am aware of the fact that the direct inclusion of the measures of entrepreneurship would make the innovation variable more complete; however, due to the lack of comparable data on entrepreneurship, I will have to consent with including entrepreneurship only in an indirect way into the analysis.

Independent Variables

The independent variable of the analysis is ethnolinguistic diversity. This variable intends to measure the ethnolinguistic fractionalization of the country. Its purpose is to provide an indication of how societies differ between each other with respect to the ethnolinguistic diversity. I would like to include two dimensions of ethnolinguistic diversity in the analysis. The first dimension relates to the ethnolinguistic differentiation stemming from old, indigenous minorities. The second dimension relates to ethnolinguistic differentiation stemming from the more recent waves of immigration.

The immigration aspect of diversity has not yet been included in the analysis of other scholars concerning the impact of diversity on the economic outcomes. I would like to include this measure in order to see whether the effects of indigenous diversity are similar to the effects of diversity stemming from immigration.

Despite the fact that diversity stemming from immigration might be smaller in magnitude than indigenous diversity, its effect on innovativeness might be comparable to the effect of indigenous diversity. It could be due to the fact that the diversity coming from immigration is more fresh or new. Therefore, it might carry an even stronger creativity potential than the diversity coming from old minorities, which might be already strongly assimilated into the dominant culture.

Intervening Variables

Besides the independent and the dependent variables, the theory calls for inclusion of the intervening variable, which is the Right Context variable. It is supposed to act as a catalyst for the positive relationship between the ethnolinguistic diversity and innovativeness. Based on the research of diversity in organizational science, as well as on application of that research to the country level, there are three main elements of the right context: (1) *democratic pluralism*—value in diversity, and within value in diversity: (a) integration and learning perspective, (b) verification of personal self-views, (c) simultaneous verification of personal and social self-views; (2) *growth- and innovation-focused strategy*; and (3) *interaction between diverse individuals*.

Ideally, all of the elements of the right context should be included into our analysis. However, due to the problems with data availability, it is impossible to do so. This analysis is designed as a quantitative analysis. Therefore, it can include only those elements of the right context that can be measured in a quantitative way.

Unfortunately, a lot of the elements of the right context require qualitative measures and are hard to measure quantitatively. Such elements include the democratic pluralism (with the exception of the integration and learning perspective, which can be somehow measured quantitatively), and the interaction between diverse individuals.

Thus, out of all the elements of the right context indicated by the theory, only the integration and learning perspective, as well as the growth- and innovation-focused strategy, can be measured confidently in a quantitative way. Therefore, the analysis directly includes only those two intervening variables, and they indicate the existence of the right context.

However, since the democratic pluralism has been identified by the theory as crucial for translating diversity into innovativeness, I have tried to incorporate it into the analysis in an indirect manner. In order to do so, I have included in the analysis only those countries that can be considered as plural democracies. I purposely have limited the sample size and use only the OECD countries as a sample for the analysis. In that way, democratic pluralism also is integrated into the analysis; however, not directly as a variable, but indirectly as a constant.

It is important to note that there are differences between the OECD countries with respect to the quality of democratic pluralism. However, all of them, more or less, can be qualified as plural democracies. Therefore, all are potentially in the position to exploit the benefits of ethnolinguistic diversity.

Model

Sample Size

The 30 OECD countries constitute a sample for this analysis. I am aware of the fact that such a small sample size for a cross-country regression weakens the validity of the results. However, the goal of the analysis is not to provide robust proof for the hypothesis, but rather to make a preliminary check of whether the hypothesis is plausible. Since, until now, there has been no attempt in the literature to test such a hypothesis, I would like to make a first step in that direction. It is left to future research to assess whether this specific hypothesis holds when the sample size is enlarged and more countries are included into the analysis.

The choice of the OECD countries was dictated by two reasons. While the first reason was dictated by the need to include democratic pluralism into the analysis, the second reason was related to data availability. The OECD collects broad and extensive data for its members, which allows for a greater choice of variables. For many of the variables that are used in the analysis, there is either no data or only very limited data available outside of the OECD countries. Choosing the OECD countries as a sample allowed the analysis to be more profound and comprehensive.

Method

An empirical quantitative analysis was used to test the proposed hypothesis. I used single cross-country regression analyses to evaluate the influence of ethnolinguistic diversity on innovativeness. Most importantly, I used single cross-country regressions to assess the impact of the right context on the relationship between diversity and innovativeness.

However, before testing the hypothesis with the regression analysis, I used the factor analysis to identify the independent, dependent, and intervening variables. First, I chose a number of variables, which appear to capture in the best way the various dimensions of ethnolinguistic diversity, innovativeness, and right context. Then, I conducted factor analyses to see whether there are underlying factors among those variables.

Where there were underlying factors, and if they were consistent in terms of content, I grouped the variables that form the separate factors into distinct single scales. The scales were then used as the independent, dependent, and intervening variables in the regression analyses. In the case when there were no underlying factors, I had to choose single variables as a measure for the independent, dependent, and the intervening variables.

Regression Framework

The proposed hypothesis states that the relationship between ethnolinguistic diversity and innovativeness is not unconditional, but is a significant function of the right context variable. In order to test that hypothesis, I conducted the same two regressions for each of the dependent, independent, and intervening variables.

In the equation of the model, the dependent variable is represented by the generic variable: Innovation (*I*); the independent variable by the generic variable: Diversity (*Div*); and the intervening variable by the generic variable: Right Context (*RC*). The two regressions were conducted for all the dependent, independent, and intervening variables that are identified by the factor analysis.

The aim of the first regression was to establish whether there is a relationship between diversity and innovativeness, even without the right context in place. The aim of the second regression was to test the hypothesis and to establish whether the positive relationship between diversity and innovativeness is indeed a function of the right context variable.[11]

The first regression is represented with the following generic equation:

$$I = \alpha_0 + \alpha_1 \, Div \qquad (1)$$

If not a specific choice of the sample, I would have expected the first regression to be insignificant because, according to the hypothesis, the relationship between diversity and innovativeness is only positive and significant when the right context is in place. However, due to the choice of the OECD countries as a sample for the analysis, I should have already expected a positive and significant relationship between diversity and innovativeness.

The choice of the OECD countries purports that one of the right context variables, which is democratic pluralism, is already accounted for in the analysis. Therefore, in this group of countries the relationship between diversity and innovativeness should be already positive and significant. In other words, I expected that for plural democracies, diversity matters unconditionally (alone) for innovativeness. However, the significance might not be very strong because the other right context variables are still missing from the equation.

Given that the results of the first regression show some positive significance, and thus give basis for the claim that in plural democracies, ethnolinguistic diversity leads to higher innovativeness, I carry on with the second regression. The second regression is represented with the following generic equation:[12]

$$I = \alpha_0 + \alpha_1\, Div + \alpha_2\, DivRC \qquad (2)$$

The second regression equation has been derived in the following way:

$$I = \alpha_0 + \alpha_1\, Div$$

$$\alpha_1 = (\gamma_0 + \gamma_1\, RC)$$

hence,

$$I = \alpha_0 + (\gamma_0 + \gamma_1\, RC)\, Div$$

$$I = \alpha_0 + \gamma_0\, Div + \gamma_1\, RCDiv \ \text{ or } \ I = \alpha_0 + \alpha_1\, Div + \alpha_2\, DivRC$$

The second regression was the actual test of the proposed hypothesis. It tested whether the relationship between diversity and innovativeness is indeed conditioned by the existence of the right context. In other words, it tested whether the significance of the relationship between diversity and innovativeness is indeed a positive function of the right context variable.

In order to test the conditionality argument of the right context variable, I introduced into the second regression an interaction term of diversity and the right context variable *DivRC*. The interaction term of diversity and the right context show how diversity matters at different levels of the right context. Thus, looking at the interaction term shows whether the importance of diversity for innovativeness indeed increases with the presence of the right context. Thus, it reveals whether the relationship between diversity and innovativeness is indeed conditioned by the existence of the right context variable.

If the interaction term α_2 would be statistically less significant than the coefficient on diversity α_1, then it would mean that the relationship between diversity and innovativeness is not dependent on the right context. However, if the interaction term α_2 would be statistically more significant than the coefficient on diversity α_1, then it would mean that diversity matters more for innovativeness when it is combined with the right context. In other words, it would mean that the relationship between diversity and innovativeness is a function of the right context.

Furthermore, the coefficient on diversity would indicate the impact of diversity on innovativeness when the right context is at a level of zero. Thus, it would reveal what the relationship between diversity and innovativeness is without the existence of the right context. Therefore, the second regression should not only tell us how the importance of diversity for innovativeness changes with the existence of the right context, but also reveal the relationship between diversity and innovativeness when the right context is not present.

To conclude, I applied a two-regression model to test the hypothesis. The model was employed for each of the dependent, independent, and intervening variables that were distinguished through the factor analyses. The first regression was just a preliminary step to test the grounds for further analyses. The second regression was the actual test of the hypothesis. Therefore, the results of the second regression are crucial for assessing the plausibility of the hypothesis, which states that the relationship between ethnolinguistic diversity and innovativeness is a positive function of the right context variable.

ENDNOTES

1. A question arises whether having more ideas in a heterogenous group is likely to produce only positive results in terms of creativity? Having more ideas does not necessarily mean that they are only good ones. It is the *quality* of the ideas and not necessarily the *quantity* that would matter for reaching the optimal solution. Therefore, it is essential to consider the quality of the ideas rather than their quantity, and that is the research approach adopted by the scholars of organizational science. The *value-in-diversity* scholars focus on measuring the impact of diversity on the quality of ideas generated by diverse groups, and their results show that the impact is positive.
2. The scholars studying ethnic diversity in organizations mention that there has been relatively little research conducted on ethnic/race diversity and its impact on organizations; greater emphasis has been placed on diversity with respect to age, gender, and tenure (Williams & O'Reilly, 1998).
3. The *resource-based* theory argues that the sources of sustainable competitive advantage must be valuable, imperfectly imitable, and rare; since ethnic diversity meets these requirements, it may serve as a source of advantage.
4. Here, innovation is not understood in the full Schumpeterian sense, but it is understood as creativity.
5. In Richard's (2000) article, the term "cultural diversity" refers to racial diversity; the two terms are used interchangeably throughout the article.
6. The study of Richard et al. (2003) used the terms "racial diversity" and "cultural diversity" interchangeably.
7. The research is in accordance with the earlier writings in the organizational science, which stated that the effects of diversity may depend on the nature of the group's task (Hambrick, Davison, Snell, & Snow, 1993; Iles & Hayers, 1996; Jackson, 1992). According to these earlier writings, diversity is best suited for creative tasks, while homogeneity is more desirable for routine tasks. If the task requires creativity and divergent thinking, then diversity is desirable and beneficial because it provides the varied perspectives and the consideration of a broader range of options and alternatives, and thus greater stimulation and creativity. However, if the task is defined, structured, and routine, then diversity might be less beneficial or even impairing to the effectiveness of the group. In routine tasks, the need for creativity is low but a need for group cohesiveness is high, and diversity brings the opposite to what is needed for a routine task.

8. In that point, Harles disagreed with Kymlicka, who argued that Canada is the most successful in the integration of immigrants, closely followed by Australia; Harles argued that the United States is as successful as the other two.
9. Some scholars of political science (e.g., Will Kymlicka, 2001) put in question the concept of ethnocultural neutrality of the liberal democratic states. They argued that the claim that civic nations are ethnoculturally neutral is a myth that is false both historically and conceptually. They argued that, at one point or another, virtually all liberal democracies have attempted to diffuse a single societal culture throughout all of its territory, and United States is not an exception in that regard. The U.S. government deliberately engaged in the process of establishing the hegemony of English and designing the boundaries of the states to ensure that Anglophones would be a majority in each of the 50 states. Those decisions were not unintended, but were made with the intention of promoting integration into what we call *societal culture*. However, it is important to stress that Kymlicka understood societal culture in a very thin sense, as a conception of culture, which focuses on a common language and societal institution. And his use of the term *culture* is in conflict with the way it is used in most academic disciplines, where culture is defined in a more thick sense, referring to the sharing of specific history, rituals of life, folk customs, and habits. I argue that if the term *culture* is defined in a more thick way, which is in accordance with the prevailing orthodoxy in most academic disciplines, then we can still talk about the neutrality of the liberal democratic state.
10. If the entrepreneurship variable would have been directly included in the analysis, it would have measured the commercialization of new knowledge.
11. In all of the regressions, the error term was omitted.
12. Ideally, the second regression should also include a separate Right Context variable *RC* and have the following shape: $I = \alpha_0 + \alpha_1 Div + \alpha_2 RC + \alpha_3 DivRC$. However, it is impossible to run such a regression due to the problem of high multicolinearity (e.g., for the variables *I, Div, RCi, DivRCi*, the *mean vif* equals 27.57). Hence, I had to run the interacted regression without a separate *RC* variable.

CHAPTER 4

EMPIRICAL ANALYSIS

MEASUREMENT OF VARIABLES

Except for two cases, I rely on the OECD data for the analysis. The OECD has collected very comprehensive data sets for its member states. Since all of the countries in the sample belong to the OECD, using the OECD data ensures the most complete and coherent data for the analyses.

Non-OECD data has been used to measure the ethnolinguistic diversity stemming from old minorities, because the OECD does not have data for it. To measure the indigenous ethnolinguistic diversity, I have used two measures. The first one is the Ethnolinguistic Fractionalization (ELF) index, which has been widely used in the previous studies concerning the impact of ethnic diversity on economic outcomes. The second one is the measure of ethnolinguistic fractionalization created by Alberto Alesina, which is a more recent measure.

The non-OECD data is used in relation to Internet technology. This is because the data published by the OECD does not include the data on generic top level domains (gTLDs) when counting the country-related

Internet hosts. The OECD bases its country-related Internet hosts data on the registrations under the country code top level domains (ccTLDs) (OECD, 2005a, 2005f).[1] It induces a problem of data adequacy because the gTLDs constitute 64% of all the registrations (in the United States specifically, it is 95%). Thus, excluding the gTLDs from the count significantly distorts the picture of Internet diffusion between countries.

For that reason, I use an alternative source of data for Internet technology, which is the World Telecommunication Indicators Database published by the International Telecommunication Union (ITU).[2] The ITU data takes into account both the ccTLDs and the gTLDs, and it has been broadly used as an indicator of Internet technology diffusion.

However, the ITU data is not free from problems. It assumes that the majority of gTLDs are U.S.-based registrations, and it assigns all of the codes that are not country codes to the United States. Therefore, as noted in the "ITU Technical Notes" (n.d.), the number of Internet hosts can be considered only as an approximation. Still, the distortion of data is smaller than in the case when the gTLDs are entirely removed from the data.

Concerning the time reference of the data, I use the latest data available. In the cases when there is missing data for some of the countries for a given year, I utilize the latest data available from the previous years. Overall, I apply yearly data. However, in certain cases (such as patents), I make use of data averaged over a period of time to provide a more balanced view of the production of patents. I also bring in time averages in situations when that form of data is available for the biggest number of countries (e.g., the contribution of ICT capital to GDP growth).

Measurement of Dependent Variables

I chose an array of variables to measure each of the dependent variables: creativity, openness to change, and innovation. Several measures have been selected for each of the dependent variables because there is no established canon of how to measure them. Bringing in a lot of diverse measures ensures that the different dimensions of creativity, openness to change, and innovation are captured by the analysis.

Creativity

The creativity variable is intended to measure the creativity and inventiveness of a given country. It should measure the invention part of the innovation process. Thus, the creativity variable should measure the new thinking, the novelty of the ideas, and (in general) the creation of new knowledge in the society.

There are several indicators that have been used by the researchers to measure the creation of new knowledge in the society. One of them is the literature-based innovation output indicator. The indicator measures the value and importance of the new knowledge. It consists of data on scientific publications, also referred to as *bibliometrics*. Originally, the bibliometrics measure was limited only to collecting data on numbers of scientific articles and other publications. However, recently more sophisticated and multidimensional techniques, based on citations of articles (and more recently, also patents), have been developed (OECD, 2002).

I use one of the OECD scientific output indicators, which is the relative prominence of cited scientific literature indicator, to measure both the value and importance of the new knowledge created in a given country. The relative prominence of cited scientific literature weighs the volume of published articles by the frequency of citations. It is measured by comparing a country's share of cited literature with its world share of scientific articles, and a country's citation of its own literature is excluded. The citations attest not only to the productivity but also to the influence of scientific literature. Moreover, the international citations highlight the visibility of scientific research beyond national boundaries (OECD, 2005f). Therefore, the relative prominence of cited scientific literature is a good indicator of the magnitude of valuable new knowledge produced in a country (Acs, Anselin, & Varga, 2002).

Other than literature-based indicators, the other indicators that have been used by the researchers to measure the creation of new knowledge in the society are the patent counts. Patents are exclusive rights issued by authorized bodies to inventors to make use of and exploit their inventions for a limited period of time (OECD, 2004a). The patent counts are actually the most frequently used country-related measure of the inventive output. The literature-based indicators are less frequently used in the literature because they are relatively expensive to produce; thus, they are available only for selected years and for selected countries (Acs et al., 2002).

Patents have been widely used as a proxy for innovative output, but the measure has well-known drawbacks. First, many patents have no technological or economic value while others do, but those differences are not reflected in the patent counts. The patent counts assume all patents to be of generally equal value, and that is very misleading. Second, many innovations are not patented, and others are covered by multiple patents. That again makes patent counts a misleading measure of the inventive capacity of a country (OECD, 2005e). Due to the drawbacks of patent data, the publications suggest that the number of patents should be used only in conjunction with other indicators (OECD, 2002).

I would like to point to another drawback of patent counts, which is their low utility for measuring the inventions in the services sector. The patent system was developed under very different circumstances than the current ones (Kahin, 2004). The system was created in the realm of an industrial economy to measure the inventions of the most vibrant sector of the economy that, at that time, was the manufacturing sector. Those inventions were tangible in nature.

The situation is different now. In the last few decades, there has been a major change in the structure of the economy. The importance of the manufacturing industry has declined, and services have become the most vital sector of the economy. There has been a shift of the economic activities between sectors and the associated reallocation of jobs.

According to the OECD reports, the advanced economies have become richer, and an increasing proportion of consumption and production has taken place in the services sector. The services sector has expanded rapidly over the last 20–30 years and currently accounts for over two thirds of the whole OECD business activity, 70% of jobs, and 70% of total OECD value added (OECD, 1998; Tamura, Sheehan, Martinez, & Kergroach, 2005).

Traditionally, the services have been considered less innovative than manufacturing. However, the most recent studies have shown that the services are more innovative than previously considered. In some areas, such as knowledge-intensive business services, they are even more innovative than the manufacturing industry (Tamura et al., 2005).

Despite the fact that many services sectors are considered highly innovative, however, their inventive output is very hard to measure (OECD, 2000a). The shift toward a service economy has not been accompanied by a better understanding of how to measure the inventions in the services sector, which are mostly intangible in their nature.

Recently, the service sector firms started to employ the formal mechanism of intellectual property (IP) protection, such as patents, copyrights, and trademarks, to protect their invention from imitation. This is especially true in relation to software patents and "business methods" patents. However, a host of innovative activity in services is organizational and disembodied in their nature, and thus it is very hard to capture by the standard measures of innovation (Tamura et al., 2005). Therefore, still most inventions in the services sector are not patented, and so they are not accounted for by the patent data (OECD, 2000).

Since the invention in the services sector is not well accounted for by the patent statistics, and since the services play a key role in the economy, I have decided to employ some indicative measures of the magnitude and the quality of the inventive activities that take place in the services sector. I use the development of the services sector in general as an indicator of the inventive activities that take place in that sector.

An additional reason for which it is important to include the data on services is that the services rely heavily on human capital in their innovative effort. As stressed in the OECD publications, human capital is a pillar of the innovative process in the labor-intensive services sector. Furthermore, human capital appears to be more important for the innovative process in the services sector than it is in the manufacturing sector. According to the third European Community Innovation Survey (CIS3), the share of employees with higher education is, in general, larger in market services than in manufacturing (Tamura et al., 2005).[3]

Since the services sector relies heavily on human capital for its innovation process, the impact of ethnolinguistic diversity should then be especially evident in the development of the services sector. Because of this, it seems sensible to include the data on the development of the services sector into our analysis.

At the same time, I would like to also include the data on the development of the manufacturing sector in order to test the soundness of the argument that the inventions in the manufacturing sector are much more "patentable" than the inventions in the services sector. If the argument has any basis, then I would expect the countries with a stronger manufacturing sector to have a higher number of patents than the countries with a weaker manufacturing sector, but with a stronger services sector. If the argument has no basis, then I would not expect any relationship between the development of the manufacturing and the services sectors, and the number of patents.

I adhere to the OECD database to extract the data on the development of the services and the manufacturing sector, as well as the data on the patents. As for the patent data, I use the patent counts relative to the population of the country. In order to have the most comprehensive coverage of patent data, I first include several categories of patent counts starting from the triadic patent families[4] and then go through the different groups of patent counts from the European Patent Office (EPO) and the U.S. Patent & Trademark Office (USPTO).[5] The EPO and USPTO patent counts consist of the following categories: the patents as a whole, the information and communication technology (ICT) patents, and the biotechnology patents.

As for the data on the development of the services sector, I use the following indicators: the share of knowledge-intensive market services in total gross value added, the contribution of the services sector to productivity growth, and the share of services in total value added. The development of the manufacturing sector is measured by the following: the share of high and medium-high technology manufactures in total gross value added, and the share of manufacturing in total value added.

I use two other measures that give an additional indication on the magnitude and quality of new knowledge created in the economy. These measures include the following: the technology balance of payments (TBP) as percent of GDP and the contribution of ICT capital to GDP growth.

The technology receipts and payments constitute the main form of disembodied technology diffusion (OECD, 2005f), thus the technology balance of payments should be a good indicator of the inventions that take place not only in the manufacturing sector but also in the services sector (at least those related to technology). The TBP measures different aspects of international technology transfers: license fees, patents, purchases and royalties, know-how, research, and technical assistance. The trade in technology is composed of four main categories: transfer of techniques; transfer of design, trademarks and patterns; services with technical content; and industrial R&D (OECD, 2005f). The fees associated with the technology transfers relate to production-ready technologies. Thus, the TBP is a good indicator of the quality of the inventions. It is also a good indicator of the magnitude of the new knowledge created in a country because it measures the amount of technology sold to other countries.

The contribution of ICT capital to GDP growth is a measure that has been developed within the OECD framework (Colecchia & Shreyer, 2002; Shreyer, 2000). It uses a well-established growth accounting framework to assess the role of ICTs as capital inputs and the contribution of these capital inputs to output growth (Shreyer). It seems to be a good indicator of the creativity of a given country because it shows how creative the countries are in applying the new technologies into productive uses.

There have been differences observed among the OECD countries concerning the contribution of ICT capital to GDP growth. While both the investment in and use of information technology have been widely spread among all the OECD countries, some countries were much better than others in turning the new technology into productive uses.

One of the reasons for this could be the difference in creativity potential between countries. Most probably, some countries are simply more creative than others in finding productive applications of the new technology, and thus seizing the benefits of the new knowledge. In my analysis, the differences in creativity levels between countries are attributed to the differences in ethnolinguistic diversity existing in those countries. Based on the hypothesis, I would expect the more ethnolinguistically diverse countries to be more creative in applying the new knowledge than the more homogeneous countries.

To conclude, I have identified 15 variables to measure the different dimensions of creativity, which are listed as follows: relative prominence of cited scientific literature, triadic patents per population, EPO patents per population, USPTO patents per population, ICT patents EPO per population, ICT patents USPTO per population, biotech patents EPO per population, biotech patents USPTO per population, share of knowledge-intensive market services in total gross value added, share of high and medium-high technology manufactures in total gross value added, contribution of the services sector to productivity growth, share of services in total value added, share of manufacturing in total value added, TBP as percent of GDP, and the contribution of ICT capital to GDP growth (in percentage points). All those variables are intended to provide an estimation of the creation of new knowledge in the society.

Openness to Change

The openness to change variable is intended to measure the openness of the society to new ideas and knowledge that is produced by the creative minds of the human society. Thus, the openness to change variable should measure the ability of a society to adapt to both changing technological trends and new emerging technologies. Therefore, while the creativity variable is intended to measure the creation of new knowledge, the openness to change variable is intended to measure the diffusion of new knowledge in the society.

The diffusion of new knowledge in the society is usually measured by the diffusion of ICT in the economy. According to the OECD publications, the core indicator of ICT diffusion is the investment in ICT (OECD, 2003). Therefore, I use the investment in ICT as one of the indicators of knowledge diffusion. I also add an extra variable related to ICT investment, which is the investment in software. Both of those measures indicate how the society is absorbing the new technology by investing in that new technology.

The other indicators, which are widely used to measure the diffusion of ICT in the society, are the indicators of Internet and computer diffusion. The ones that are the most commonly used are the secure servers, Internet hosts, and Internet users. I also add the indicator that measures the number of personal computers (PCs).[6] All those indicators measure the uptake of the ICT technology in the society.

The secure servers indicator measures the number of servers that use secure software for purchasing goods and services or transmitting privileged information over the Internet, for example, credit cards details. Therefore, the secure servers have been widely used as the indicators for the development of electronic commerce (OECD, 2000). The Internet hosts and Internet users measure Internet penetration in the society, while the number of PCs indicator measures the spread of personal computers in the society.

As for the Internet hosts, a host is a domain name associated with an Internet protocol (IP) address. This includes any computer or device connected to the Internet via a full-time, part-time, direct, or dial-up connection. The hosts, however, are no longer necessarily individual devices as they used to be. Therefore, the host counts tend to be lower and should be seen rather as an indicator of the minimum size of the Internet. Still, they are often used to indicate the extent of growth in Internet-hosting activities (OECD, 2005f).

As for the Internet users, the data is based on nationally reported data regarding Internet users. The data has been gathered from national surveys—or, if the country does not have surveys, from the reports of subscriber counts by the Internet service providers. As for the number of PCs, the data shows the estimated number of personal computers. The figures for PCs come from the annual questionnaire supplemented by other sources ("ITU Technical Notes," n.d.). The measures of Internet users and the number of PCs are good indicators of the extent to which the new technology is adopted by the society.

To conclude, I have identified six variables to measure the openness to change of different countries. These variables indicate the diffusion of new knowledge in the society. They include the following: investment in ICT as percent of gross fixed capital formation, software investment as percent of nonresidential gross fixed capital formation, secure servers per 100,000 inhabitants, Internet hosts per 100 inhabitants, Internet users per 100 inhabitants, and PCs per 100 inhabitants. All of these variables are intended to denote the openness of the society to both new knowledge and changes in technological trends.

Innovation

The innovation variable is intended to measure the innovativeness of countries. Since the concept of innovation can be seen as being three-dimensional, the innovation variable should include all the three dimensions of innovation, which are creativity, openness to change, and entrepreneurship. However, because of the lack of comprehensive and comparable data on entrepreneurship, more specifically on the business start-ups, the innovation variable does not contain the entrepreneurship dimension. It only includes the creativity and the openness to change variables.

In order to encompass the two dimensions, the innovation variable combines together all the measures of creativity and openness to change, which have been previously identified. Then, a factor analysis is conducted to establish whether all of those variables, could be grouped together into one innovation scale or have to be divided into several scales.

Measurement of Independent Variables

Several variables have been chosen to measure the ethnolinguistic diversity of countries. The first group of variables measures the older diversity coming from old ethnic minorities, while the second group measures the newer diversity coming from immigration. In relation to the first group, I rely on the data that has been used previously in the studies concerning the impact of ethnolinguistic diversity on economic growth. In relation to the second group, I utilize the immigration data from the OECD database.

Ethnolinguistic Diversity—Old Ethnic Minorities

I use two sources of data to measure the ethnolinguistic diversity coming from old ethnic minorities: the ELF index, created in the beginning of the '60s, and the more recent fractionalization indices developed by Alberto Alesina et al. (2003a).

The ELF index has been compiled for 129 countries, and its broad coverage is one of the principal reasons why it has been used in the vast majority of cross-national quantitative analyses regarding the impact of ethnic diversity on economic growth (Canning & Fay, 1993; Collier, 2001; Easterly & Levine, 1997; Mauro, 1995). It is based on Soviet data collected in the early 1960s and published in the *Atlas Narodov Mira* (1964). Subsequently, the index was included in Taylor and Hudson's *Handbook of Political and Social Indicators* (1972).[7]

The ELF index makes the distinction between different ethnolinguistic groups on the basis of ethnic, linguistic, and religious differences between those groups. It measures the probability that two randomly selected people from a given country will belong to different ethnolinguistic groups. The index is calculated using a simple Herfindahl concentration formula:

$$ELF = 1 - \sum_i s_i^2$$

The problem with the Herfindahl formula is that it does not account for the variations in the ethnic diversity of the countries. It does not distinguish between dominance and fractionalization in ethnic diversity. For example, it gives the same score (0.5) to countries with two big groups of equal size that it does to countries with three groups containing two thirds, one sixth, and one sixth of the population, respectively.

The different spread of ethnic diversity might have a different impact on innovativeness. Generally, one would expect higher fractionalization to be more encouraging for creativity because it would provide more diverse backgrounds, and thus more stimulation for diverse ideas. However, the goal of this analysis is not to assess the impact of different types of ethnic diversity on innovativeness, but to assess the impact of ethnic diversity in general. Therefore, the data on diversity calculated with the Herfindahl index does not pose a problem.

The second source of data for indigenous ethnolinguistic diversity comes from the publication of Alesina et al. (2003a), where a new measure of ethnic fractionalization was developed. The researchers created a new measure of ethnic fractionalization in order to revisit the question of the impact of ethnic diversity on the quality of government and economic growth. They have developed three separate indices to measure the diversity of countries, which include linguistic fractionalization, religious fractionalization, and ethnic fractionalization. Their main goal was to clearly distinguish between ethnic, religious, and linguistic heterogeneity, as well as to avoid lumping the data together into one ethnolinguistic variable—as it has been done for the ELF index (Alesina et al., 2003a).

Their data uses the Herfindahl concentration formula in the same way that the ELF index does. Therefore, their indices measure the probability that two individuals in a given country will come from different ethnic, linguistic, or religious groups. However, their indices are based on alternative sources of data derived from *Encyclopedia Britannica* (2001), *CIA World Factbook* (2000), *Ethnic Groups Worldwide* by Levinson (1998), and the *Minority Rights Group International* (1997). Hence, their data is more recent than the ELF index.

Since Alesina et al. (2003a) use different sources of data, their observations do not have the same year of reference. The time coverage in their dataset varies from 1981 to 2001. However, the authors argued that it does not present a problem because "ethnic fractionalization displays tremendous time persistence" (p. 7). They stated that the group shares are sufficiently stable, especially within a 30-year horizon; therefore, the changes within that horizon have a minor impact on fractionalization measures.[8]

Ethnolinguistic Diversity—Immigration

The measures of ethnolinguistic fractionalization either do not take into account recent immigration (ELF) or take it into account only to a limited extent (see Alesina et al., 2003a, index).[9] Thus, in order to account for immigration, I have to include into the analysis a separate measure for immigration.

I use the OECD immigration database, which has been recently revised to make the data on immigration more comparable across countries (Dumont & Lemaître, 2005; OECD, 2004b). Before the revision, there has been a lack of comparability in the migration estimates due to the differences between countries in defining the immigrant population. The main settlement countries (Australia, Canada, New Zealand, and the United States) report statistics on foreign-born people (a criterion based on the place of birth), while the European and Asian OECD countries report statistics on foreigners (a criterion based on nationality) (OECD, 2004b).

The foreign-born population covers persons who are first-generation immigrants. They might have already acquired the citizenship of the new country of residence, but they are accounted for in the statistics as immigrants. Thus, the foreign-born population consists of both foreign and national citizens. The foreign population, however, includes immigrants who have kept the nationality of their home country, as well as second- and third-generation immigrants born in the host country (OECD, 2004b). It does not account for immigrants who have already acquired a nationality of the new country, because those are no longer considered foreign. It creates a problem of comparability, and it distorts the data on immigration stocks between countries, especially for countries with high rates of naturalization such as Australia, Canada, the United States, the Netherlands, and Sweden.

In order to remove the problems of comparability in the immigration data, the OECD has undertaken a project to harmonize the reported statistics on immigration. It launched a data collection project across the OECD with the aim of incorporating the question on both the country of birth and the nationality of persons enumerated. The undertaking has resulted in a new database concerning immigrants in OECD countries, which was first published in 2004. The new database is the first internationally comparable data set with detailed information on the foreign-born population for almost all the OECD countries (Dumont & Lemaître, 2005).

I use three indicators to measure the level of immigration in the OECD countries. The first indicator measures the stocks of foreign-born population as percent of the total population (OECD, 2004b). It is intended to measure the size of the immigrant population in the respective countries. However, since the indicator is based on the data of foreign-born people, it does not include the immigrants who were born already in the new country of residence but still do not have the nationality of that country, and thus still remain immigrants. In Europe and Asia, when the citizenship at birth is based on that of the parents (*jus sanguinis*), there might be still a big number of such immigrants. Therefore, in order to account also for those immigrants, I use a second indicator that measures the number of noncitizens as percent of total population (OECD). It gives an indication of the amount of immigrants without the citizenship of the country of residence.

A third indicator, which is used in relation to immigration, is one that measures the stocks of foreign or foreign-born labor force as percent of total labor force (OECD, 2004b). It assesses the size of the labor force composed of foreigners and immigrants. I decided to include this measure into the analysis because it denotes how much of the immigrant population is actually employed in the labor force. Therefore, it specifies the impact of the creative potential carried by the immigrants on the total labor force. In the end, it is the workplace that is an important platform where the diverse individuals can meet, interact, and exchange ideas, and thus stimulate higher creativity.

To conclude, seven variables have been identified to measure the ethnolinguistic diversity of the countries in the sample. Four of them measure the ethnolinguistic fractionalization coming from old ethnolinguistic minorities and they include the ELF index, the Alesina Fractionalization Index on Ethnicity, the Alesina Fractionalization Index on Language, and the Alesina Fractionalization Index on Religion. The remaining three variables measure the ethnolinguistic diversity coming from immigration and they are composed of the following measures: stocks of foreign-born population as percent of total population, noncitizens as percent of total population, and the stocks of foreign or foreign-born labor force as percent of total labor force. All of those variables are intended to provide estimations of the extent of ethnolinguistic diversity, both old and new, that is present in the countries of the sample.

Measurement of Intervening Variables

As previously established, out of all the elements of the right context, there are only two elements that can be measured in a quantitative way, and thus can be incorporated directly into our analysis. Those elements include the integration and learning perspective on diversity, as well as the growth- and innovation-focused strategy. I rely on the OECD data and identify several variables to measure those two right context elements.

Value in Diversity—Integration and Learning Perspective on Diversity

The countries that have an integration and learning perspective on diversity perceive ethnolinguistic diversity as a potentially valuable resource, which can be utilized by the society for its well-being. The policies that reveal the integrative approach toward diversity consist of inclusive citizenship laws and multicultural policies. And the policies that reveal a learning approach toward diversity include openness toward high-skilled immigration, favorable conditions for labor market access, and social mobility for minorities.

Two from the list of integration and learning policies, which are the multicultural policies and the policies that favor social mobility of minorities, have to be left out from the analysis because they are very hard to measure in a quantitative way. For all the other policies, I have found quantitative data that can be used in the analysis.

A country can be considered as having an inclusive citizenship law if it promotes the acquisition of citizenship among the immigrants. I have chosen two measures to assess the rate of acquisition of nationality in different countries. The two measures include the naturalization/acquisition of nationality as percentage of foreign population (OECD, 2004b)[10] and the percentage of foreign born with the citizenship of country of residence (OECD, 2004b). Both of those measures indicate the magnitude of naturalizations taking place in different countries, and thus indicate the inclusiveness of their citizenship laws.

Openness toward high-skilled immigration can be assessed based on whether the country encourages either high-skilled or low-skilled immigration. There are two indicators that are used to assess it: the percentage of high-skilled foreign born and low percentage of low-skilled foreign born (OECD, 2004b).[11] Those two measures give an indication of the shares of both the high-skilled and low-skilled immigration present in a given country.

In order to evaluate the conditions for labor market access for ethnically diverse people, I choose two types of indicators: those that indicate low unemployment of foreign-born people and those that indicate high labor participation rate of foreign-born people.[12] The low unemployment among immigrants is measured by two indicators: the low percentage of foreign-born unemployment rate, as well as the small percentage gap in unemployment between foreign born and natives (OECD, 2004b).

The high labor participation rate of foreign-born people is assessed by two measures: the percentage of foreign-born labor participation rate and the small percentage gap in foreign-born people to native-labor participation rate (OECD, 2004b). All of those measures indicate the participation of immigrants in the labor force, as well as the differences in the labor participation between the immigrants and the natives. As a result, they assess the conditions for labor market access for immigrants existing in different countries.

Growth- and Innovation-Focused Strategy

A growth- and innovation-based strategy is present when a country pursues a strategy that aims at strengthening the competitiveness and the innovativeness of the economy. A good indication of the existence of a growth-focused strategy on a country level is the presence of a good business climate and flexible labor markets. The existence of the innovation-focused strategy is indicated by high levels of spending on innovation.

The competitiveness of the business climate is measured by the following three indicators: low economic regulations in business, low administrative regulations in business (OECD, 2005g),[13] and low barriers to entrepreneurship (p. 33). The flexibility of labor markets is indicated by the low level of employment protection legislation (EPL) (OECD, 2006).[14]

The innovation-focused strategy is measured by the level of spending on research and development (R&D). I use an OECD indicator, which is the gross domestic expenditure on R&D as percentage of GDP (GERD), to compare the level of R&D spending between different countries. GERD is defined as a total intramural expenditure on R&D performed on the national territory during a given period (OECD, 2002).[15] As noted by the *OECD Frascati Manual* (2002), GERD and the GERD matrix are the basis of international comparison of R&D expenditures.

To conclude, 13 variables have been identified to measure the different intervening variables of the right context. Eight of those variables measure the existence of the integration and learning perspective on diversity, and they include the following: naturalization/acquisition of nationality as a percentage of foreign population, percentage of foreign born with the citizenship of country of residence, percentage of high-skilled foreign born, low percentage of low-skilled foreign born, low percentage of foreign born unemployment rate, small percentage gap in unemployment between foreign-born people and natives, foreign-born labor participation rate, and small percentage gap in labor participation rate between foreign-born people and natives.

The remaining five variables measure the growth- and innovation-focused strategy: low economic regulations in business, low administrative regulations in business, low barriers to entrepreneurship, low level of EPL, and R&D expenditure as percentage of GDP (GERD). All of those variables are intended to provide estimations of the existence of the right context in different countries. Appendix A lists all the variables, their respective Stata names, and the years for which the data is reported.[16]

Factor Analysis—Creating Single Scales for the Variables

Having identified the list of variables, I conduct factor analyses to assess whether it is possible to create single scales for each of the dependent, independent, and intervening variables. The aim of the factor analyses is to achieve data reduction and construct single scales, which can be used in further analysis. The underlying idea of the factor analytic approach is the assumption that some underlying factors, which are smaller in number than the observed variables, are responsible for the covariation among the observed variables (Kim & Mueller, 1978). Conducting the factor analysis allows one to identify those common factors and to group the variables into separate single scales.

The first step of the factor analysis involves an examination of the interrelationships among the variables. For that purpose, a correlation matrix is created, and the correlations among the variables are examined to determine whether there might be some underlying factors among the variables. If the correlation table would indicate the existence of common factors, then the factor analysis would be conducted to identify those factors and to distinguish which variables are associated with which factors. Finally, the variables that constitute each of the factors are grouped into single scales and used as the dependent, independent, and intervening variables in the regression analysis.

Creating Scales for Dependent Variables

Creativity Factor Analysis

A correlation matrix of the creativity variables reveals that there are many high correlations between the variables indicating that there could be some underlying factors present among the variables. A principal components factor analysis that was performed on those variables has determined that there are two underlying factors among the creativity variables. The factors have been identified based on the eigenvalues, scree chart, percent of variance explained, factor loadings, content validity, and alpha reliability. A detailed summary of the correlations and the factor analysis is presented in Appendix B. Table 1 shows the list of variables constituting Factor 1 and Factor 2 for the creativity factor analysis.

When examining the content of the two lists of variables, Factor 1 contains variables that relate to the patents in general and to the ICT patents, as well as to the manufacturing sector. The factor analysis indicates that all the variables constituting Factor 1 have very similar

TABLE 1. Creativity—variables constituting Factor 1 and Factor 2.

Factor 1	Factor 2
1. Triadic patents per population	1. Relative prominence of cited scientific literature
2. EPO patents per population	2. Biotech patents EPO per population
3. USPTO patents per population	3. Biotech patents USPTO per population
4. ICT patents EPO per population	4. Share of knowledge-intensive market services in total value added
5. ICT patents USPTO per population	5. Share of services in total value added
6. Share of high and medium technology manufactures in total value added	6. Technology balance of payments as percent of GDP
7. Share of manufacturing in total value added	7. Contribution of ICT capital to GDP growth

variation patterns. This implies that countries with high levels of patents in general and high levels of patents related to the ICT would also have relatively large manufacturing sectors.

Factor 2, on the other hand, contains the variables associated with a high level of scientific citations, biotechnology patents, relatively large services sector, high technology balance of payments, and a strong contribution of the ICT to GDP growth. Again, the factor analysis indicates that all of those variables have similar variation patterns. That means that the countries with high levels of biotechnology patents, relatively positive technology balance of payments, and high ICT contribution to GDP growth also have a relatively large services sector.

Since the development of the services sector occurs after the development of the manufacturing sector in the process of economic progress, the countries with more developed services sectors can be considered as more modern or advanced in their economic development. At the same time, the countries with more developed manufacturing sectors can be considered as being more traditional in their development.

Concurrently, the biotechnology patents are considered to be much more cutting-edge technology than either the general patents or the ICT patents.[17] Again, the countries that have relatively high levels of biotechnology patents can be considered as more modern in their focus, while the countries that have relatively high levels of general and ICT patents can be considered as more traditional.

And finally, the countries with a relatively high technology balance of payments and high ICT contribution to the productivity growth can be also considered as more modern in their technological development than the countries with a low technology balance of payments and where the ICT has a low contribution to the productivity growth. Having a high technology balance of payments suggests that a given country is successful in selling its technology, as well as that its technology is highly demanded by other countries. Being able to reach higher productivity growth from ICT means that a country is more advanced in using and applying the new knowledge than other countries where the ICT contribution to GDP growth is lower.

In light of the aforementioned, I call the factor scale created from Factor 1 a Traditional Creativity Scale, and the factor scale created from Factor 2 is called a Modern Creativity Scale. The scales are formed by summing all the variables constituting each of the factors. Table 2 presents the two scales and the variables that compose those two scales.

Based on the content, it is the Modern Creativity Scale, rather than the Traditional Creativity Scale, which is a more appropriate measure of creativity. The variables that constitute the Modern Creativity Scale are better indicators of creativity because they relate to a more forefront, novel, and modern creativity than the variables comprising the Traditional Creativity Scale. Therefore, the true spirit of creating novel ideas is better captured by the Modern Creativity Scale.

Figure 1 (on p. 114) presents the scores on the Traditional Creativity Scale and the Modern Creativity Scale for all the OECD countries.[18] The countries that are the highest on the Traditional Creativity Scale are Switzerland, Japan, Finland, Sweden, and Germany. And the countries that are the highest on the Modern Creativity Scale are the United States,

Table 2. Variables constituting the Traditional Creativity Scale and Modern Creativity Scale.

Traditional Creativity Scale	Modern Creativity Scale
1. Triadic patents per population	1. Relative prominence of cited scientific literature
2. EPO patents per population	2. Biotech patents EPO per population
3. USPTO patents per population	3. Biotech patents USPTO per population
4. ICT patents EPO per population	4. Share of knowledge-intensive market services in total value added
5. ICT patents USPTO per population	5. Share of services in total value added
6. Share of high and medium technology manufactures in total value added	6. Technology balance of payments as percent of GDP
7. Share of manufacturing in total value added	7. Contribution of ICT capital to GDP growth

Denmark, Switzerland, Luxemburg, and Belgium. Some of the countries, such as the United States, Switzerland, the Netherlands, and Sweden, are relatively high on both of the scales. Other countries exhibit a strong preponderance on the side of the Traditional Creativity Scale, and those countries include Ireland, Japan, Finland, South Korea, Germany, Czech Republic, and Sweden. There are also countries that exhibit a strong preponderance on the side of the Modern Creativity Scale, and those countries include Denmark, Luxemburg, Australia, the United States, the United Kingdom, Belgium, and New Zealand.

Openness to Change Factor Analysis

A correlation matrix of the openness to change variables reveals that there are many high correlations between the variables. That indicates that there could be some underlying factors present among those variables. A principal components factor analysis was performed on those

FIGURE 1. Modern Creativity Scale and Traditional Creativity Scale.

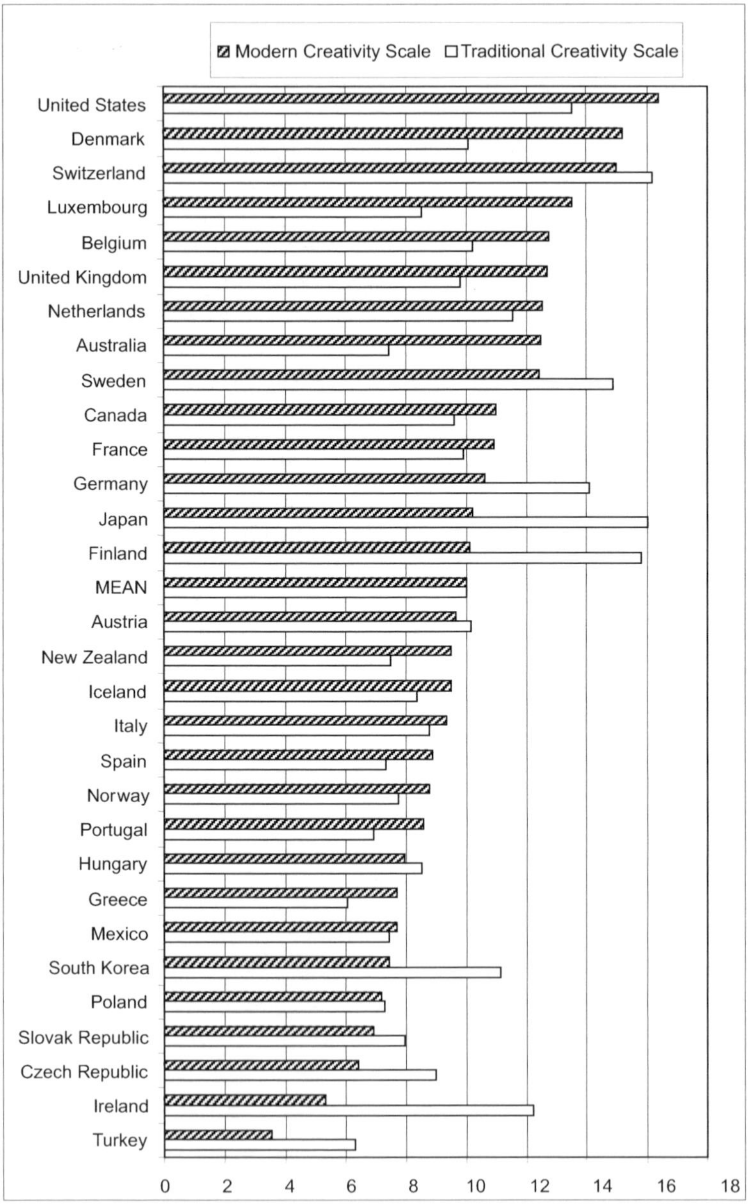

TABLE 3. Variables constituting the Openness Scale.

Openness Scale
1. Investment in ICT as percent of gross fixed capital formation
2. Software investment as percent of nonresidential gross fixed capital formation
3. Secure servers per 100,000 inhabitants
4. Internet hosts per 100 inhabitants
5. Internet users per 100 inhabitants
6. Personal computers per 100 inhabitants

variables to determine the common factors. A detailed summary of the correlations and the factor analysis is presented in Appendix C.

The examination of the eigenvalues, scree chart, percent of variance explained, factor loadings, content validity, and alpha reliability has shown that there is one underlying factor present among the openness to change variables. That means that all of the variables that have been chosen as the indicators of openness show similar patterns of variation. Thus, they can be grouped into one single scale. The scale created from those variables is named the Openness Scale. Table 3 lists all the variables that are part of the Openness Scale.

Figure 2 on the following page presents the scores on the Openness Scale for all the OECD countries.[19] The countries that are the highest on the Openness Scale are the United States, Iceland, Sweden, Denmark, and Australia, while the lowest are Turkey, Mexico, Greece, Poland, and Hungary.

Innovation Factor Analysis

Since the concept of innovation includes the dimensions of both creativity and openness, it is sensible to check whether we can combine those variables into a single Innovation Scale. That would be possible if there is a common underlying factor among the creativity and openness variables.

A principal components factor analysis that was performed on those variables reveals that there are two meaningful underlying factors among

FIGURE 2. Openness Scale.

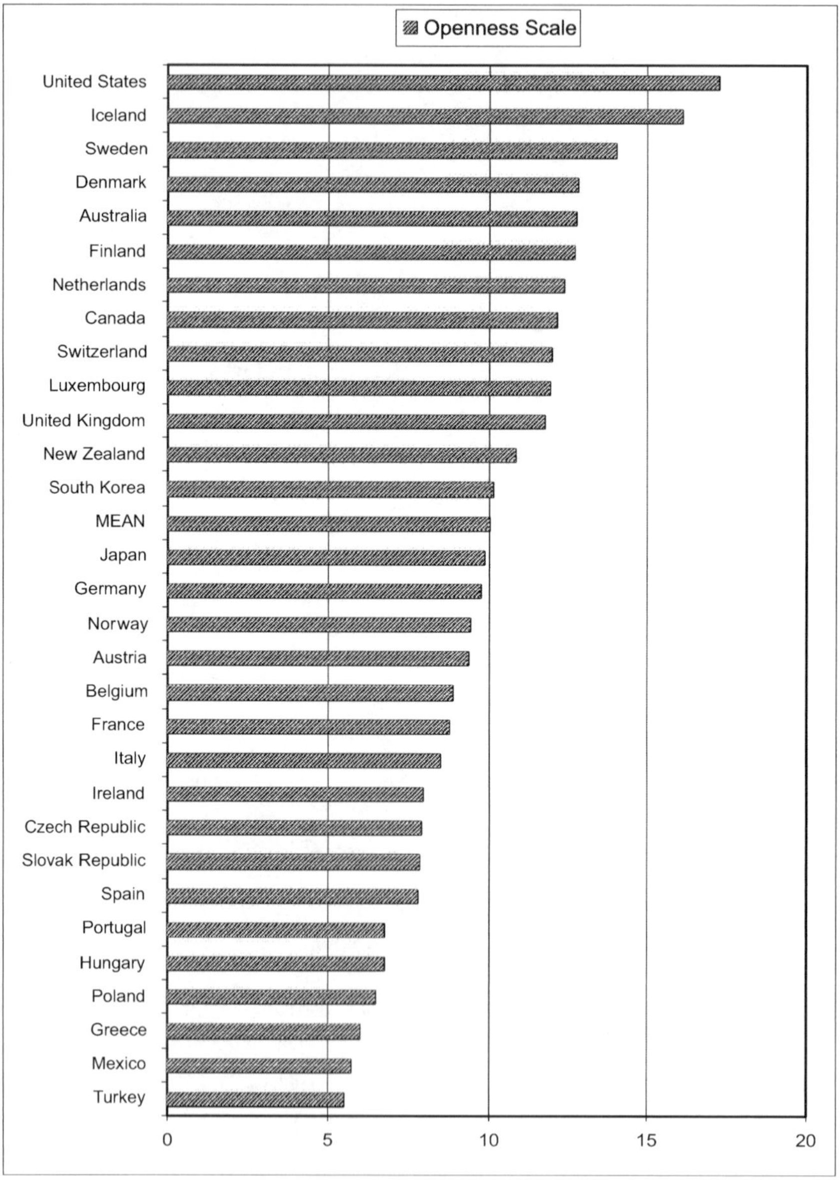

the variables. The two common factors have been determined based on the eigenvalues, scree chart, percent of variance explained, factor loadings, content validity, and alpha reliability. A detailed summary of the correlations and the factor analysis is presented in Appendix D. Table 4 shows the list of variables comprising the Factor 1 and Factor 2 for the innovation factor analysis.

When examining the content of the two factors, one notices that the variables that are listed under Factor 1 are actually the variables that compose the Modern Creativity Scale and the Openness Scale.[20] Conversely, the

TABLE 4. Innovation—variables constituting Factor 1 and Factor 2.

Factor 1	Factor 2
1. Relative prominence of cited scientific literature	1. Triadic patents per population
2. Biotech patents EPO per population	2. EPO patents per population
3. Biotech patents USPTO per population	3. ICT patents EPO per population
4. Share of knowledge-intensive market services in total value added	4. ICT patents USPTO per population
5. Contribution of the services sector to productivity growth	5. Share of high and medium technology manufactures in total value added
6. Share of services in total value added	6. Share of manufacturing in total value added
7. Technology balance of payments as percent of GDP	
8. Contribution of ICT capital to GDP growth	
9. Investment in ICT as percent of gross fixed capital formation	
10. Software investment as percent of nonresidential gross fixed capital formation	
11. Secure servers per 100,000 inhabitants	
12. Internet hosts per 100 inhabitants	
13. Internet users per 100 inhabitants	
14. Personal computers per 100 inhabitants	

variables listed under Factor 2 are the variables that constitute the Traditional Creativity Scale. Such a turnout is consistent with the notion that creativity and openness are parts of a broader concept of innovation. It is also consistent with a previous assertion that the Modern Creativity Scale, rather than the Traditional Creativity Scale, is a better measure of creativity.

The purpose of running the innovation factor analysis was to see whether it is possible to combine some of the creativity and openness variables together into a single Innovation Scale. The results of that analysis show that not just some, but rather *all* of the modern creativity and openness variables share a common pattern of variance. Therefore, it is possible to create an Innovation Scale that combines the variables from the Modern Creativity Scale and the Openness Scale.[21] Table 5 presents the list of variables included in the Innovation Scale.

TABLE 5. Variables constituting the Innovation Scale.

Innovation Scale
1. Relative prominence of cited scientific literature
2. Biotech patents EPO per population
3. Biotech patents USPTO per population
4. Share of knowledge-intensive market services in total value added
5. Contribution of the services sector to productivity growth
6. Share of services in total value added
7. Technology balance of payments as percent of GDP
8. Contribution of ICT capital to GDP growth
9. Investment in ICT as percent of gross fixed capital formation
10. Software investment as percent of nonresidential gross fixed capital formation
11. Secure servers per 100,000 inhabitants
12. Internet hosts per 100 inhabitants
13. Internet users per 100 inhabitants
14. Personal computers per 100 inhabitants

Figure 3 presents the scores on the Innovation Scale for all the OECD countries.[22] The countries that are the highest on the Innovation Scale are the United States, Denmark, Switzerland, Sweden, and Iceland. The countries with the lowest scores on the Innovation Scale are Turkey, Ireland, Mexico, the Czech Republic, and Greece.

FIGURE 3. Innovation Scale.

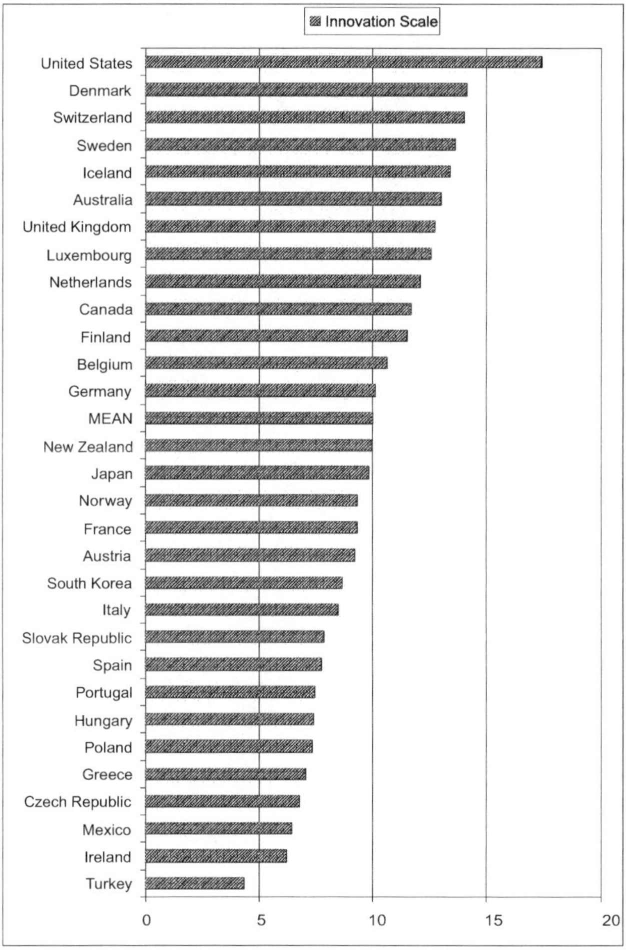

Creating Scales for Independent Variables

Diversity Factor Analysis

Having constructed the scales for the dependent variables, we turn to the independent variables. The list of the diversity variables consists of seven variables. A correlation matrix reveals that there are many high correlations between the variables; these correlations indicate that there could be some underlying factors present within them.

A principal components factor analysis was performed on the diversity variables. The examination of the eigenvalues, scree chart, percent of variance explained, factor loadings, content validity, and alpha reliability

TABLE 6. Diversity—variables constituting Factor 1 and Factor 2.

Factor 1	Factor 2
1. Stocks of foreign-born population as percent of total population	1. ELF index
2. Noncitizens as percent of total population	2. Alesina's Ethnic Fractionalization Index
3. Stocks of foreign or foreign-born labor force as percent of total labor force	3. Alesina's Linguistic Fractionalization Index
	4. Alesina's Religious Fractionalization Index

TABLE 7. Variables constituting the Immigration Diversity Scale and Old Minorities Diversity Scale.

Immigration Diversity Scale	Old Minorities Diversity Scale
1. Stocks of foreign-born population as percent of total population	1. ELF index
2. Noncitizens as percent of total population	2. Alesina's Ethnic Fractionalization Index
3. Stocks of foreign or foreign-born labor force as percent of total labor force	3. Alesina's Linguistic Fractionalization Index
	4. Alesina's Religious Fractionalization Index

reveal that there are two underlying factors among them. A detailed summary of the correlations and the factor analysis is presented in Appendix E. Table 6 shows the list of variables constituting the Factor 1 and Factor 2 for the diversity factor analysis.

When examining the content of the two lists of variables, one should notice that Factor 1 contains the variables related to immigration, while Factor 2 contains the variables related to indigenous diversity stemming from the existence of old minorities. Therefore, based on the factor analysis, I create two separate scales: the Immigration Diversity Scale and the Old Minorities Diversity Scale. The Immigration Diversity Scale indicates the diversity coming from recent immigration. The Old Minorities Diversity Scale indicates the diversity coming from the old minorities present in the country. Table 7 presents the two diversity scales and the list of variables comprising each of the scales.

Figure 4 on the following page presents the scores on the Old Minorities Diversity Scale and the Immigration Diversity Scale for all the OECD countries.[23] The countries that are the highest on the Old Minorities Diversity Scale are Canada, the United States, Switzerland, Belgium, and Spain. And the countries with the highest scores on the Immigration Diversity Scale are Luxemburg, Switzerland, New Zealand, Australia, and Canada.

Creating Scales for Intervening Variables

Right Context Factor Analysis

Having constructed the scales for the independent and dependent variables, we turn to the intervening variables, which are the right context variables. The list of the right context variables is composed of 13 variables. A correlation matrix reveals that there are many high correlations between the variables, indicating that there could be some underlying factors present within those variables.

However, the correlation matrix also reveals that there are too many missing values in the data set, to the extent that we can only retain 14 out of 30 observations for the factor analysis. Such a low number cannot

FIGURE 4. Old Minorities Diversity Scale and Immigration Diversity Scale.

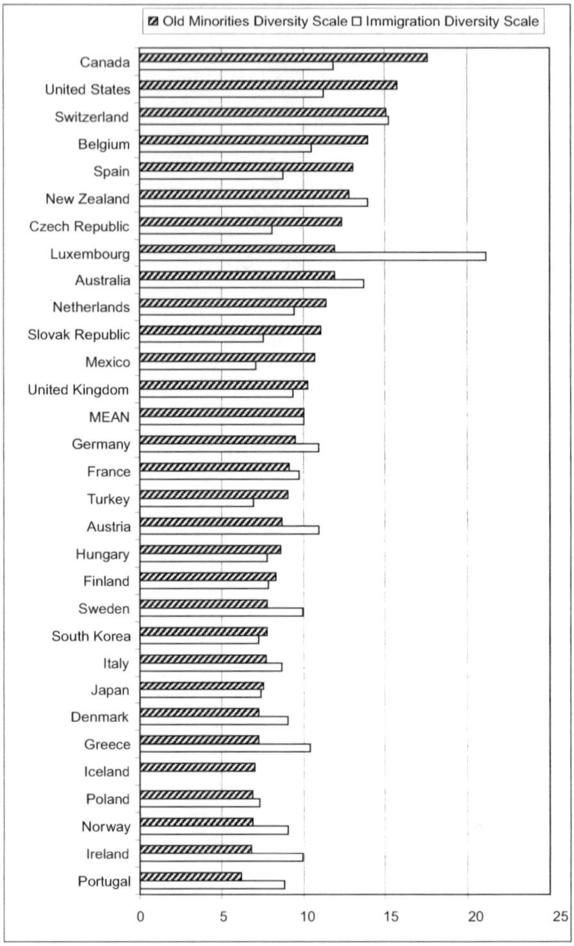

be considered representative of the whole sample because it constitutes less than half of the observations in the sample. Therefore, I decided to increase the number of observations in the analysis to at least 20 observations, which would constitute two thirds of the sample, and thus can be considered representative for the whole sample. In order to do so,

I decided to drop those variables from the analysis that have the highest number of missing values.

Four variables, which had eight or more missing values, were dropped, and the goal of increasing the number of observations was reached.[24] In result, 21 out of 30 observations were retained, which constitutes more than two thirds of the sample, and thus can be considered representative. Those dropped variables include the naturalization/acquisition of nationality as a percentage of foreign population, percentage of foreign born with the citizenship of country of residence, low percentage of foreign-born unemployment rate, and the small percentage gap in unemployment between foreign-born people and natives.

Having identified the final list of variables that are used for the right context factor analysis, I conducted a principal factor components analysis to determine if there are any common factors among those variables. A detailed summary of the correlations and the factor analysis is presented in Appendix F.

The rotated factor loadings indicated the existence of two factors. However, the alpha reliability score for the second factor was too low to create a reliable scale based on that factor.[25] Furthermore, there were only two variables that loaded on the second factor, and that provided an additional reason for not creating a scale based on the second factor.[26] In result, I had to drop the variables composing the second factor from the analysis.

Based on the eigenvalues, scree chart, percent of variance explained, factor loadings, content validity, and alpha reliability, I identified one reliable common factor among the right context variables. Table 8 shows the list of variables comprising that factor.

When examining the content of the list of variables constituting Factor 1, most of the variables relate to the growth-focused strategy. However, there are two variables on the list that have been categorized before as the indicators of the perception of diversity as a value. Those variables include the percentage of high-skilled foreign-born people and the low percentage of low-skilled foreign born.

Since the two variables have fallen into the same group with the growth-focused strategy variables, it means that they exhibit a common

TABLE 8. Right context—variables constituting Factor 1.

Factor 1
1. Percent of high-skilled foreign born
2. Low percent of low-skilled foreign born
3. Low economic regulations in business
4. Low administrative regulations in business
5. Low barriers to entrepreneurship
6. Low level of employment protection legislation (EPL)

variation pattern. Therefore, I decided to consider whether there is a way of looking at those variables as growth-focused strategy variables.

One could actually argue that countries that invite relatively more high-skilled immigrants are more oriented toward competitiveness and growth. By inviting them, those countries increase the competition in the sectors of the economy that employ high-skilled workers. Those countries want the knowledge and talent of foreign workers to contribute to the growth of the economy. Therefore, welcoming high-skilled immigration not only indicates perceiving diversity as a value but also reveals a growth-focused orientation. Thus, it seems plausible to combine the variables constituting Factor 1 into a single scale and call it a Growth-Focused Strategy Scale.

It is important to note that there was one variable that did not load positively on any of the factors. That is the variable that measures the levels of R&D expenditure as percentage of GDP. This variable has been previously identified as an indicator of the innovation-focused strategy. I rather expected it to show a common pattern of variance with the indicators of the growth-focused strategy, but it did not.

The factor analysis reveals that the R&D expenditure variable has a distinct character and captures different dimensions of the right context than those of the growth-focused strategy variables. From the theoretical perspective, it is essential to explore those distinct dimensions of the innovation-focused strategy. Therefore, I would like to create a separate

Table 9. Variables constituting the Growth-Focused Strategy Scale and the Innovation-Focused Strategy Measure.

Growth-Focused Strategy Scale	Innovation-Focused Strategy Measure
1. Percent of high-skilled foreign born	1. R&D expenditure as percent of GDP
2. Low percent of low-skilled foreign born	
3. Low economic regulations in business	
4. Low administrative regulations in business	
5. Low barriers to entrepreneurship	
6. Low level of employment protection legislation (EPL)	

measure, which is based on that variable and denotes a country's focus on innovation. I call it an Innovation-Focused Strategy Measure and incorporate it into the regression analysis as one of the right context variables.

To conclude, as a result of the factor analysis I created a Growth-Focused Strategy Scale and an Innovation-Focused Strategy Measure, both of which are used in the regression analysis as separate indicators of the right context. However, contrary to my expectations, I was not able to create a value in diversity scale. Already from the outset, due to the excessive number missing values, I had to drop four variables, which were originally on the value in diversity list. Those variables were the indicators of the integration and learning perspective on diversity. The remaining value in diversity variables did not form a single scale because either they had very low alpha reliability scores, or they grouped together with the growth-focused strategy variables. Consequently, I was not able to create a value in diversity scale.

Table 9 lists all the variables that are part of the two measures based on the factor analysis, which include the Growth-Focused Strategy Scale and the Innovation-Focused Strategy Measure.

Figure 5 presents the scores of the Innovation-Focused Strategy Measure and the Growth-Focused Strategy Scale for all the OECD countries.[27] The countries that are the highest on the Innovation-Focused Strategy

FIGURE 5. Innovation-Focused Strategy Measure and Growth-Focused Strategy Scale.

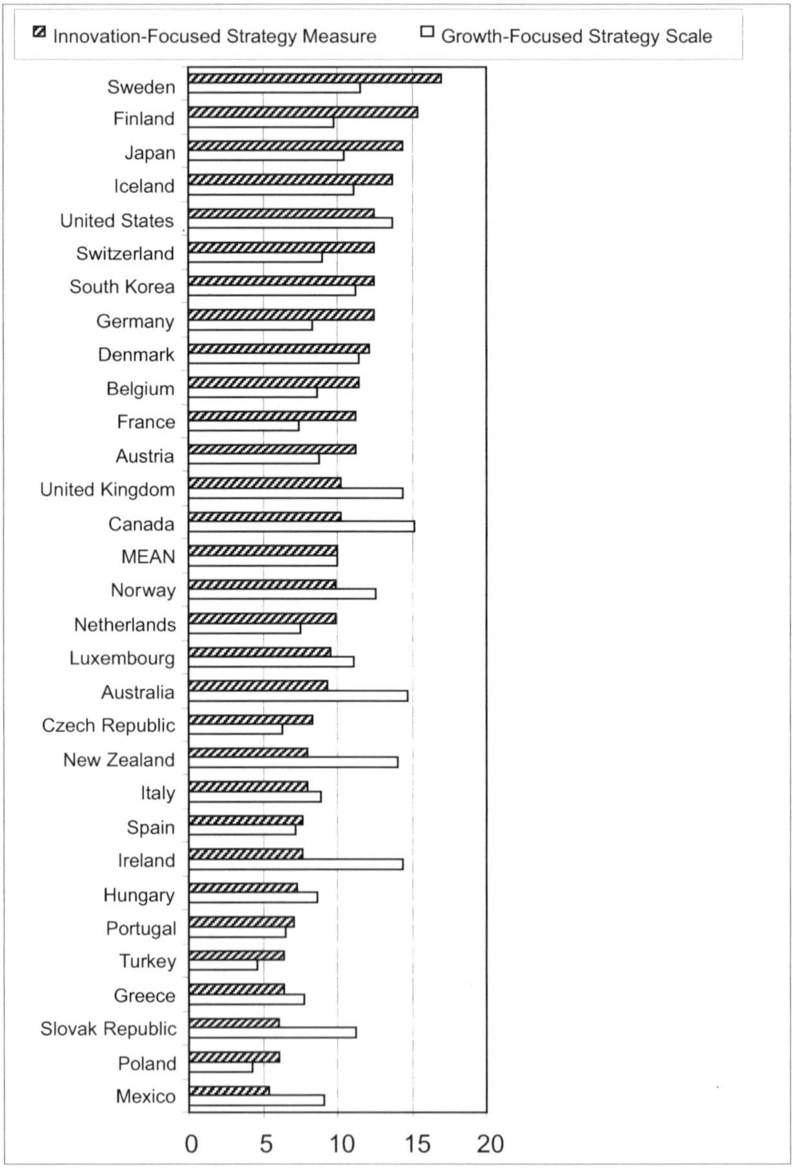

Measure are Sweden, Finland, Japan, Iceland, and the United States. And the countries with the highest scores on the Growth-Focused Strategy Scale are Canada, Australia, Ireland, United Kingdom, and New Zealand.

Results of the Factor Analysis

As intended, the factor analysis has led to a significant data reduction and to the creation of single scales, or measures, for the independent, dependent, and intervening variables. The following scales and measures were created: the Traditional Creativity Scale, the Modern Creativity Scale, the Openness Scale, the Innovation Scale, the Old Minorities Diversity Scale, the Immigration Diversity Scale, the Growth-Focused Strategy Scale, and the Innovation-Focused Strategy Measure. All of the scales and measures are used in the regression analysis.[28]

The scales and measures appear in the regression analysis with abbreviated names. The Traditional Creativity Scale is denoted as *T_C* for *traditional creativity*, while the Modern Creativity Scale is denoted as *C* for *creativity*. The reason why I denote the Modern Creativity Scale simply as *creativity* is because, as previously discussed, it is the Modern Creativity Scale that is the right indicator of creativity. As for the other scales representing the independent variables, the Openness Scale is denoted as *O* for *openness*, and the Innovation Scale is denoted as *I* for *innovation.*

The scales created for the dependent variables are denoted by the following abbreviations. The Old Minorities Diversity Scale is represented by the abbreviation *Div* for *Diversity*, and the Immigration Diversity Scale is denoted by the abbreviation *Imm* for *Immigration Diversity*. I label the Old Minorities Diversity Scale simply as *Diversity* because it is the indigenous diversity that has been used in the previous studies as an indicator of the ethnolinguistic diversity of countries. The Immigration Diversity Scale is an additional measure of ethnolinguistic diversity introduced in this study. Hence, the Old Minorities Diversity Scale (*Div*) is treated in this study as the main measure of diversity, while the Immigration Diversity Scale (*Imm*) is treated as an additional measure of diversity.

As for the intervening variables, they are represented in the regression analysis by the names that have the *RC* abbreviation, for the *Right*

TABLE 10. Abbreviated names for the scales and measures.

Traditional Creativity Scale	*T_C*
Modern Creativity Scale	*C*
Openness Scale	*O*
Innovation Scale	*I*
Old Minorities Diversity Scale	*Div*
Immigration Diversity Scale	*Imm*
Growth-Focused Strategy Scale	*RCg*
Innovation-Focused Strategy Measure	*RCi*

Context, in front of them. Thus, the Growth-Focused Strategy Scale is denoted as *RCg*, which means *Right Context—Growth-Focused Strategy*, and the Innovation-Focused Strategy Measure is denoted as *RCi*, which means *Right Context—Innovation-Focused Strategy*.

Table 10 presents the abbreviated names of all the scales and measures that are used in the regression analysis.

REGRESSION ANALYSIS—TESTING THE HYPOTHESIS

At this point, having identified the scales and measures for the regression analysis, I test the hypothesis to see whether the relationship between diversity and innovativeness is indeed a positive function of the right context.

I use the two-step regression framework developed earlier in the study. As a first step, I test the significance of the relationship between diversity and innovativeness without the right context in place. In the second step, which is the crucial one for testing the hypothesis, I test the significance of the relationship between diversity and innovativeness (but as a function of the right context). The two-step regression framework is applied for each of the dependent, independent, and intervening variables that have been identified by the factor analysis. Figure 6 presents the structure of the model with all the dependent,

FIGURE 6. Model design with the dependent, independent, and intervening variables.

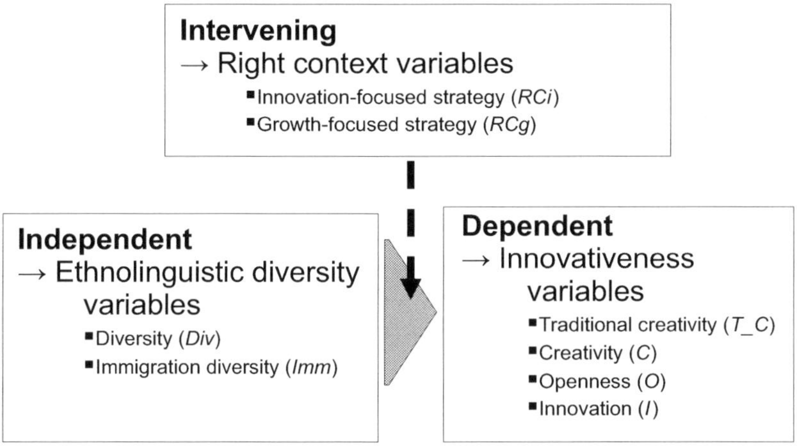

independent, and intervening variables that are used in the regression analyses.

Traditional Creativity—Regression Results

The results of the regression analyses with the traditional creativity *T_C* as a dependent variable do not provide support for the proposed hypothesis. In the first-step regressions, the diversity variable *Div* is not statistically significant (*t*-stat 0.53). That indicates that there is no significant relationship between diversity and traditional creativity (Table 11, regression 1a). This is also true when I use the immigration diversity variable *Imm* as a measure of diversity (regression 1b). Table 11 presents the results of the first-step regressions for traditional creativity *T_C* as the dependent variable.

Since the results of the first-step regressions have shown that there is no relationship between the different forms of diversity and traditional creativity, there is no basis for running the second-step regressions, which would test whether the positive relationship between diversity

TABLE 11. Relationship between diversity, immigration, and traditional creativity (dependent variable: traditional creativity *T_C*).

Variable	1a	1b
Div	0.09	–
	(0.53)	–
Imm	–	0.06
	–	(0.34)
number of observations	30	29
adj. R^2	–0.03	–0.03

Note. t-stat in parentheses.

and creativity is moderated by the existence of the right context. The results of the first-step regressions indicate that there are no foundations in the claim that diversity might have a positive impact on creativity, at least not when creativity is measured by the traditional creativity variable.

Creativity—Regression Results

When I use the Modern Creativity Scale as the dependent variable, which I simply call creativity *C*, the results of the regressions are diametrically different from the ones for traditional creativity *T_C*. The diversity variable *Div* already shows statistical significance in the first-step regression, which tests the impact of diversity on creativity, yet without the existence of the right context. The *Div* variable, in the first-step regression, is significant at the 0.05 significance level and has the anticipated positive sign. However, the model as a whole accounts only for 16% of the variance of creativity (adj. R^2 is 0.16), which is not a very satisfying amount. Still, the first regression provides some basis for the argument that ethnic diversity by itself has a positive impact on creativity, but the impact is not yet highly significant.

TABLE 12. Relationship between diversity and creativity (dependent variable: creativity *C*).

Variable	1	*RCg* 2g	*RCi* 2i
Div	0.43	0.09	–0.27
	(2.54)	(0.36)	(–1.44)
DivRCg	–	0.41	–
	–	(1.48)	–
DivRCi	–	–	0.94
	–	–	(4.91)
number of observations	30	30	30
adj. R^2	0.16	0.19	0.54

Note. t-stat in parentheses.

Those results are in accordance with what I have expected. Due to the choice of the sample, I would already expect diversity to have a positive and somehow significant impact on creativity. Since all the OECD countries can be more or less considered plural democracies, they already fulfill one of the right context requirements, which is the existence of plural democracy. Therefore, in this sample, I would already expect a positive relationship between diversity and creativity. Nevertheless, since the other right context elements are still missing from the model, I would not expect the relationship to be highly significant, as is the case.

Given the results of the first-step regression which suggest the existence of a positive relationship between diversity and creativity, I can run the second-step regressions which test the influence of the right context on that relationship. I start with the growth-focused strategy, *RCg*, as a measure of the right context.

When the *Div* and *RCg* variables are combined in an interaction term *DivRCg*, and regressed together with *Div* on creativity *C*, none of the explanatory variables show statistical significance (Table 12, regression 2g). Similar results are achieved when the immigration diversity *Imm* variable is used as the independent variable (Table 13, regression 2g). Therefore, based on those results, the growth-focused strategy variable *RCg* cannot be considered as having a positive moderating effect on the relationship between diversity and creativity. The regressions conducted with the *RCg* variable do not provide support for the hypothesis, which states that the right context has an enabling impact on the positive relationship between diversity and creativity.

The situation changes entirely when I use the innovation-focused strategy variable *RCi* as a measure of the right context. The results of the second-step regression (Table 12, regression 2i) are striking in their support of the hypothesis. The interaction term of diversity and the innovation-focused strategy, *DivRCi*, has a positive sign and is highly significant ($p < 0.001$). Furthermore, the second-step regression with the innovation-focused strategy as the right context variable has a very high coefficient of determination. The adjusted R^2 of the second model is 0.54. It signifies that more than half of the variance of creativity *C* is explained by the model, which is a highly satisfying amount.

TABLE 13. Relationship between immigration diversity and creativity (dependent variable: creativity *C*).

Variable	1	*RCg* 2g	*RCi* 2i
Imm	0.54	0.34	–0.15
	(3.31)	(1.14)	(–0.76)
ImmRCg	–	0.24	–
	–	(0.79)	–
ImmRCi	–	–	0.9
	–	–	(4.49)
number of observations	29	29	29
adj. R^2	0.26	0.25	0.57

Note. t-stat in parentheses.

The results of the second-step regression with *RCi* also show that the regression coefficient on *Div* is negative and not significant. The coefficient on *Div* indicates the impact of diversity on creativity when *RCi* equals zero. An insignificant coefficient on *Div* implies that diversity, without the existence of the right context, would not have any significant effects on creativity. This provides a further support for the hypothesis, which implies that ethnolinguistic diversity would have either negative or insignificant impact on creativity in the situation when the right context is not present.

Therefore, the results of the second-step regression, with the innovation-focused strategy *RCi* as a measure of the right context, provide a strong support for the proposed hypothesis. They show that the higher the level of the right context *RCi*, the more important diversity *Div* becomes. Furthermore, they indicate that if the right context *RCi* is not present, then diversity loses both its significance and its positive impact on creativity. Hence, the results of the second regression with *RCi* show that the relationship between diversity and creativity is indeed a positive function of the right context, and that the relationship is highly significant. Table 12 presents the regression results for the creativity variable *C* and the diversity variable *Div*.

The results of the regressions with the immigration diversity *Imm* as the independent variable (Table 13, regression 2i) show a similar pattern. The first-step regression reveals that the relationship between immigration diversity *Imm* and creativity *C*, yet without the right context, is even stronger and more significant than in the case of *Div*. Furthermore, the second-step regression with immigration diversity *Imm* explains 57% of the variance of creativity, which is even slightly bigger than in the case of *Div*. Finally, the interaction term *ImmRCi* has the anticipated positive sign and is highly significant at a 0.001 level.

Therefore, the results of the regressions conducted with *Imm* as the independent variable reinforce the results of the previous regressions conducted with the *Div* variable, and they also provide a strong support for the proposed hypothesis. Table 13 presents the regression results for the creativity variable *C* and the immigration diversity variable *Imm*.

In conclusion, the regressions conducted with the creativity variable *C* as the dependent variable indicate that there are strong foundations in the claim that the relationship between diversity and creativity is a function of the right context. The regression results with the innovation-focused strategy *RCi* variable provide a strong support for the hypothesis. They indicate that increasing the levels of innovation-focused strategy significantly strengthens the positive impact of diversity *Div* on creativity *C*. Furthermore, they demonstrate that the lack of innovation-focused strategy nullifies the positive impact of diversity on creativity. At the same time, the regression results reveal that the growth-focused strategy, indicated by the *RCg* variable, cannot be considered as having a moderating effect on the relationship between diversity and creativity.

Openness—Regression Results

The regressions conducted with the openness *O* variable as the dependent variable also provide support for the hypothesis. However, as shown in the first-step regression (Table 14, regression 1), the relationship between diversity *Div* and openness *O* seems to be weaker than the relationship between diversity *Div* and creativity *C*. When *Div* is a sole explanatory variable for openness *O*, it is significant only at a 0.1 level, and the model as a whole accounts only for 6% of the variance of openness *O*. Still, the results of the first regression provide some basis for the claim that there is a positive relationship between diversity and openness. Therefore, I run the second-step regressions to test if that relationship is moderated by the existence of the right context variables.

This time, the regression outcomes for the growth-focused strategy *RCg* as the moderating variable provide some support for the hypothesis (Table 14, regression 2g). The interaction term *DivRCg* has a positive sign, as anticipated by the hypothesis, and it is statistically significant (*t*-stat is 3.2). However, the overall explanatory power of the model is quite low (adj. R^2 is 0.29), which means that the model explains less than 30% of the variance of openness *O*. That makes the results of the regressions with the growth-focused strategy relatively weak.

TABLE 14. Relationship between diversity and openness (dependent variable: openness *O*).

Variable	1	*RCg* 2g	*RCi* 2i
Div	0.3	−0.37	−0.52
	(1.67)	(−1.41)	(−2.89)
DivRCg	–	0.83	–
	–	(3.2)	–
DivRCi	–	–	1.09
	–	–	(6.05)
number of observations	30	30	30
adj. R^2	0.06	0.29	0.59

Note. t-stat in parentheses.

The results are much stronger when the innovation-focused strategy *RCi* is used as an indicator of the existence of the right context (Table 14, regression 2i). The results of the second-step regression with the openness *O* variable provide a strong support for the hypothesis, in a similar way as it was in the case of creativity *C*. The interaction term of diversity and the innovation-focused strategy, *DivRCi*, has a positive sign and is highly significant (*t*-stat is 6.05), as anticipated by the hypothesis. The model explains 59% of the variance of openness (adj. R^2 is 0.59), which is a very satisfying amount.

The results of the second-step regression also show that when the innovation-focused strategy *RCi* is at a level of zero, the impact of diversity on openness is negative and significant (*t*-stat is 2.89). Those results carry an even stronger message, concerning the effect of diversity in the absence of the right context, than the results with creativity as the dependent variable. In the regressions with the creativity variable *C*, the lack of the right context made the diversity variable simply insignificant. The regressions with the openness variable demonstrate that the relationship between diversity *Div* and openness *O*, in the absence of the right context *RCi*, is even negative and significant.

Table 14 presents the results for the openness variable *O* and the diversity variable *Div*.

The results of the analysis with the immigration diversity *Imm* as the independent variable reinforced the results obtained with the diversity *Div* variable (Table 15). Actually, the positive relationship between openness *O* and the diversity coming from immigration *Imm* is even stronger and more significant (*t*-stat is 2.5) than in the case of indigenous diversity *Div*. The coefficient of determination (adj. R^2) for the first-step regression is also higher in the case of *Imm* than in the case of *Div*, and it equals 17% (Table 15, regression 1). As for the second-step regression, the results follow similar patterns as in the case of *Div*; therefore, they also provide support for the hypothesis. Table 15 presents the results for the openness variable *O* and the immigration diversity variable *Imm*.

To conclude, the results of the regression analysis conducted with both the openness variable *O* as the dependent variable and the innovation-focused strategy *RCi* as the right context intervening variable provide a strong support for the hypothesis, which claims that the relationship between diversity and openness is a positive function of the right

TABLE 15. Relationship between immigration diversity and openness (dependent variable: openness O).

Variable	1	*RCg* 2g	*RCi* 2i
Imm	0.41	–0.22	–0.34
	(2.58)	(–0.86)	(–1.9)
ImmRCg	–	0.76	–
	–	(2.94)	–
ImmRCi	–	–	0.97
	–	–	(5.44)
number of observations	29	29	29
adj. R^2	0.17	0.35	0.59

Note. t-stat in parentheses.

context. The hypothesis is also somewhat supported in the case when the right context variable is indicated by the growth-focused strategy. However, due to the low coefficient of determination (adj. R^2 is 0.29), this support is relatively weak.

The outcome of the second-step regression with the innovation-focused strategy *RCi* as the intervening variable shows that diversity matters more at higher levels of the right context. It means that for countries with higher levels of innovation-focused strategy *RCi*, diversity has a stronger positive impact on openness *O* than for countries with lower levels of *RCi*. Furthermore, the results of the second-step regression demonstrate that diversity can act as a double-edged sword. In the presence of the right context, diversity can have a significant positive effect, but if the right context is not present it can have a significant negative effect on the openness of countries.

Innovation—Regression Results

As a final step in the regression analysis, I use the innovation variable *I* as the dependent variable, which combines both the creativity and the openness variables together into a single measure of innovation. In line with the expectations, the results of the regressions with the innovation variable *I* also provide support for the hypothesis. Again, the results point to the innovation-focused strategy *RCi* as the strongest moderator of the positive relationship between diversity and innovation. The growth-focused strategy *RCg* also appears to be a moderator of that relationship, but the results are relatively weaker.

The sole impact of diversity *Div* on innovation *I*, as presented in the first-step regression (Table 16, regression 1), has the anticipated positive sign and is statistically significant with *t*-statistics of 2.14. The coefficient of determination (adj. R^2) of the first-step regression, however, is very low and equals 11%. Still, the results of the first regression provide some foundations for the claim that there is a positive relationship between diversity and openness. Therefore, I run the second-step regression to test whether that relationship might be conditioned by the existence of the right context variables.

TABLE 16. Relationship between diversity and innovation (dependent variable: innovation *I*).

Variable	1	*RCg* 2g	*RCi* 2i
Div	0.37	–0.19	–0.43
	(2.14)	(–0.75)	(–2.54)
DivRCg	–	0.71	–
	–	(2.69)	–
DivRCi	–	–	1.08
	–	–	(6.25)
number of observations	30	30	30
adj. R^2	0.11	0.27	0.62

Note. t-stat in parentheses.

The results of the second-step analyses, with the innovation variable *I* as the dependent variable, the diversity variable *Div* as the independent variable, and the growth-focused strategy variable *RCg* as the intervening variable, provide some support for the hypothesis. The interaction term *DivRCg* is positive and statistically significant (*t*-stat is 2.69), as anticipated by the hypothesis. However, the overall explanatory power of the model is rather low (adj. R^2 is 0.27). That means that the model explains only a small portion of the variance of innovation *I*. Therefore, the results with the growth-focused strategy appear relatively weak.

The results of the second-step regressions become significantly stronger when the innovation-focused strategy *RCi* is brought into play as an indicator of the right context. In that case, the results provide a very strong support for the proposed hypothesis. The coefficient of determination is the highest among all the regressions that have been conducted in this analysis. The adjusted R^2 is 0.62, which means that the model explains 62% of the variance of innovation *I*. Furthermore, the statistical significance of the interaction term is very high, with *t*-statistics of 6.25, which again is the highest among all the regressions.

Finally, the diversity variable *Div* in the second-step regression (Table 16, regression 2i) has a negative sign and is statistically significant (*t*-stat is –2.54). This entails that, in the absence of the innovation-focused strategy *RCi*, the relationship between diversity *Div* and innovation *I* is negative and statistically significant. That result is in agreement with the hypothesis. Table 16 presents the results for the innovation variable *I* and the diversity variable *Div*.

The regressions with the immigration diversity *Imm* as the independent variable (Table 17) reinforce the results obtained with the diversity *Div* variable. The only difference appears in the second-step regression with *RCi*, where the immigration diversity variable *Imm* does have a negative sign—but it is not statistically significant. This suggests that in the case when the right context variable *RCi* is not present, immigration diversity *Imm* has an insignificant, rather than a negative, impact on innovation *I*. Table 17 presents the results for the innovation variable *I* and the immigration diversity variable *Imm*.

To conclude, the regressions with the innovation variable *I* as the dependent variable, the diversity variable *Div* as the independent variable, and the innovation-focused strategy *RCi* as the intervening variable

TABLE 17. Relationship between immigration diversity and innovation (dependent variable: innovation *I*).

Variable	1	*RCg* 2g	*RCi* 2i
Imm	0.49	0.01	–0.27
	(3.0)	(0.05)	(–1.47)
ImmRCg	–	0.57	–
	–	(2.01)	–
ImmRCi	–	–	0.98
	–	–	(5.35)
number of observations	30	30	30
adj. R^2	0.22	0.30	0.62

Note. t-stat in parentheses.

provide the strongest support for the hypothesis among all the regressions conducted in this study. The hypothesis is also somewhat supported in the case of the growth-focused strategy *RCg* as the right context variable, but the results are considerably weaker, which makes them less credible.

The strongly significant results with the innovation-focused strategy *RCi* as the right context variable signify that the relationship between diversity and innovation *I* is indeed a positive function of the right context. The results demonstrate that the positive impact of diversity on innovation *I* occurs only in the presence of the right context. If the right context is not present, the impact of diversity is insignificant or even negative. Furthermore, the positive effect of diversity on innovation *I* increases together with the levels of the right context; the higher the level of the right context *RCi*, the stronger and more significant the impact of diversity. This implies that diversity matters more at higher levels of the innovation-focused strategy *RCi*. Those results hold for both forms of diversity—the indigenous diversity *Div* and the immigration diversity *Imm*.

ROBUSTNESS OF THE RESULTS

I have to consider an alternative explanation for the results because it is possible that there could be another influence that is driving them. There is one obvious alternative influence that could be driving the results, and that is the income level of countries.[29] It is very probable that what I am really capturing in the results is not the relationship between innovativeness and diversity, but rather the relationship between innovativeness and income level.

The innovativeness variables, in the way that I have measured them, may be more dependent on the level of per capita income than on diversity, and the expenditure on R&D (*RCi*) might be just a proxy for per capita income levels. It is very likely that the level of R&D spending (*RCi*) is strongly dependent on the level of per capita income. Therefore, the results of the regressions might actually be capturing the relationship between innovativeness and income, instead of between innovativeness and diversity moderated by the R&D spending (*RCi*).

In order to rule out such a possibility, I have to control for the level of per capita income in all the regressions that provided support for the existence of the positive relationship between innovativeness and diversity moderated by the right context. I have to include the measure of per capita income, which I call the income variable *Inc* (OECD, 2005d),[30] into the respective regressions to see whether the relation of interest still holds. In order to do so, I apply the following regression model for all the relevant measures of innovativeness and diversity:[31]

$$I = \alpha_0 + \alpha_1 \, Div + \alpha_2 \, Div\, RC + \alpha_2 \, Inc$$

The results of the regressions with the income variable (Tables 18 and 19) and the innovation-focused strategy (*RCi*) as the right context variable have shown that even when we control for the per capita income levels, the relationship between innovativeness and diversity is still a significant function of the right context variable. The relationship of interest still holds for all the relevant measures of innovativeness, which are creativity, openness, and innovation, as well as for both measures of diversity, which are diversity and immigration diversity.

For the regressions with diversity as the independent variable and creativity as the dependent variable, introducing the income measure into the regressions decreases the significance of the interaction term *DivRCi*; however, the term still remains statistically significant at the 0.05 level. For the regressions with diversity on one side, and the openness and innovation variables on the other side, the interaction term *DivRCi* remains highly statistically significant at the 0.001 level. The income variable *Inc* has a slightly weaker statistical significance than the interaction term *DivRCi* in the case of the regressions with the creativity variable, and it is considerably weaker in the case of the regressions with the openness and the innovation variables.

For all the regressions with diversity, the introduction of the income variable increases the overall explanatory power of the models in comparison to the previous models that did not include the *Inc* variable (for creativity, the adj. R^2 is 0.63; for openness, the adj. R^2 is 0.64; and for innovation, the adj. R^2 is 0.69). The results also show that the diversity variable, when not accompanied by the right context variable *RCi*, is either insignificant or negatively significant for the relationship between diversity and innovativeness. Therefore, those results are in line with the previous results, which did not include the income variable. Table 18 presents the results of the regressions for diversity as the independent variable, and creativity, openness, and innovation as the dependent variables.

The results of the regressions with the immigration diversity *Imm* as the independent variable and the innovation-focused strategy *RCi* as the intervening variable also show that the relationship of interest still holds even when we control for the income level. For all of the different measures of innovativeness, the interaction term *ImmRCi* remains statistically significant at considerable levels. The introduction of the income variable also increases the overall explanatory power of the models. However, what makes the results with the *Imm* variable different from the results with the *Div* variable is that the income variable does not show statistical significance in the regressions with the immigration variable. Furthermore, the immigration variable actually increases its statistical significance in comparison to the previous regressions, which do not include the income variable. Table 19 presents the regression results for diversity as the independent variable, and creativity, openness, and innovation as the dependent variables.

The situation is different in the case of the growth-focused strategy *RCg* as the right context variable. The introduction of the income variable *Inc* increases the overall explanatory power of the models, but at the same time, it decreases the statistical significance of the interaction terms *DivRCg* and *ImmRCg*. The income variable *Inc* shows statistical significance in all the models. However, only the interaction terms in the models with openness as the dependent variable remain

TABLE 18. Relationship between diversity and innovativeness controlled for income, with innovation-focused strategy *RCi* (dependent variables: creativity *C*, openness *O*, and innovation *I*).

Variable	*C* 2a	*O* 2b	*I* 2c
Div	−0.12	−0.40	−0.30
	(−0.64)	(−2.24)	(−1.84)
DivRCi	0.61	0.84	0.80
	(2.97)	(4.11)	(4.24)
Inc	0.39	0.30	0.33
	(2.8)	(2.2)	(2.57)
number of observations	30	30	30
adj. R^2	0.63	0.64	0.69

Note. t-stat in parentheses.

TABLE 19. Relationship between immigration and innovativeness controlled for income, with innovation-focused strategy *RCi* (dependent variables: creativity *C*, openness *O*, and innovation *I*).

Variable	*C* 2a	*O* 2b	*I* 2c
Imm	−0.22	−0.41	−0.33
	(−1.08)	(−2.33)	(−1.79)
ImmRCi	0.72	0.78	0.82
	(3.10)	(3.82)	(3.83)
Inc	0.29	0.34	0.27
	(1.41)	(1.77)	(1.43)
number of observations	29	29	29
adj. R^2	0.58	0.63	0.63

Note. t-stat in parentheses.

statistically significant. In the models with openness, the statistical significance of the interaction term *DivRCg* is just on the borderline with the *t*-statistics equal to 1.97. The statistical significance of the interaction term *ImmRCg* is 2.24, which is a slight decrease compared to the model without *Inc*.

TABLE 20. Relationship between diversity and innovativeness controlled for income, with growth-focused strategy *RCg* (dependent variables: creativity *C*, openness *O*, and innovation *I*).

Variable	*C* 2a	*O* 2b	*I* 2c
Div	0.31	−0.19	−0.01
	(1.41)	(−0.87)	(−0.04)
DivRCg	−0.02	0.48	0.32
	(−0.12)	(1.97)	(1.35)
Inc	0.63	0.49	0.55
	(4.27)	(3.27)	(3.73)
number of observations	30	30	30
adj. R^2	0.51	0.48	0.51

Note. t-stat in parentheses.

Thus, in the case of the models with the growth-focused strategy *RCg* as the right context variable, only the models with the openness variable withstand the robustness test, which controls for the income level. In the case of innovation as the dependent variable and the growth-focused strategy *RCg* as the intervening variable, the models do not pass the robustness test. Tables 20 and 21 present the regression results for the models with the growth-focused strategy *RCg* and the income variable *Inc*.

To conclude, I have considered the per capita income level as a competitive explanation for the results obtained in this study. I have shown empirically that the relationship of interest still holds in the case of the innovation-focused strategy *RCi* as the right context variable, but it does not hold in the case of the growth-focused strategy *RCg*, except for the openness variable. Therefore, the results with the *RCg* have to be taken with caution. This turnout does not constitute a real harm to this study because, from the outset, the results with the *RCg* did not show a very strong statistical significance. The main support for the hypothesis is derived from

TABLE 21. Relationship between immigration and innovativeness controlled for income, with growth-focused strategy *RCg* (dependent variables: creativity *C*, openness *O*, and innovation *I*).

Variable	*C* 2a	*O* 2b	*I* 2c
Imm	0.11	–0.42	–0.19
	(0.42)	(–1.80)	(–0.73)
ImmRCg	–0.02	0.53	0.33
	(–0.08)	(2.24)	(1.25)
Inc	0.63	0.55	0.57
	(2.97)	(3.05)	(2.83)
number of observations	29	29	29
adj. R^2	0.43	0.51	0.45

Note. t-stat in parentheses.

the regression results with the innovation-focused strategy *RCi* as the right context variable, and those results turned out to be robust.

There are some other variables that might have an impact on the level of innovativeness of countries and could be considered in future research as the additional control variables. Such variables would include, for example, the level of education, the availability of finance, and the ideological diversity existing in the country. One can easily imagine how those variables might have an impact on the creativity, flexibility, and innovativeness of countries. They would most likely increase the level of innovativeness. However, due to the limited sample size, and in order to keep the study within a manageable scope, those issues have to be left to further research.

ENDNOTES

1. The U.S. domains include the following: .us; .edu; .mil; .gov.
2. Except for the data on secure servers, as the ITU does not compile the data for it. Thus, for the secure servers I use the OECD data. For all the other Internet technology variables, such as Internet hosts, Internet users, and number of PCs, I use the ITU data (http://www.itu.int).
3. The Community Innovation Survey aims to gather information on business innovation across the European Union (EU) area.
4. The indicator of triadic patent families has been recently developed by the OECD in order to improve the quality and international comparability of patent-based indicators. It was created in order to eliminate the "home advantage" bias and to generally represent patents of high value. The triadic patent families are defined as a set of patents taken at the European Patent Office (EPO), the Japanese Patent Office (JPO), and the U.S. Patent & Trademark Office (USPTO) that share one or more priorities.
5. The reason why I do not include separate JPO counts of patents is because the OECD does not carry that type of data. The JPO counts are only included in the triadic patent families.
6. All those Internet and computer diffusion measures are reported relative to the country population.
7. The ELF index has some problems associated with it: first, the problems that stem from the underlying ethnographic data from which it is calculated, and second, the problems that arise from attempting to summarize a country's ethnic diversity with a single measure. For more on that topic, see Posner (1999).
8. The statement could indeed be true in the case of indigenous groups; however, it might not be true in the case of immigration.
9. Alesina's index captures some of the effects of immigration because it is based on the data from the last 10 to 20 years. However, it does not make a distinction between the indigenous groups and the immigrants. For example, in the case of Switzerland, apart from the four big groups (the German, the French, the Italian, and the Romaine groups), the rest are lumped into an "Other Swiss" group, without a distinction whether this group is related to indigenous ethnic groups or immigrants.
10. The statistics on the rates of naturalization/acquisition of nationality cover all means of acquiring the nationality of a country, except where otherwise

indicated. The naturalization rate gives the number of persons acquiring the nationality of the country as a percentage of the stock of foreign population at the beginning of the year.

11. High-skilled immigrants are those with "tertiary" education, and low-skilled immigrants are those with "less than upper secondary" education.
12. The two measures relate to immigration diversity and do not take into account the conditions for indigenous minorities. It is due to the lack of data on the labor market access for indigenous minorities.
13. The administrative regulations include reporting, information and application procedures, and the burdens on business start-ups, implied by both economy-wide and sector-level requirements. The economic regulations include all other domestic regulatory provisions affecting private governance and product market competition (such as state control and legal barriers to entry in competitive markets).
14. Employment protection legislation (EPL) measures the restrictiveness of protection legislation on regular employment.
15. GERD includes both the defense and civil spending on R&D. For more details on the definition of GERD, see OECD (2002, p. 121).
16. Stata is a general-purpose statistical software package. Most of its users work in research, especially in the fields of economics, sociology, political science and epidemiology. The name "Stata" was formed by blending "statistics" and "data" (it is not an acronym).
17. The ICT patents were still considered as cutting edge a couple of years ago; however, now it is no longer the case because other more advanced technologies have appeared, such as biotechnology and nanotechnology, which took the cutting edge position away from the ICT. The same applies to the high and medium technology manufactures, which once were considered as distinctive of a country's advancement but not anymore, because the real cutting edge progress is taking place in different sectors of the economy.
18. For the reason of comparability, and in order to avoid negative values, the two scales have been standardized so that the mean equals 10 and standard deviation equals 3.
19. See endnote 18.
20. There is one variable, services contribution to productivity, which is not part of the modern creativity scale, but it is a part of Factor 1. This variable was also on the list of creativity variables and was considered for the factor analysis. However, the loading on that variable was too low to include it into the modern creativity scale. Now, when we conduct the analysis of creativity and openness variables together, the services contribution

to productivity variable loads 0.5 on the first factor, which is just enough to include it with Factor 1. Also, the alpha reliability score supports that decision.

21. There will be no scale created for the constituting Factor 2 because, apart from one variable, all the variables are the same as in the traditional creativity scale. Thus, creating a new scale would not add any explanatory value to our analysis.
22. See endnote 18.
23. See endnote 18.
24. The variables that were dropped indicate the existence of the integration and learning perspective on diversity, and they included the following: naturalization/acquisition of nationality as percentage of foreign population, percentage of foreign-born people with the citizenship of country of residence, low percentage of foreign-born unemployment rate, small percentage gap in unemployment between foreign-born people and natives.
25. The alpha reliability score for the second factor is 0.73, while the required threshold is 0.8.
26. The two variables that loaded on Factor 2 include the foreign born labor participation rate, as well as the small percentage gap in labor participation rate between foreign born and natives.
27. See endnote 18.
28. The scales and the measure have been standardized in order to allow for the comparability between them. They all have the mean of 10 and the standard deviation of 3.
29. I have also empirically checked the impact of the right context variable *RCi* as a separate explanatory variable, together with the *Div* variable, on the level of innovativeness of countries. I did it in order to assess whether the inclusion of the *RCi* variable does not take away the significance of the diversity variable. One possible explanation of the results of the second-step regression with the interaction term is that the *RCi* variable is so strongly related to the innovativeness variables that—no matter what I would interact it with—the interaction term would still show statistical significance. In order to contest such an explanation, I have to show that the diversity variable possesses a significant explanatory power on its own, which is not related to the *RCi* variable. If that is the case, then I can argue that the interaction term *DivRCi* indeed reflects the combined effect of *Div* and *RCi*, and not only the overwhelming effect of *RCi*. The results of the regressions conducted with *Div* and *RCi* as the separate explanatory variables have shown that both of the variables constitute significant explanations

for the variance of creativity, openness, and innovation (all *t*-stats above the statistically significant threshold). The same was in the case when the *Imm* variable was used as a measure of diversity. Therefore, the results of the regressions conducted with *RCi* as a separate explanatory variable have shown that *Div* and *Imm* possess a significant explanatory power on their own, which is independent of the *RCi* variable. Thus, the results have provided support for the claim that the interaction terms *DivRCi* and *ImmRCi* reflect the combined effects of *Div* and *RCi*, or *Imm* and *RCi*, and not only the strong effect of *RCi* on the level of innovativeness.

30. The income variable *Inc* is measured by GDP per capita in the year 2002. The measurement is based on the data from the *OECD Factbook 2005* (OECD, 2005d).
31. Ideally, we should have also included a separate term for the right context variable RC. However, it is not possible due to very high multicolinearity (for the models with the *Div* variable, *vif* = 22; for the models with the *Imm* variable, *vif* = 35).

Chapter 5

Discussion of the Results

Discussion of the Factor Analysis Results

There are two important outcomes of the factor analysis. First, the factor analysis led to a significant data reduction and to the creation of reliable factor scales, which were then explored in the regression analysis as the independent, dependent, and intervening variables. Second, it revealed that there is an evident divide between the creativity variables. Those variables did not form one single scale, but they split between two factors and formed two separate single scales. One group of creativity variables exhibited a different pattern of variation than the other group. Therefore, the factor analysis uncovered that the variables that were chosen to measure creativity refer to two different types of creativity, which are significantly distinct from one another.

The existence of two underlying factors among the creativity variables necessitated the creation of two creativity scales. The examination of the content of the two scales reveals that one of the scales is related to a more traditional type of creativity, while the other refers to a more modern type of creativity. The first scale, which was named the Traditional Creativity Scale, concentrates more on the inventive activities in the old sectors of the economy. The other scale, which was named the Modern Creativity Scale, focuses more on the developments in the new sectors of the economy.

The variables that constitute the Traditional Creativity Scale refer to patents both in general and specifically in the ICT sector, as well as to the overall development of the manufacturing sector. The variables that form the Modern Creativity Scale relate to prominent scientific citations, biotechnology patents, strong ICT contribution to GDP growth, high technology balance of payments, and the development of the services sector.

This finding is worth a stronger notice because the current research does not differentiate between those two distinct types of creativity. It mainly uses the patent counts as indicators of the creative output of countries. The factor analysis reveals that such approach is no longer valid because most of the patents do not measure the creativity that takes place in the whole economy, but rather measure the creativity that takes place mainly in the manufacturing sector. That leaves all the inventions in the services sector unaccounted for.

The patent counts might have been good indicators of inventiveness at the time of industrial economy when manufacturing was the key sector of the economy, but it is no longer true in the era of the knowledge economy. At the moment, the share of the services sector in the economy is constantly growing, and in most of the advanced countries it has gone above 70%. It is the services sector that is now the key sector of modern economies. Therefore, a measure such as patent counts, which focuses mainly on the inventions in the manufacturing sector, loses its credibility as a measure of the creativity of countries. Currently, in the era of the knowledge economy, in order to measure the creative output of countries we have to focus on the services sector. The factor analysis suggests that we can also employ additional indicators that measure the creativity of countries such as the prominent scientific citations, biotechnology patents, the technology balance of payments, and the ICT contribution to GDP.

The distinction between the two types of creativity, uncovered by the factor analysis, seems to be very important for measuring the creative output of countries in the era of the knowledge economy. The distinction did prove important for evaluating the impact of diversity on the creativity of countries. When the creativity was measured in the traditional way using the Traditional Creativity Scale, the impact of diversity on creativity was found to be not significant. However, when the creativity was measured by the Modern Creativity Scale, the impact of diversity on creativity appeared to be significant and positive. Therefore, the distinction between the two types of creativity contributed to portraying diversity in a different light.

Discussion of the Regression Analysis Results

The results of the regression analysis showed that the ethnolinguistic diversity can constitute a resource of creativity, openness, and innovation for countries. At the same time, they demonstrated that this positive potential of diversity can be unleashed only in the presence of the right context. Therefore, the results provided support for the hypothesis, which stated that, given the right context in place, the countries that are ethnolinguistically more heterogeneous are expected to have higher levels of innovativeness than the countries that are more homogeneous.

The positive impact of diversity on innovativeness was not asserted in the case of the traditional creativity variable. The results of the first-step regression for this variable showed that there is no significant relationship between diversity and traditional creativity. I have just explained the main reason for such a turnout on the occasion of discussing the results of the factor analysis. To reiterate, the lack of the positive relationship is related to the fact that the traditional creativity variable refers to innovativeness that takes place in the older sectors of the economy such as manufacturing. Therefore, it does not really capture the creative spirit existing in a modern economy. It is the modern creativity variable, denoted simply as creativity, which truly captures the creative spirit of a contemporary economy.

There is also an additional explanation of why we see a positive relationship between diversity and creativity, but not between diversity and traditional creativity. It is related to the differences that exist in the mechanism of new knowledge creation between the manufacturing and the services sector. The innovation process of the manufacturing sector is more dependent on a specialized scientific knowledge, while in the services sector the human resources play a much more important role (OECD, 2005c; Tamura et al., 2005).

In the manufacturing sector, the generation of new ideas takes place in more structured and formal settings, and it requires much more conventional research and development. The novel ideas are mainly related to the invention of new products and to the improvement of the existing products and processes. The new ideas are created by a group of researchers, or even an individual researcher, specialized on the topic. Thus, the invention in the manufacturing sector is more heavily dependent on a specialized scientific knowledge.

In the services sector, however, a lot of the novel ideas are related to the invention of new services and the improvement in the quality of the existing services and processes. A lot of the innovative activities are more organizational and disembodied in nature, and they relate to organizational arrangements, changes in processes, and markets (Tamura et al., 2005). Since a lot of the inventions in the services are nontechnical, they do not require much formal research and development (Tamura et al.). They are based more on the knowledge of the area, as well as a creative and adaptive approach toward the topic. The generation of new ideas takes place in a much more informal setting with a big involvement of teamwork. Thus, in the services sector, the human resources are the key element of the innovation efforts.

Since human resources are the main channel through which the creative potential of ethnolinguistic diversity is carried through to the economy, the impact of diversity should be especially evident in the development of the services sector, rather than the manufacturing sector. This further explains why the regression results assert the existence of a positive relationship between diversity and creativity, but not between diversity and traditional creativity.

Except for the traditional creativity variable, all the other dependent variables show a positive relationship with the diversity variables already in the first-step regression. However, only the addition of the right context variable as the moderator of that relationship, in the second-step regression, made the relationship statistically significant. This outcome underlined the crucial importance of the right context variable for the existence of the positive relationship between diversity and innovativeness. The results of the regressions show that only in the presence of the right context can the ethnolinguistic diversity lead to higher levels of creativity, openness, and innovation.

Furthermore, the results of the second-step regressions show that the impact of diversity becomes stronger with higher levels of the right context (*RCi*). At the same time, they reveal that if the right context is absent, diversity loses its significance and positive effect on innovativeness. When diversity is not accompanied by the right context, its sole effect on the innovativeness of countries becomes insignificant and even negative.[1]

The regression results mainly point to the innovation-focused strategy as the right context variable, which acts as a moderator of the relationship between diversity and innovativeness. It has proven consistently throughout the analysis to be the most significant variable, which conditions the positive impact of diversity. The conditioning effect of the innovation-focused strategy is strongly supported by the regression results for all the innovativeness variables, which included creativity, openness, and innovation, as well as for both of the diversity variables, which included diversity and immigration diversity.

The results of the regressions show that the more a country pursues an innovation-focused strategy, the more it benefits from a diverse workforce. Having a strategy that emphasizes innovation allows the country to orient itself in a way that enables it to extract the resource of innovation embedded in the ethnolinguistic diversity. Therefore, the results of the regressions reveal that the claim made by the scholars of organizational science in relation to firms is also valid in relation to countries: "Simply put, ethnolinguistic diversity is beneficial to innovators" (Richard et al., 2003, p. 114).

The other right context element, which (based on the analysis) can be considered as having a positive impact on the relationship between diversity and innovativeness, is the plural democracy. The plural democracy has been accounted for in the analysis by the specific choice of the sample that included only those countries which can be considered, more or less, plural democracies. The sample was limited only to the OECD countries, in order to control for plural democracy. Therefore, the results of the regressions can be interpreted as valid only for plural democracies.

An additional confirmation for the moderating effect of plural democracy on the relationship between diversity and innovativeness has been provided by the results of the first-step regressions in the model. They show that the relationship between diversity and innovativeness is already positive and somewhat significant, even when the other right context variables are not yet added to the equation. This means that for countries that are plural democracies, diversity already exhibits some positive effects on innovativeness.

However, in order to directly test the conditionality argument of the right context in relation to plural democracy, one would have to also include into the analysis those countries that are not plural democracies. One would have to use democratic pluralism as one of the intervening variables in the regressions to then see whether the results of the second-step regression provide any support for the conditionality argument of the right context. However, it is beyond the scope of this study, and it has to be left for the consideration of future research.

The right context variable that, opposite to expectations, does not show a very strong moderating impact on the relationship between diversity and innovativeness is the growth-focused strategy. The results of the regressions with the growth-focused strategy variable are much weaker than the results with the innovation-focused strategy variable. In the case of openness and the innovation, the growth-focused strategy shows some moderating effect on the relationship between diversity and innovativeness. However, in both cases, the model as a whole did not exhibit enough significance to make the results very plausible. Furthermore, the results—except for the ones relating to openness—did not pass the robustness test that controlled for the income level. Still, the results with the growth-focused strategy show some statistical significance; therefore, they should not be disregarded.

The reason why the growth-focused strategy did not show a strong moderating effect on the relationship between diversity and innovativeness might be related to the fact that I was not able to include the entrepreneurship variable in the analysis. Most variables that constitute the Growth-Focused Strategy Scale are actually the facilitators of a good climate for entrepreneurship. Therefore, they might not be as important for the positive relationship between diversity and the other innovativeness variables (such as creativity and openness) as they might be for the positive relationship between diversity and entrepreneurship. Future research should assess whether the significance of the growth-focused strategy as the conditioning right context variable would increase when the entrepreneurship variable is added into the analysis.

The final comment concerns the regression results for the different types of diversity. The regression outcomes show that the economic benefits of increased innovativeness coming from diversity are related to both indigenous diversity and the diversity coming from immigration. The results with the immigration diversity as the independent variable exhibit a very similar pattern as the results with the diversity variable, which relates to old minorities. They demonstrate that the diversity coming from immigration, when set in the right context, also increases the creativity, openness, and innovativeness of countries. That implies that the source of ethnolinguistic diversity is not relevant for the positive effects of diversity to take place. It is the fact of having diversity that increases the levels of creativity, openness, and innovativeness of countries. Hence, the results of this analysis show that it is not the *type* of diversity, but rather the *diversity itself* that matters for innovation.

ENDNOTE

1. In relation to the innovation-focused strategy *RCi*, which passes the robustness tests, the sole effects of ethnolinguistic diversity are insignificant in the case of creativity as the dependent variable, and they are negative in the case of openness and innovation.

Conclusions

The objective of this study was to assess whether ethnolinguistic diversity can constitute an economic benefit for countries. The hypothesized positive effects of diversity were associated with the increases in creativity, openness, and innovativeness. The proposed hypothesis stated that, given the right context in place, the countries that are ethnolinguistically more heterogeneous would reach higher levels of innovativeness than countries that are more homogeneous.

The hypothesis was examined in the context of advanced economies and, overall, the results of the empirical analysis provided support for the hypothesis. The cross-country regression analysis, conducted on the sample of thirty OECD countries, shows that ethnolinguistic diversity indeed leads to higher levels of creativity, openness to change, and innovativeness of countries. However, that is only true when diversity is accompanied by the right context.

The main implication of the results is that countries that fulfill the requirements of the right context, which are plural democracy and an innovation-focused strategy, can seize economic benefits from ethnolinguistic diversity. For those countries, the ethnolinguistic diversity constitutes not just a potential, but rather a *real* economic advantage. The economic benefit comes from increased creativity, openness to change, and innovation.

The results of the analysis also imply that at a certain level of development, having ethnolinguistic diversity provides a competitive advantage to countries, while not having it constitutes a disadvantage. Once the countries develop plural democratic systems and an orientation toward innovation, those that are more ethnically diverse are privileged in terms of innovative outcomes versus the ones that are more homogeneous. The more homogeneous countries have a shortage of the resource of innovation, which is the ethnolinguistic diversity. Therefore, despite the high levels of spending on innovation, they are not able to obtain comparably good results as other countries with the same level of spending but with a higher level of ethnolinguistic diversity. The more heterogeneous countries are more successful in reaching the higher levels of creative thinking, openness to change, and innovation because they possess the resource of innovation: diversity.

At the same time, the countries that are ethnically heterogeneous, but do not have the right context in place, cannot experience the positive impact of diversity. For those countries, the effects of diversity are either insignificant or even negative. That might be the reason why many of the cross-country studies reported the negative effects of ethnic diversity. In those studies, a lot of the countries in the sample did not have the right context in place.

The results of this study are reassuring in their message. They imply that if the right context is added to the equation, ethnic diversity will bring economic benefits to countries that possess it; countries that are ethnolinguistically diverse should not focus on obliterating their diversity—they should rather aim at establishing the right context for diversity. Such approach should ensure a long-term economic benefit for them.

When more countries become plural democracies and increase their focus on innovation, the positive impact of ethnolinguistic diversity, which currently can be observed in the OECD countries, should also be observed in other parts of the world. Therefore, as the countries become more democratized and more focused on innovation, ethnolinguistic diversity (as a resource of creativity) and flexibility can constitute an important source of economic growth, as well as significantly contribute to the increasing of the welfare of the world economy.

It is important to notice that the results of this study reinforced the findings from the organizational science concerning the impact of diversity on the performance of firms. The scholars of organizational science asserted that ethnolinguistic diversity can increase the flexibility and creativity of firms, but only if it is placed in the right context. Based on the research conducted on the level of firms and organizations, they found that diversity has the nature of a double-edged sword. It can have either a positive or negative impact, depending on the context in which it is placed. They pointed to the value-in-diversity perspective, the growth- and innovation-based strategy, and the interaction between diverse individuals as the elements essential for establishing the right context for diversity.

This study used the organizational science research as the theoretical foundations for the analyses and applied it to countries in order to assess whether the same mechanism holds also on the level of countries. The results of the analysis reinforce the findings from the level of firms with respect to the innovation-focused strategy and the value in diversity perspective represented on the level of countries by democratic pluralism. The results provide some support for the growth-focused strategy, but it is relatively weaker. Furthermore, the outcome of the regressions reveal that, also on the level of countries, diversity exhibits a double-edged sword nature and can lead to higher innovativeness only if it is accompanied by the right context. Therefore, the results of this study show that, indeed, the findings from the level of firms also apply to the level of countries.

The conclusions of this study have a direct relevance for the discussion taking place in the field of international political economy concerning the matter of state unity. In the academic debate, those scholars (e.g., Alesina, Spolaore, and La Ferrara) who perceive diversity mainly as a cost to society advocate for secessions and for the breaking up of multiethnic states into smaller and more homogeneous units. Conversely, the scholars (e.g., Doran and Collier) who perceive diversity rather as a benefit advocate against secessions. They are in favor of keeping the multiethnic countries united and heterogenous.

The results of the empirical analysis provide support on the side of those scholars who perceive diversity as a value and advocate against secessions, especially in relation to advanced countries. The results clearly show that diversity, when accompanied by the right context, confers a real economic benefit for countries in terms of higher innovativeness. Therefore, the secessionist breakup of states into smaller and more homogeneous units would sacrifice the rich cultural, ethnic, and social diversities, which have proven to be essential for the creativity of the modern state.

Thus, the findings do not support the theoretical analysis presented by Alesina and Spolaore (2003), which stated that there are no significant economic costs associated with secessions. According to the findings of this study, secession is not free of economic costs because it is associated with losing the resources of diversity essential for the creativity, flexibility, and innovativeness of the societies. Alesina and Spolaore stated that small, homogeneous countries can profit from an integrated and open-trade system just as well as the large and heterogeneous countries; therefore, there are very little costs associated with secessions. However, the authors did not take into account the cost associated with losing ethnolinguistic diversity and, therefore, losing the capacity to innovate and to exploit novelty in production.

According to this study, the more homogeneous states, created as a result of secessions, would be disadvantaged toward the heterogeneous states because they would not possess the resource of innovation provided by ethnolinguistic diversity. Therefore, it is more economically viable, at least for more advanced countries (e.g., those that are part of the OECD), to be heterogeneous rather than homogeneous. Thus, secessions do not really make economic sense, at least for countries that have already reached a certain level of development.

The results of this study provide support on the side of those scholars who argued that the tensions arising from ethnic diversity should not be resolved through secessions but should rather be managed using the institutions of democratic pluralism. According to Doran (2001), the adherence to democratic pluralism instead of secessions is especially important in the current times, when the populations within states become increasingly mixed. The increased diversification of populations within states is particularly vivid within the advanced countries due to the increased flows of immigration and emigration, as well as differential growth rates across populations of differing cultural backgrounds. The system of democratic pluralism is vital because it provides effective instruments to manage the tensions arousing in culturally diverse societies, and it allows the creation of an environment in which diverse people can peacefully interact with each other. The results of this study support that view and suggest that instead of resorting to secessions, the countries should explore the possibilities of establishing the right context for ethnolinguistic diversity.

At the same time, one has to keep in mind that since the analysis considered only the OECD countries, the results can be interpreted as valid only for the more advanced economies. There is a need for further research that would test the hypothesis proposed by this study on a broader range of countries. Only an analysis using a sample composed of both advanced and developing countries would be able to assess whether the positive effects of diversity, moderated by the existence of the right context, are also valid for economically less advanced countries.

There are also other issues that should become a subject of further research. The future research should try to incorporate into the quantitative analysis the right context elements, which were identified by the theoretical part of the study but could not be included into the empirical analysis due to the lack of quantitative data. Future research should also try to create a reliable quantitative measure of democratic pluralism and include it into the analysis as a distinct regression variable. Furthermore, whenever more internationally comparable data on entrepreneurship becomes available, the entrepreneurship variable should be incorporated into the analysis. The future research may also consider designing a model that would test the hypothesis using qualitative measures. This would be especially important if the quantitative data for the right context elements that have been omitted would not become available.

In summary, the results of this study demonstrated that ethnolinguistic diversity constitutes an economic benefit for countries. For the countries with the right context in place, diversity proved to be a resource of increased creativity, openness to change, and innovation. The results suggest that the existence of democratic pluralism and a strategy oriented toward innovation allow the countries to take advantage of their ethnolinguistic diversity and to significantly increase the level of their innovative output. This implies that as the countries progress in their development and in the establishing of the right context, the heterogeneous states will achieve a competitive advantage in terms of innovation over the more homogeneous ones.

Those results provide an important insight for the discussion concerning the unity of multiethnic states. They give leverage to the claim that secessions should be treated with caution, especially in reference to advanced economies. The findings of this study demonstrate that cultural diversity present in multiethnic states, if placed in the right context, can lead to higher levels of creativity, flexibility, and innovation. Therefore, the existence of heterogeneous states, especially in relation to advanced economies, should be encouraged by the international community. This would profit the entire world economy because it would allow the multiethnic states to facilitate the generation of the enormous innovative output of which they are capable in the 21st century.

Appendix A

List of Variables

Table A-1. List of dependent variables: Creativity.

CREATIVITY (Creation of new knowledge)		
Variables	**Stata names**	**Years**
Scientific Articles		
Relative prominence of cited scientific literature	C_citat_scien	2001
Patents per million population		
Triadic patents per population	C_triadic	Ø1991–2001
EPO patents per population (applications)	C_EPO	Ø1991–2002
*USPTO patents per population (granted)	C_USPTO	Ø1991–2001
ICT patents EPO per population	C_ICT_EPO	Ø1991–2001
ICT patents USPTO per population	C_ICT_USPTO	Ø1991–1999
Biotech patents EPO per population	C_BT_EPO	Ø1991–2001
Biotech patents USPTO per population	C_BT_USPTO	Ø1991–1999
Services and Manufacturing		
Share of knowledge-intensive market services in total gross value added	C_serv_know	2002
Share of high and medium-high techn. manufactures in total gross value added	C_manuf_hmtech	2002
**Contribution of the services sector to productivity growth	C_serv_contrib	Ø1990–2001
Share of services in total value added	C_serv_va	2003
Share of manufacturing in total value added	C_manuf_va	2003
Other		
Technology balance of payments as percent of GDP	C_techbal	2003
Contribution of ICT capital to GDP growth (in percentage points)	C_ICT_contrib	Ø1995–2003

*Variables that were not included in the Innovation Scale due to inadequate factor loadings, low alpha reliability, or missing data. **Variables that were not included into the scales either due to inadequate factor loadings.

TABLE A-2. List of dependent variables: Openness to change.

Openness to Change (Diffusion of new knowledge)		
Variables	**Stata names**	**Years**
ICT Investment		
Investment in ICT as percent of gross fixed capital formation	O_Inv_ICT	2003
Software investment as percent of nonresidential gross fixed capital formation	O_Inv_Soft	2003
Internet and PCs		
OECD Data		
Secure servers per 100,000 inhabitants	O_SecServ	2004
ITU Data		
Internet hosts per 100 inhabitants	O_itu_Hosts	2004
Internet users per 100 inhabitants	O_itu_Users	2004
PCs per 100 inhabitants	O_itu_PCs	2004

TABLE A-3. List of independent variables: Ethnolinguistic diversity.

Ethnolinguistic Diversity		
Variables	**Stata names**	**Years**
Old Ethnolinguistic Minorities		
ELF (Ethnolinguistic Fractionalization index), *Atlas Narodov Mira*	ELF	1961
Alesina Fractionalization Index—Ethnic	A_ethnic	*within* 1998–2001
Alesina Fractionalization Index—Language	A_language	*within* 1998–2001
Alesina Fractionalization Index—Religion	A_religion	*within* 1998–2001
Immigration		
Stocks of foreign-born population as percent of total population	IMM_fborn_stock	2003
Noncitizens as percent of total population	IMM_noncitizens	2003
Stocks of foreign or foreign-born labor force as percent of total labor force	IMM_laborforce_stock	2003

Table A-4. List of intervening variables: Right context.

Right Context		
Variables	**Stata names**	**Years**
Value in Diversity (Integration and Learning Perspective on Diversity)		
Acquisition of Nationality (Naturalization)		
*Naturalization/acquisition of nationality as percent of foreign population	RC_naturaliz	2001
*Percent of foreign-born people with the citizenship of country of residence	RC_fb_citiz	Ø2000–2003
High Level of High-Skilled Immigration		
Percent of high-skilled foreign-born people	RC_HS_fb	Ø2000–2003
Low percent of low-skilled foreign-born people	RC_low_LS	Ø2000–2003
Low Unemployment of Foreign Born		
*Low percent foreign-born unemployment rate	RC_low_unem_fb	2003
*Small percent gap in unemployment between foreign-born people and natives	RC_small_unem_gap	2003
High Labor Participation Rate of Foreign-Born People		
*Percent foreign-born labor participation rate	RC_labpa_fb	2003
*Small percent gap in labor participation rate between foreign-born people and natives	RC_small_labpa_gap	2003
Growth-Focused Strategy		
Competitive Business Climate		
Economic regulations in business	RC_low_econ_busreg	2003

(*continued on next page*)

TABLE A-4. *(continued)*

Right Context		
Variables	**Stata names**	**Years**
Administrative regulations in business	RC_low_adm_busreg	2003
Barriers to entrepreneurship	RC_low_barr_entr	2003
Flexible Labor Markets		
Low level of employment protection legislation (EPL) (Low restrictiveness of protection legislation on regular employment)	RC_low_EPL	2003
Innovation-Focused Strategy		
High Expenditure on R&D		
R&D expenditure as percent of GDP (GERD) (GERD—Gross domestic expenditure on R&D as a percentage of GDP)	RC_ExpRD	2002–2003

*Variables that were not included into the scales either due to inadequate factor loadings, low alpha reliability, or missing data.

Appendix B

Creativity Factor Analysis

Standardization of the Variables

In order to be able to create single scales using different variables, all the variables have been standardized into *normed* variables with a mean equal to 0 and a standard deviation equal to 1. I do not lose any generality by dealing with the *standardized* variables (Kim & Mueller, 1978). The standardized variables are denoted by a small letter *s* in front of their name. Since the standardized variables are perfectly correlated with the original variables, they can be used interchangeably in the correlation and factor analysis. The following Stata command was used to standardize all the variables. Table B-1 refers to the creativity variables, but the same standardization procedure was employed for the openness to change, innovation, diversity, and right context variables.

Creativity Factor Analysis

The list of the creativity variables is composed of 15 variables. A correlation matrix reveals that there are many high correlations between the variables, indicating that there could be some underlying factors present among the variables.

Table B-1. Stata: Standardization of the creativity variables.

```
• for var C_citat_scien C_triadic C_EPO C_USPTO C_ICT_EPO C_
ICT_USPTO C_BT_EPO C_BT_USPTO C_serv_busi C_serv_know C_manuf_
hmtech C_serv_contrib C_serv_va C_manuf_va C_serv_em C_manuf_em
C_techbal C_ICT_contrib C_triadic C_EPO: egen sX = std(X)
```

TABLE B-2. Stata: Creativity—correlation matrix.

```
• corr sC_citat_scien sC_triadic sC_EPO sC_USPTO sC_ICT_EPO sC_ICT_USPTO sC_BT_EPO sC_BT_USPTO
SC_serv_know sC_manuf_hmtech sC_serv_contrib sC_serv_va sC_manuf_va sC_techbal sC_ICT_contrib;
(obs = 20)
```

	sC_cit~n	sC_tri~c	sC_EPO	sC_USPTO	sC_IC~PO	sC_IC~TO	sC_BT~PO	sC_BT~TO	sC_ser~w
sC_citat_s~n	1.0000								
sC_triadic	0.5691	1.0000							
sC_EPO	0.6666	0.9194	1.0000						
sC_USPTO	0.4779	0.7723	0.5419	1.0000					
sC_ICT_EPO	0.5376	0.8954	0.8764	0.6128	1.0000				
sC_ICT_USPTO	0.2213	0.6897	0.3933	0.9315	0.5859	1.0000			
sC_BT_EPO	0.7482	0.5134	0.5898	0.4123	0.4225	0.2076	1.0000		
sC_BT_USPTO	0.6518	0.3938	0.3494	0.6155	0.2724	0.4093	0.8504	1.0000	
sC_serv_know	0.5604	0.2086	0.1786	0.3436	0.1098	0.2186	0.2927	0.2944	1.0000
sC_manuf_h~h	0.1016	0.5474	0.5389	0.4293	0.4676	0.4460	0.1329	0.0336	0.1402
sC_serv_co~b	0.0735	0.0975	-0.0117	0.2720	0.0385	0.1913	0.1399	0.3282	-0.0110
sC_serv_va	0.5808	0.2862	0.2814	0.2497	0.1659	0.0747	0.4712	0.4661	0.5795
sC_manuf_va	-0.1119	0.3567	0.3498	0.2268	0.3532	0.3156	-0.0614	-0.1631	-0.0327
sC_techbal	0.5841	0.3330	0.2850	0.3300	0.2674	0.2114	0.5479	0.4875	0.3545
sC_ICT_con~b	0.2709	0.0673	-0.1018	0.3287	-0.0345	0.2700	0.3318	0.4863	0.3623

	sC_man~h	sC_ser~b	sC_ser~a	sC_man~a	sC_tec~l	sC_ICT~b
sC_manuf_h~h	1.0000					
sC_serv_co~b	-0.1491	1.0000				
sC_serv_va	-0.2047	-0.0239	1.0000			
sC_manuf_va	0.8701	-0.2386	-0.3676	1.0000		
sC_techbal	-0.1057	0.3529	0.5214	-0.2314	1.0000	
sC_ICT_con~b	-0.1562	0.5045	0.1705	-0.2374	0.3108	1.0000

A principal components factor analysis was performed on those variables[1] to determine if there are any underlying relationships that might be used to create factor scales for the creativity variables. Results were obtained as seen in Table B-3.

Although in this case there are four eigenvalues that exceed the threshold level of 1.0, the last two are very close to the threshold. This means that the last two factors probably do not explain much more of the total variance for this list of variables than a single variable does. Therefore, the two-factor solution is the most probable one.

To further examine the eigenvalues, it is useful to graph them on a scree chart, as seen in Figure B-1.

TABLE B-3. Stata: Creativity—principal components factor analysis.

```
• factor sC_citat_scien sC_triadic sC_EPO sC_USPTO sC_ICT_EPO
sC_ICT_USPTO sC_BT_EPO sC_BT_USPTO sC_serv_know sC_manuf_hmtech
sC_serv_contrib sC_serv_va sC_manuf_va sC_techbal sC_ICT_contrib,
pcf;
Factor analysis/correlation                    Number of obs = 20

    Method: principal-component factors
    Rotation: (unrotated)
```

Factor	Eigenvalue	Difference	Proportion	Cumulative
Factor1	**6.05516**	2.86738	0.4037	0.4037
Factor2	**3.18778**	1.52739	0.2125	**0.6162**
Factor3	1.66039	0.53970	0.1107	0.7269
Factor4	1.12068	0.28229	0.0747	0.8016
Factor5	0.83839	0.15915	0.0559	0.8575
Factor6	0.67924	0.17839	0.0453	0.9028
Factor7	0.50085	0.14787	0.0334	0.9362
Factor8	0.35298	0.07729	0.0235	0.9597
Factor9	0.27569	0.15055	0.0184	0.9781
Factor10	0.12514	0.00848	0.0083	0.9864
Factor11	0.11666	0.05195	0.0078	0.9942
Factor12	0.06470	0.04669	0.0043	0.9985
Factor13	0.01802	0.01552	0.0012	0.9997
Factor14	0.00249	0.00067	0.0002	0.9999
Factor15	0.00183	.	0.0001	1.0000

FIGURE B-1. Stata: Creativity—scree plot of eigenvalues.

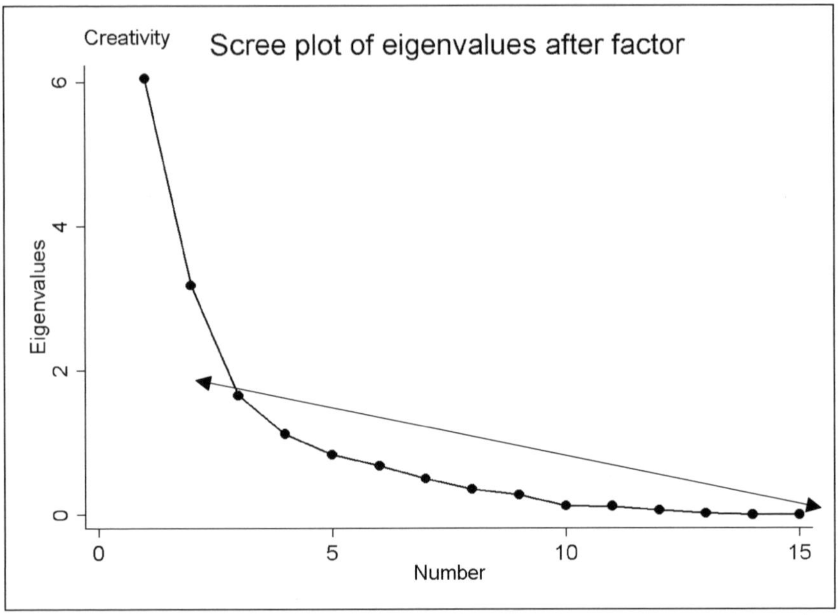

Again, the scree chart indicates that a two-factor solution is the most appropriate, as the line of eigenvalues makes a definite turn at the second factor. In addition, Factor 3 and beyond appear to lie in a straight line, indicating that they do not individually account for a substantial amount of variance. Besides, a two-factor solution would explain 61% of the total variance (cumulative 0.6162), which is a very satisfying amount.[2]

In order to construct factor scales, it is necessary to examine the loadings of each of the variables on the retained factors. Maximization of these loadings for each factor can be obtained by rotating for a two-factor solution.

The rotated loadings indicate that Factor 1 is composed of the following variables: sC_triadic, sC_EPO, sC_USPTO, sC_ICT_EPO, sC_ICT_USPTO, sC_manuf_hmtech, and sC_manuf_va. Each of these

TABLE B-4. Stata: Creativity—rotated factor loadings.

```
• rotate, factors(2);

Rotated factor loadings (pattern matrix) and unique variances
```

Variable	Factor1	Factor2	Uniqueness
sC_citat_s~n	0.3915	**0.7596**	0.2698
sC_triadic	**0.8908**	0.3243	0.1013
sC_EPO	**0.8346**	0.2787	0.2258
sC_USPTO	**0.7152**	0.4533	0.2830
sC_ICT_EPO	**0.8447**	0.2142	0.2406
sC_ICT_USPTO	**0.6988**	0.2356	0.4561
sC_BT_EPO	0.3524	**0.7351**	0.3355
sC_BT_USPTO	0.2511	**0.7987**	0.2990
sC_serv_know	0.1443	**0.5432**	0.6841
sC_manuf_h~h	**0.8234**	-0.2831	0.2419
sC_serv_co~b	-0.0810	0.4153	0.8209
sC_serv_va	0.0085	**0.7238**	0.4761
sC_manuf_va	**0.6986**	-0.4984	0.2636
sC_techbal	0.0993	**0.7428**	0.4383
sC_ICT_con~b	-0.1067	**0.6062**	0.6211

variables has a loading of at least 0.5 on Factor 1, which is the required threshold, and a lower loading on Factor 2.

As for the second factor, the rotated loadings indicate that Factor 2 is composed of the following variables: sC_citat_scien, sC_BT_EPO, sC_BT_USPTO, sC_serv_know, sC_serv_va, sC_techbal, and sC_ICT_contrib. Correspondingly, each of these variables has a loading of at least 0.5 on Factor 2 and a lower loading on Factor 1.

The variable sC_serv_contrib cannot be included with any of the factors because it does not have sufficient loadings that would exceed the 0.5 threshold on any of the factors.[3] Therefore, the sC_serv_contrib variable has to be excluded from further analyses.

Before I combine the aforementioned groups of variables into single factor scales, I have to test if the factors meet the reliability requirement, which means that their alpha reliabilities have to meet the threshold of 0.8. In the case of both factors, the alpha reliability scores exceed the required threshold. The alpha reliability for Factor 1 is 0.85, and the alpha

TABLE B-5. Stata: Creativity—factor alpha reliability.

```
Factor 1
• alpha sC_triadic sC_EPO sC_USPTO sC_ICT_EPO sC_ICT_USPTO sC_
manuf_hmtech sC_manuf_va, std;

Test scale = mean (standardized items)
Average interitem correlation:        0.4670
Number of items in the scale:              7
Scale reliability coefficient:        0.8598

Factor 2
• alpha sC_citat_scien sC_BT_EPO sC_BT_USPTO sC_serv_know sC_serv_
va sC_techbal sC_ICT_contrib, std;

Test scale = mean (standardized items)
Average interitem correlation:        0.3833
Number of items in the scale:              7
Scale reliability coefficient:        0.8131
```

TABLE B-6. Stata: Creativity—composition of Factor 1 and Factor 2.

Factor 1	Factor 2
1. sC_triadic	1. sC_citat_scien
2. sC_EPO	2. sC_BT_EPO
3. sC_USPTO	3. sC_BT_USPTO
4. sC_ICT_EPO	4. sC_serv_know
5. sC_ICT_USPTO	5. sC_serv_va
6. sC_manuf_hmtech	6. sC_techbal
7. sC_manuf_va	7. sC_ICT_contrib

reliability for Factor 2 is also 0.81. Thus, the variables that constitute both Factor 1 and Factor 2 can be combined into single factor scales.

Based on the eigenvalues, scree chart, percent of variance explained, factor loadings, content validity, and alpha reliability, it appears that a two-factor solution is the optimum for this list of variables. Table B-6 shows the list of variables that constitute Factor 1 and Factor 2.

Based on the content, the factor scale created from Factor 1 is called a Traditional Creativity Scale, and the factor scale created from Factor 2

TABLE B-7. Stata: Creativity—country scores.

	country	Tradit~e	Modern~e
1.	Australia	-.8587102	.8212423
2.	Austria	.0607597	-.1130001
3.	Belgium	.0663868	.9157087
4.	Canada	-.1404294	.3332053
5.	Czech Republic	-.3460682	-1.199009
6.	Denmark	.0236853	1.725698
7.	Finland	1.919657	.0349351
8.	France	-.0244431	.3029757
9.	Germany	1.362179	.2159656
10.	Greece	**-1.318565**	-.7647616
11.	Hungary	-.4890213	-.6889915
12.	Iceland	-.5564587	-.175026
13.	Ireland	.7329665	-1.566148
14.	Italy	-.4118076	-.2269301
15.	Japan	2.003642	.0687582
16.	Luxembourg	-.4954347	1.168649
17.	Mexico	-.8650987	-.765833
18.	Netherlands	.5205733	.851833
19.	New Zealand	-.8319475	-.1744358
20.	Norway	-.752692	-.4088477
21.	Poland	-.916362	-.9521215
22.	Portugal	-1.033989	-.4721033
23.	Slovak Republic	-.6775781	-1.036336
24.	South Korea	.3756968	-.8622352
25.	Spain	-.8868657	-.3683997
26.	Sweden	1.610437	.8131769
27.	Switzerland	**2.055137**	1.657856
28.	Turkey	-1.240791	**-2.141528**
29.	United Kingdom	-.0616451	.8955433
30.	United States	1.176786	**2.11016**

is called a Modern Creativity Scale. They are denoted in the quantitative analysis as Tradit_Creat_Scale and Modern_Creat_Scale, respectively. The scales are formed by summing all the variables for each factor in respect to every country.[4]

Table B-7 presents the scores on both creativity scales for all of the 30 OECD countries. The scales are standardized so that the mean equals 0 and the standard deviation is 1. Thus, all the countries with the scores below zero on both of the creativity scales are below the average in relation to other countries. Therefore, the minus value does not mean that the countries have negative creativity, it only means that they are below the mean value on the scale. The bolded entries indicate the lowest and the highest values on the scale. For the Traditional Creativity Scale, the maximum value is 2.05 (Switzerland) and the minimum value is –1.31 (Greece). For the Modern Creativity Scale, the maximum value is 2.11 (United States) and the minimum value is –2.14 (Turkey).

APPENDIX C

OPENNESS TO CHANGE FACTOR ANALYSIS

The list of the openness to change variables consists of six variables. A correlation matrix (Table C-1) reveals that there are many high correlations between the variables, indicating that there could be some underlying factors present among the variables.

A principal components factor analysis was performed on those variables to determine if there are any underlying relationships that might be used to create factor scales for the openness variables.[5] The results of the factor analysis are seen in Table C-2.

There is one eigenvalue that exceeds the threshold of 1.0, which suggests that there is one underlying factor among those variables, and thus I check for a one-factor solution. To further examine the eigenvalues, I graph them on a scree chart, as seen in Figure C-1.

Again, the scree chart indicates that a one-factor solution is the most appropriate, as the line of eigenvalues makes a definite turn after the first factor. In addition, a one-factor solution would explain 70% of the total variance (cumulative 0.70), which is a very satisfying amount.

TABLE C-1. Stata: Openness—correlation matrix.

```
• corr O_Inv_ICT O_Inv_Soft O_SecServ O_itu_Hosts O_itu_Users
O_itu_PCs (obs = 21)
```

	O_Inv_~T	O_Inv_~t	O_SecS~v	O_Hosts	O_Users	O_PCs
O_Inv_ICT	1.0000					
O_Inv_Soft	0.9032	1.0000				
O_SecServ	0.5912	0.5456	1.0000			
O_Hosts	0.6594	0.6151	0.6931	1.0000		
O_Users	0.5966	0.6588	0.5777	0.4463	1.0000	
O_PCs	0.5600	0.7153	0.7225	0.5678	0.7540	1.0000

TABLE C-2. Stata: Openness—principal components factor analysis.

```
• factor O_Inv_ICT O_Inv_Soft O_SecServ O_Hosts O_Users O_PCs, pcf

Factor analysis/correlation                  Number of obs = 21
Method: principal-component factors
```

Factor	Eigenvalue	Difference	Proportion	Cumulative
Factor1	**4.20930**	3.56517	0.7016	**0.7016**
Factor2	0.64413	0.02553	0.1074	0.8089
Factor3	0.61860	0.37162	0.1031	0.9120
Factor4	0.24697	0.01030	0.0412	0.9532
Factor5	0.23668	0.19236	0.0394	0.9926
Factor6	0.04432	.	0.0074	1.0000

FIGURE C-1. Stata: Openness—scree plot of eigenvalues.

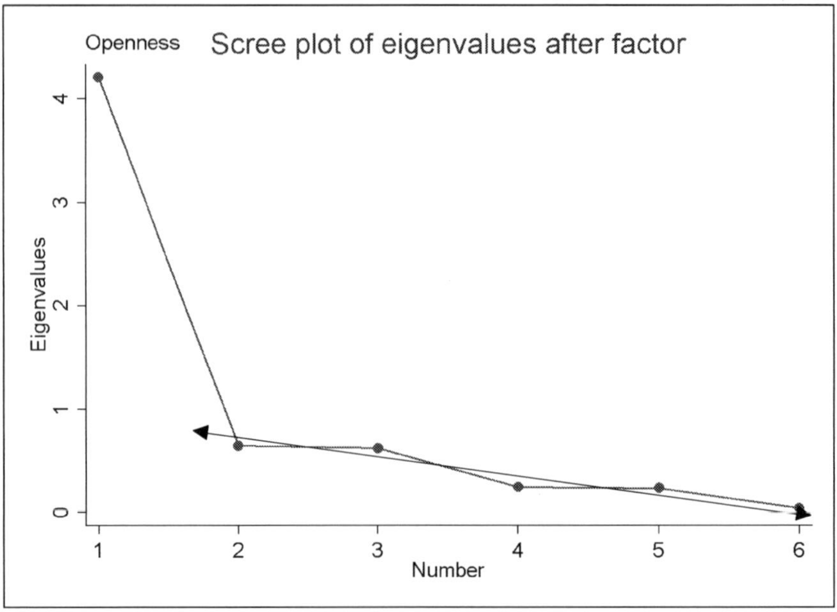

In order to construct factor scales, it is necessary to examine the loadings of each of variables on the retained factor. Maximization of these loadings can be obtained by rotating for a one-factor solution. The rotated loadings indicate that Factor 1 is composed of the following variables: O_Inv_ICT, O_Inv_Soft, O_SecServ, O_Hosts, O_Users, and O_PCs. Each of these variables has a loading of at least 0.5 on Factor 1.

Before I can combine the aforementioned group of variables into a single factor scale, I have to test whether the alpha reliability for the variables forming the common factor meets the required threshold of 0.8. The alpha reliability for the group of variables under consideration is 0.92, and thus I can combine them into a single factor scale.

TABLE C-3. Stata: Openness—rotated factor loadings.

```
• rotate, factors (2);
(varimax rotation)
Rotated factor loadings (pattern matrix) and unique variances
```

Variable	**Factor1**	Uniqueness
O_Inv_ICT	**0.8623**	0.2565
O_Inv_Soft	**0.8893**	0.2091
O_SecServ	**0.8184**	0.3302
O_Hosts	**0.7881**	0.3789
O_Users	**0.8020**	0.3568
O_PCs	**0.8608**	0.2591

TABLE C-4. Stata: Openness—factor alpha reliability.

```
Factor 1
• alpha O_Inv_ICT O_Inv_Soft O_SecServ O_Hosts O_Users O_PCs, std
Test scale = mean (standardized items)
Average interitem correlation:        0.6574
Number of items in the scale:         6
Scale reliability coefficient:        0.9201
```

The eigenvalues, scree chart, percent of variance explained, factor loadings, content validity, and alpha reliability reveal that there is one underlying factor for the openness to change variables. Table C-5 shows the list of variables constituting the common factor.

Since all the variables forming Factor 1 are measures of the openness to change, the factor scale created from those variables is named an Openness Scale (Openness_Scale). The scale is created by summing all the variables of Factor 1 for each country.[6] The scale is standardized so that the mean equals 0 and the standard deviation equals 1. I have normalized the Openness Scale in order to acquire comparable data with all the other scales and measures that were created through the factor analysis, which are also normalized. One has to remember that the scores below zero do not indicate a negative value of the scale. They simply indicate that a country scores below the average.

Table C-6 presents the scores on the Openness Scale for all of the 30 OECD countries under investigation. The bolded entries indicate the lowest and the highest values on the scale. For the Openness Scale, the maximum value is 2.39 (United States) and the minimum value is –1.48 (Turkey).

TABLE C-5. Stata: Openness—composition of Factor 1.

	Factor 1
1.	O_Inv_ICT
2.	O_Inv_Soft
3.	O_SecServ
4.	O_Hosts
5.	O_Users
6.	O_PCs

Table C-6. Stata: Openness—country scores.

	country	Opennes~e
1.	Australia	.9099237
2.	Austria	-.2021264
3.	Belgium	-.3707289
4.	Canada	.7145699
5.	Czech Republic	-.7032301
6.	Denmark	.9286113
7.	Finland	.908183
8.	France	-.4012622
9.	Germany	-.0877217
10.	Greece	-1.33795
11.	Hungary	-1.089567
12.	Iceland	2.027394
13.	Ireland	-.6777037
14.	Italy	-.5054116
15.	Japan	-.0535039
16.	Luxembourg	.6461054
17.	Mexico	-1.422054
18.	Netherlands	.7878476
19.	New Zealand	.2831869
20.	Norway	-.1970822
21.	Poland	-1.168125
22.	Portugal	-1.078923
23.	Slovak Republic	-.7252399
24.	South Korea	.0423151
25.	Spain	-.7355864
26.	Sweden	1.32955
27.	Switzerland	.671427
28.	Turkey	**-1.489872**
29.	United Kingdom	.5980528
30.	United States	**2.398922**

Appendix D

Innovation Factor Analysis

Since I argue that the creativity and openness are the composites of a broader concept of innovation, I would like to check whether there is a common factor among the creativity and openness variables. If yes, then I could combine those variables that exhibit a common variance pattern into one scale called innovation.

There are 15 variables related to creativity and 6 variables related to openness, which gives 21 variables in total. A correlation matrix (Table D-1) has revealed that there are many high correlations between the variables, indicating that there could be some underlying factors present within the variables.

A principal components factor analysis was performed on those variables[7] to determine if there are any underlying factors that might be used to create a single scale for innovation. The results of the factor analysis are seen in Table D-2.

Although in this case there are five eigenvalues that exceed the threshold level of 1.0, the last three are quite close to the threshold. This means that the last three factors probably do not explain much more of the total variance for this list of variables than a single variable does. The third eigenvalue is slightly above 2; however, a three-factor solution does not seem plausible because adding an extra factor to a two-factor solution would increase the explained variance only by 10%, which is very low and not a satisfying amount. Such a low percentage of additional explained variance indicates that the additional factor does not individually account for a substantial amount of the variance.

To further examine the eigenvalues and make the decision about the number of meaningful factors existing among the variables under

TABLE D-1. Stata: Innovation—correlation matrix.

```
• corr sC_citat_scien sC_triadic sC_EPO sC_USPTO sC_ICT_EPO sC_ICT_USPTO sC_BT_EPO sC_BT_USPTO
sC_serv_know sC_manuf_hmtech sC_serv_contrib sC_serv_va sC_manuf_va sC_techbal sC_ICT_contrib
sO_Inv_ICT sO_Inv_Soft sO_SecServ sO_Hosts sO_Users sO_PCs;
(obs = 20)
```

	sC_cit~n	sC_tri~c	sC_EPO	sC_USPTO	sC_IC~PO	sC_IC~TO	sC_BT~PO	sC_BT~TO	sC_ser~w
sC_citat_s~n	1.0000								
sC_triadic	0.5691	1.0000							
sC_EPO	0.6666	0.9194	1.0000						
sC_USPTO	0.4779	0.7723	0.5419	1.0000					
sC_ICT_EPO	0.5376	0.8954	0.8764	0.6128	1.0000				
sC_ICT_USPTO	0.2213	0.6897	0.3933	0.9315	0.5859	1.0000			
sC_BT_EPO	0.7482	0.5134	0.5898	0.4123	0.4225	0.2076	1.0000		
sC_BT_USPTO	0.6518	0.3938	0.3494	0.6155	0.2724	0.4093	0.8504	1.0000	
sC_serv_know	0.5604	0.2086	0.1786	0.3436	0.1098	0.2186	0.2927	0.2944	1.0000
sC_manuf_h~h	0.1016	0.5474	0.5389	0.4293	0.4676	0.4460	0.1329	0.0336	0.1402
sC_serv_co~b	0.0735	0.0975	-0.0117	0.2720	0.0385	0.1913	0.1399	0.3282	-0.0110
sC_serv_va	0.5808	0.2862	0.2814	0.2497	0.1659	0.0747	0.4712	0.4661	0.5795
sC_manuf_va	-0.1119	0.3567	0.3498	0.2268	0.3532	0.3156	-0.0614	-0.1631	-0.0327
sC_techbal	0.5841	0.3330	0.2850	0.3300	0.2674	0.2114	0.5479	0.4875	0.3545
sC_ICT_con~b	0.2709	0.0673	-0.1018	0.3287	-0.0345	0.2700	0.3318	0.4863	0.3623
sO_Inv_ICT	0.6266	0.4783	0.4004	0.6359	0.4908	0.4879	0.5014	0.6556	0.4876
sO_Inv_Soft	0.7337	0.6577	0.6051	0.6996	0.6594	0.5632	0.6011	0.6674	0.4548

(continued on next page)

TABLE D-1. *(continued)*

	sC_cit~n	sC_tri~c	sC_EPO	sC_USPTO	sC_IC~PO	sC_IC~TO	sC_BT~PO	sC_BT~TO	sC_ser~w
sO_SecServ	0.5808	0.2257	0.1365	0.5419	0.1634	0.3495	0.4427	0.6705	0.4363
sO_Hosts	0.5217	0.3083	0.2241	0.6451	0.3200	0.5304	0.4984	0.7448	0.3474
sO_Users	0.4497	0.3436	0.3377	0.3707	0.3460	0.2903	0.4318	0.4089	0.3905
sO_PCs	0.6696	0.5197	0.4784	0.5923	0.4363	0.4458	0.5599	0.5612	0.4967

	sC_man~h	sC_ser~b	sC_ser~a	sC_man~a	sC_tec~l	sC_ICT~b	sO_Inv~T	sO_Inv~t	sO_Sec~v
sC_manuf_h~h	1.0000								
sC_serv_co~b	-0.1491	1.0000							
sC_serv_va	-0.2047	-0.0239	1.0000						
sC_manuf_va	0.8701	-0.2386	-0.3676	1.0000					
sC_techbal	-0.1057	0.3529	0.5214	-0.2314	1.0000				
sC_ICT_con~b	-0.1562	0.5045	0.1705	-0.2374	0.3108	1.0000			
sO_Inv_ICT	0.2281	0.4776	0.3627	0.0870	0.4242	0.6616	1.0000		
sO_Inv_Soft	0.3963	0.3319	0.3547	0.2020	0.4010	0.5266	0.8951	1.0000	
sO_SecServ	-0.1863	0.5067	0.2260	-0.2616	0.4168	0.6437	0.6725	0.6004	1.0000
sO_Hosts	-0.0762	0.2774	0.2344	-0.2337	0.1615	0.4696	0.6546	0.6028	0.7198
sO_Users	0.2910	0.1706	-0.0679	0.2977	0.1571	0.4842	0.5477	0.6261	0.6408
sO_PCs	0.2736	0.3198	0.0866	0.0323	0.2838	0.5434	0.5966	0.7440	0.7266

	sO_Hosts	sO_Users	sO_PCs
sO_Hosts	1.0000		
sO_Users	0.4240	1.0000	
sO_PCs	0.5735	0.7899	1.0000

TABLE D-2. Stata: Innovation—principal components factor analysis.

```
• factor sC_citat_scien sC_triadic sC_EPO sC_USPTO sC_ICT_EPO sC_ICT_USPTO sC_BT_EPO sC_BT_USPTO
sC_serv_know sC_manuf_hmtech sC_serv_contrib sC_serv_va sC_manuf_va sC_techbal sC_ICT_contrib
sO_Inv_ICT sO_Inv_Soft sO_SecServ sO_Hosts sO_Users sO_PCs, pcf;

Factor analysis/correlation                              Number of obs = 20
   Method: principal-component factors
```

Factor	Eigenvalue	Difference	Proportion	Cumulative
Factor1	**9.26884**	5.70286	0.4414	0.4414
Factor2	**3.56598**	1.47915	0.1698	**0.6112**
Factor3	2.08682	0.73117	0.0994	0.7106
Factor4	1.35566	0.27926	0.0646	0.7751
Factor5	1.07640	0.11055	0.0513	0.8264
Factor6	0.96585	0.25173	0.0460	0.8724
Factor7	0.71412	0.15319	0.0340	0.9064
Factor8	0.56093	0.17476	0.0267	0.9331
Factor9	0.38617	0.02403	0.0184	0.9515
Factor10	0.36213	0.12740	0.0172	0.9687
Factor11	0.23473	0.05531	0.0112	0.9799
Factor12	0.17942	0.05353	0.0085	0.9884
Factor13	0.12588	0.07605	0.0060	0.9944
Factor14	0.04983	0.00900	0.0024	0.9968
Factor15	0.04083	0.02060	0.0019	0.9987
Factor16	0.02023	0.01495	0.0010	0.9997
Factor17	0.00528	0.00477	0.0003	1.0000
Factor18	0.00052	0.00012	0.0000	1.0000
Factor19	0.00039	0.00039	0.0000	1.0000
Factor20	0.00000	0.00000	0.0000	1.0000
Factor21	-0.00000	.	-0.0000	1.0000

consideration, it is useful to graph the eigenvalues on a scree chart, as seen in Figure D-1.

Again, the scree chart indicates that a two-factor solution is the most appropriate, as the line of eigenvalues makes a definite turn after the second factor. In addition, Factor 3 and beyond appear to lie in a straight line, indicating that they do not individually account for a substantial amount of variance. Besides, a two-factor solution would explain 61% of the total variance (cumulative 0.6112), which is a very satisfying amount.

In order to construct single factor scales, it is necessary to examine the loadings of each of the variables on the retained factors. Maximization of these loadings for each factor can be obtained by rotating for a two-factor solution.

FIGURE D-1. Stata: Innovation—scree plot of eigenvalues.

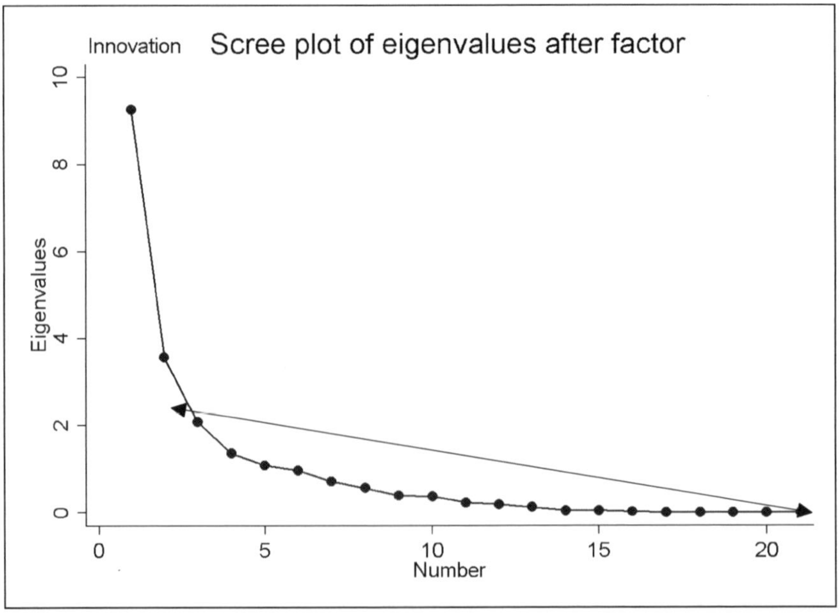

The rotated loadings indicate that Factor 1 is composed of the following variables: sC_citat_scien, sC_BT_EPO, sC_BT_USPTO, sC_serv_know, sC_serv_contrib, sC_serv_va, sC_techbal, sC_ICT_contrib, sO_Inv_Soft, sO_SecServ, sO_Hosts, sO_Users, and sO_PCs. Each of these variables has a loading of at least 0.5 on the first factor, which is the required threshold, and a lower loading on the second factor.[8]

As for the second factor, the rotated loadings indicate that it is composed of the following variables: sC_triadic, sC_EPO, sC_ICT_EPO, sC_ICT_USPTO, sC_manuf_hmtech, and sC_manuf_va. Correspondingly, each of these variables has a loading of at least 0.5 on Factor 2 and a lower loading on Factor 1.

TABLE D-3. Stata: Innovation—rotated factor loadings.

```
• rotate, factors(2);

Rotated factor loadings (pattern matrix) and unique variances
```

Variable	Factor1	Factor2	Uniqueness
sC_citat_s~n	**0.7457**	0.3348	0.3319
sC_triadic	0.3509	**0.8475**	0.1586
sC_EPO	0.2745	**0.8174**	0.2565
sC_USPTO	0.5766	0.6225	0.2801
sC_ICT_EPO	0.2710	**0.8225**	0.2501
sC_ICT_USPTO	0.3719	**0.6246**	0.4716
sC_BT_EPO	**0.6868**	0.2911	0.4436
sC_BT_USPTO	**0.8316**	0.1531	0.2851
sC_serv_know	**0.5566**	0.1082	0.6784
sC_manuf_h~h	-0.1653	**0.8605**	0.2322
sC_serv_co~b	**0.5000**	-0.1482	0.7280
sC_serv_va	**0.5268**	-0.0456	0.7204
sC_manuf_va	-0.3609	**0.7561**	0.2981
sC_techbal	**0.6070**	0.0305	0.6307
sC_ICT_con~b	**0.7287**	-0.1702	0.4401
sO_Inv_ICT	**0.7954**	0.3289	0.2592
sO_Inv_Soft	**0.7426**	0.5473	0.1489
sO_SecServ	**0.8746**	-0.0384	0.2335
sO_Hosts	**0.7628**	0.1181	0.4043
sO_Users	**0.5360**	0.3634	0.5807
sO_PCs	**0.7220**	0.3815	0.3332

The variable sC_USPTO cannot be included with any of the factors because it is split between the two factors. It loads 0.57 on the first factor and 0.62 on the second factor. The difference between the two loadings is too small (less than 10%) to include it with any of the factors. Therefore, the sC_USPTO variable has to be excluded from the factor scales created through this factor analysis.

Before I can combine the two groups of variables into single factor scales, I have to test if the factors meet the reliability requirement, which means that their alpha reliabilities have to meet the threshold of 0.8. In case of both factors, the alpha reliability scores exceed the required threshold. The alpha reliability for Factor 1 is 0.91, and the alpha reliability for Factor 2 is 0.82. Hence, the variables that form Factor 1 and Factor 2 can be combined into single factor scales.

Based on the eigenvalues, scree chart, percent of variance explained, factor loadings, content validity, and alpha reliability, it appears that there are two meaningful factors among the variables. Table D-5 shows the list of variables that constitute Factor 1 and Factor 2.

When examining the content of the two factors, one notices that all of the variables that are listed with Factor 1 are the variables that compose the Modern Creativity Scale[9] and the Openness Scale. However, all of the variables listed with Factor 2 are the variables that constitute the Traditional Creativity Scale. Such a turnout is consistent with the proposed theory, which states that creativity and openness are both part of a broader concept of innovation. Furthermore, such a turnout also supports a previous claim made in this study that the true spirit of creativity is better captured by the Modern Creativity Scale than by the Traditional Creativity Scale.

The results of the factor analysis indicate that I can create a scale that combines both the Modern Creativity Scale and the Openness Scale together; I call this an Innovation Scale.[10] It is denoted in the statistical analysis with capital letters as an INNOVATION_Scale because it combines two other scales together.

Table D-6 presents the scores on the Innovation Scale for all of the 30 OECD countries. The scales are standardized so that the mean equals 0

Table D-4. Stata: Innovation—factor alpha reliability.

```
Factor 1
. alpha sC_citat_scien sC_BT_EPO sC_BT_USPTO sC_serv_know sC_
serv_contrib sC_serv_va sC_techbal sC_ICT_contrib sO_Inv_ICT
sO_Inv_Soft sO_SecServ sO_Hosts sO_Users sO_PCs, std;

Test scale = mean(standardized items)
Average interitem correlation:          0.4240
Number of items in the scale:               14
Scale reliability coefficient:          0.9115

Factor 2
. alpha sC_triadic sC_EPO sC_ICT_EPO sC_ICT_USPTO sC_manuf_
hmtech sC_manuf_va, std;

Test scale = mean(standardized items)
Average interitem correlation:          0.4316
Number of items in the scale:                6
Scale reliability coefficient:          0.8200
```

Table D-5. Stata: Innovation—composition of Factor 1 and Factor 2.

Factor 1	Factor 2
1. sC_citat_scien	1. sC_triadic
2. sC_BT_EPO	2. sC_EPO
3. sC_BT_USPTO	3. sC_ICT_EPO
4. sC_serv_know	4. sC_ICT_USPTO
5. sC_serv_contrib	5. sC_manuf_hmtech
6. sC_serv_va	6. sC_manuf_va
7. sC_techbal	
8. sC_ICT_contrib	
9. sO_Inv_ICT	
10. sO_Inv_Soft	
11. sO_SecServ	
12. sO_Hosts	
13. sO_Users	
14. sO_PCs	

and the standard deviation is 1. Thus, all the countries with the scores below zero on the scale are below the average in relation to other countries. Hence, the minus value does not mean that the countries have negative innovation, it only means that they are below the mean value on the scale. The bolded entries indicate the lowest and the highest values on the scale. For the Innovation Scale, the maximum value is 2.45 (United States) and the minimum value is –1.9 (Turkey).

TABLE D-6. Stata: Innovation—country scores.

	country	INNOVAT~e
1.	Australia	1.000001
2.	Austria	-.2735682
3.	Belgium	.2006718
4.	Canada	.5706401
5.	Czech Republic	-1.086125
6.	Denmark	1.379172
7.	Finland	.5097174
8.	France	-.2266015
9.	Germany	.0368684
10.	Greece	-.9827402
11.	Hungary	-.8795222
12.	Iceland	1.13973
13.	Ireland	-1.268663
14.	Italy	-.5032342
15.	Japan	-.0527783
16.	Luxembourg	.849126
17.	Mexico	-1.18887
18.	Netherlands	.6959242
19.	New Zealand	-.027331
20.	Norway	-.2225483
21.	Poland	-.8942611
22.	Portugal	-.8535671
23.	Slovak Republic	-.7286234
24.	South Korea	-.4544559
25.	Spain	-.7546859
26.	Sweden	1.213426
27.	Switzerland	1.339555
28.	Turkey	**-1.902752**
29.	United Kingdom	.9061267
30.	United States	**2.459368**

Appendix E

Diversity Factor Analysis

The list of the diversity variables consists of seven variables. A correlation matrix (Table E-1) reveals that there are many high correlations between the variables, indicating that there could be some underlying factors present within the variables.

A principal components factor analysis was performed on those variables to determine if there are any underlying relationships that might be used to create factor scales for the diversity variables.[11] The results of the factor analysis are seen in Table E-2.

There are two eigenvalues that exceed the threshold of 1.0, so I check for the two-factor solution. To further examine the eigenvalues, I graph them on a scree chart, as seen in Figure E-1.

Again, the scree chart indicates that a two-factor solution is the most appropriate, as the line of eigenvalues makes a turn after the second factor. In addition, a two-factor solution would explain 82% of the total variance (cumulative 0.8249), which is a very satisfying amount.

In order to construct factor scales, it is necessary to examine the loadings of each of the variables on the retained factors. Maximization of these loadings for each factor can be obtained by rotating for a two-factor solution.

The rotated loadings indicate that Factor 1 is composed of the following four variables: IMM_fborn_stock, IMM_noncitizens, and IMM_laborforce_stock. Each of these variables has a loading of at least 0.5 on Factor 1 and a lower loading on Factor 2.

Further examination of the rotated loadings indicates that Factor 2 consists of the remaining four variables: ELF, A_ethnic, A_language, and A_religion. Two of the variables, A_ethnic and A_language, also have high loadings on Factor 1 (around 0.5); however, their loadings on Factor 2 are significantly higher (around 0.75). Therefore, they can be included with Factor 2, especially since their content validity supports such decision.[12]

TABLE E-1. Stata: Diversity—correlation matrix.

```
. corr ELF A_ethnic A_language A_religion IMM_fborn_stock IMM_noncitizens IMM_laborforce_stock;
(obs = 23)
```

	ELF	A_ethnic	A_lang~e	A_reli~n	IMM_fb~k	IMM_no~s	IMM_la~k
ELF	1.0000						
A_ethnic	0.7838	1.0000					
A_language	0.6903	0.8390	1.0000				
A_religion	0.3373	0.0315	0.2095	1.0000			
IMM_fborn_~k	0.2728	0.4751	0.6085	-0.0665	1.0000		
IMM_noncit~s	0.1910	0.5802	0.5893	-0.2411	0.8960	1.0000	
IMM_laborf~k	0.2533	0.5265	0.6023	-0.0738	0.9500	0.9246	1.0000

TABLE E-2. Stata: Diversity—principal components factor analysis.

```
• factor sELF sA_ethnic sA_language sA_religion sIMM_fborn_stock
sIMM_noncitizens sIMM_laborforce_stock, pcf;
Factor analysis/correlation                Number of obs = 23
Method: principal-component factors
```

Factor	Eigenvalue	Difference	Proportion	Cumulative
Factor1	**4.10763**	2.44115	0.5868	0.5868
Factor2	**1.66648**	0.87102	0.2381	**0.8249**
Factor3	0.79546	0.57457	0.1136	0.9385
Factor4	0.22089	0.08059	0.0316	0.9701
Factor5	0.14030	0.09644	0.0200	0.9901
Factor6	0.04386	0.01848	0.0063	0.9964
Factor7	0.02538	.	0.0036	1.0000

FIGURE E-1. Stata: Diversity—scree plot of eigenvalues.

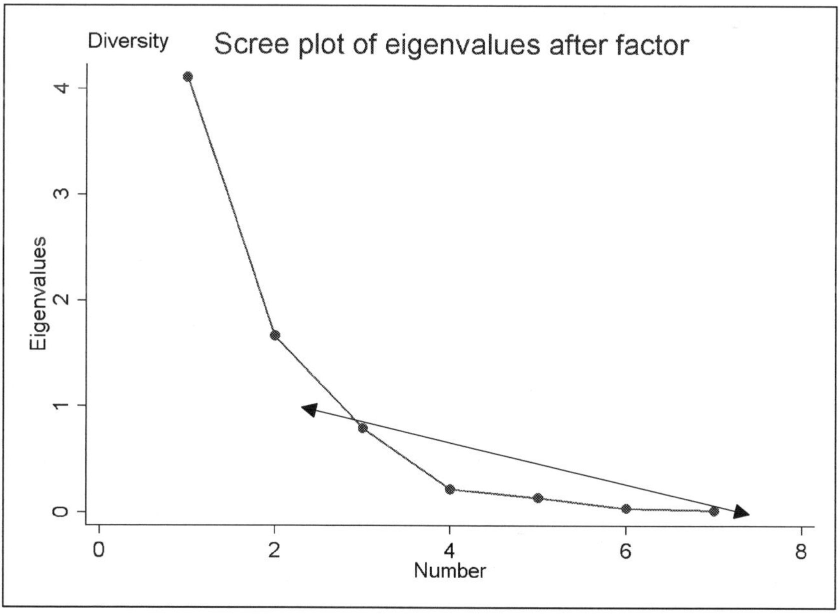

TABLE E-3. Stata: Diversity—rotated factor loadings.

```
• rotate, factors (2);
Rotated factor loadings (pattern matrix) and unique variances
```

Variable	Factor1	Factor2	Uniqueness
sELF	0.1050	**0.9172**	0.1476
sA_ethnic	0.4904	**0.7553**	0.1891
sA_language	0.5260	**0.7656**	0.1372
sA_religion	-0.3810	**0.5976**	0.4977
sIMM_fborn~k	**0.9171**	0.2035	0.1176
sIMM_nonci~s	**0.9673**	0.1281	0.0479
sIMM_labor~k	**0.9328**	0.2025	0.0889

TABLE E-4. Stata: Diversity—factor alpha reliability.

Factor 1

```
• alpha IMM_fborn_stock IMM_noncitizens IMM_laborforce_stock, std;
Test scale = mean(standardized items)
Average interitem correlation:          0.9118
Number of items in the scale:                3
Scale reliability coefficient:          0.9687
```

Factor 2

```
• alpha ELF A_ethnic A_language A_religion, std;
Test scale = mean(standardized items)
Average interitem correlation:          0.5222
Number of items in the scale:                4
Scale reliability coefficient:          0.8138
```

Before I can combine the aforementioned groups of variables into single factor scales, I have to test if the factors meet the reliability requirement, which means that their alpha reliabilities have to meet the threshold of 0.8. In the case of both factors, the alpha reliability scores exceed the required threshold. The alpha reliability for Factor 1 is 0.96, and the

TABLE E-5. Stata: Diversity—composition of Factor 1 and Factor 2.

Factor 1	Factor 2
1. IMM_fborn_stock	1. ELF
2. IMM_noncitizens	2. A_ethnic
3. IMM_laborforce_stock	3. A_language
	4. A_religion

alpha reliability for Factor 2 is 0.81. Hence, the variables constitute both Factor 1 and Factor 2 can be combined into single factor scales.

The eigenvalues, scree chart, percent of variance explained, factor loadings, content validity, and alpha reliability reveal that there are two underlying factors for the diversity variables. Table E-5 shows the list of variables constituting Factor 1 and Factor 2.

When examining the content of the two lists of variables, one should notice that Factor 1 contains the variables related to immigration, while Factor 2 contains the variables related to diversity stemming from old minorities. Therefore, I can create two single scales based on the factor analysis: the Immigration Diversity Scale and the Old Minorities Diversity Scale. The two scales are denoted in the statistical analysis as Imm_Divers_Scale and Old_Minor_Divers_Scale, respectively. The Immigration Diversity Scale indicates a country's immigration level, and thus the level of diversity coming from recent immigration. The Old Minorities Diversity Scale, however, indicates a country's degree of cultural (ethnolinguistic and religious) fractionalization coming from the old minorities present in the country.

The Immigration Diversity Scale and the Old Minorities Diversity Scale were created by summing all the variables constituting Factor 1 and Factor 2 for each country, respectively.[13] The scales are standardized (mean 0, standard deviation 1) in order to assure comparability with all the other scales that were created through the factor analysis. When examining the scores, one has to remember that the scores below zero do not indicate a negative value on the diversity scales. They simply indicate that a country scores below the average on a given scale.

Table E-6. Stata: Diversity—country scores.

	country	Imm_Div~e	Old_Min~e
1.	Australia	1.241874	.6267686
2.	Austria	.3139437	-.43277
3.	Belgium	.1559391	1.309381
4.	Canada	.6068355	**2.533146**
5.	Czech Republic	-.6457642	.7755327
6.	Denmark	-.3025227	-.9082707
7.	Finland	-.710447	-.566134
8.	France	-.079806	-.2988617
9.	Germany	.3115939	-.174901
10.	Greece	.1458918	-.9098474
11.	Hungary	-.750208	-.4690668
12.	Iceland	.	-.9887516
13.	Ireland	-.0036651	-1.056728
14.	Italy	-.4421562	-.775208
15.	Japan	-.8529758	-.8246047
16.	Luxembourg	**3.713814**	.627732
17.	Mexico	-.964711	.2326185
18.	Netherlands	-.1877402	.461873
19.	New Zealand	1.308439	.9332165
20.	Norway	-.3125996	-1.039485
21.	Poland	-.8917512	-1.029313
22.	Portugal	-.3934394	**-1.255216**
23.	Slovak Republic	-.813627	.3486507
24.	South Korea	-.9051849	-.7394558
25.	Spain	-.4194731	1.006405
26.	Sweden	-.0267374	-.7359285
27.	Switzerland	1.720263	1.675464
28.	Turkey	**-1.001741**	-.3067824
29.	United Kingdom	-.2124216	.0777549
30.	United States	.3983772	1.902781

Table E-6 presents the scores on both diversity scales for all of the 30 OECD countries. The bolded entries indicate the lowest and the highest values on the scale. For the Immigration Diversity Scale, the maximum value is 3.71 (Luxemburg) and the minimum value is –1.0 (Turkey). For the Old Minorities Diversity Scale, the maximum value is 2.53 (Canada) and the minimum value is –1.25 (Portugal).

APPENDIX F

RIGHT CONTEXT FACTOR ANALYSIS

The list of the right context variables is composed of 13 variables. A correlation matrix reveals that there are many high correlations between the variables, indicating that there could be some underlying factors present within those variables.

The correlation matrix (Table F-1) has also revealed, however, that there are too many missing values in the data set, to the extent that I could only retain 14 out of 30 observations for the analysis. Such a low number cannot be considered representative of the whole sample because it consists of less than half of the observations in the sample. Hence, I decided to drop as many variables as necessary, up to the point that I could reach at least 20 observations in the analysis. That would constitute two thirds of the sample, and thus could be considered representative for the whole sample.

Subsequently, I dropped four variables that had the highest number of missing values (8 missing values or more). Those dropped variables include the following: RC_naturaliz, RC_fb_citiz, RC_low_unem_fb, and RC_small_unem_gap. I kept nine variables for the analysis, which include the following: RC_HS_fb, RC_low_LS, RC_labpa_fb, RC_small_labpa_gap, RC_ExpRD, RC_low_econ_busreg, RC_low_adm_busreg, RC_low_barr_entr, and RC_low_EPL. As a result, I retained 21 out of 30 observations for the analysis, which is an acceptable number, since it constitutes above two thirds of the whole sample.

As a next step, I conducted a principal components factor analysis on those nine variables to determine if there are any underlying relationships that might be used to create factor scales for the right context variables. The results of the factor analysis are presented in Table F-2.

TABLE F-1. Stata: Right context—correlation matrix.

```
• corr RC_naturaliz RC_fb_citiz RC_HS_fb RC_low_LS RC_low_unem_fb RC_small_unem_gap RC_labpa_fb
RC_small_labpa_gap RC_ExpRD RC_low_econ_busreg RC_low_adm_busreg RC_low_barr_entr RC_low_EPL
(obs = 14)
```

	RC_nat~z	RC_fb_~z	RC_HS_fb	RC_low~S	RC_low~b	RC~m_gap	RC_lab~b	RC~a_gap	RC_ExpRD
RC_naturaliz	1.0000								
RC_fb_citiz	0.2953	1.0000							
RC_HS_fb	0.5175	0.2060	1.0000						
RC_low_LS	0.4452	0.2719	0.4766	1.0000					
RC_low_une~b	0.1248	0.2608	0.3470	0.4501	1.0000				
RC_small_u~p	-0.1128	0.2739	0.4037	0.2599	0.7696	1.0000			
RC_labpa_fb	-0.3579	-0.0401	0.1131	0.2257	0.3017	0.5006	1.0000		
RC_small_l~p	-0.4923	-0.1043	-0.1643	-0.1236	-0.0592	0.3336	0.7505	1.0000	
RC_ExpRD	0.2980	-0.2729	-0.0141	0.1810	-0.2789	-0.4635	-0.1590	-0.4227	1.0000
RC_low_eco~g	0.4677	0.2055	0.4364	0.0766	0.3888	0.3741	-0.3155	-0.4134	0.2087
RC_low_adm~g	0.5116	0.1824	0.6739	0.4236	0.2496	0.2868	0.0243	-0.3037	0.2919
RC_low_bar~r	0.5139	0.2241	0.6244	0.4152	0.1244	0.2197	0.1288	-0.1594	0.2616
RC_low_EPL	0.3697	-0.3616	0.4981	0.2502	0.2017	0.1246	-0.1533	-0.3373	0.3826

	R~econ~g	R~adm_~g	RC_low~r	RC_low~L
RC_low_eco~g	1.0000			
RC_low_adm~g	0.4544	1.0000		
RC_low_bar~r	0.2982	0.9657	1.0000	
RC_low_EPL	0.5623	0.3847	0.2258	1.0000

There are two eigenvalues that exceed the threshold level of 1.0. That indicates a two-factor solution. In order to further examine the eigenvalues, I graph them on a scree chart, as seen in Figure F-1.

Again, the scree chart indicates that a two-factor solution is the most appropriate, as the line of eigenvalues makes a definite turn after the second factor. In addition, a two-factor solution explains 62% of the total variance (cumulative 0.6223), which is a very satisfying amount.

In order to construct factor scales, it is necessary to examine the loadings of each of the variables on the retained factors. I obtain the maximization of these loadings for each factor by rotating for a two-factor solution.

The rotated loadings indicate that Factor 1 comprises the following variables: sRC_HS_fb, sRC_low_LS, sRC_low_econ_busreg, sRC_low_adm_busreg, sRC_low_barr_entr, and sRC_low_EPL. Each of these variables has a loading of at least 0.5 on Factor 1, which is the required threshold, and a lower loading on Factor 2.

TABLE F-2. Stata: Right context—principal components factor analysis.

```
• factor sRC_HS_fb sRC_low_LS sRC_labpa_fb sRC_small_labpa_gap
sRC_ExpRD sRC_low_econ_busreg sRC_low_adm_busreg sRC_low_barr_
entr sRC_low_EPL, pcf

Factor analysis/correlation         Number of obs = 21
    Method: principal-component factors
    Rotation: (unrotated)
```

Factor	Eigenvalue	Difference	Proportion	Cumulative
Factor1	**3.70313**	1.80566	0.4115	0.4115
Factor2	**1.89746**	0.99838	0.2108	**0.6223**
Factor3	0.89909	0.16712	0.0999	0.7222
Factor4	0.73197	0.05995	0.0813	0.8035
Factor5	0.67202	0.05029	0.0747	0.8782
Factor6	0.62173	0.30935	0.0691	0.9473
Factor7	0.31238	0.17491	0.0347	0.9820
Factor8	0.13747	0.11273	0.0153	0.9973
Factor9	0.02474	.	0.0027	1.0000

FIGURE F-1. Stata: Right context—scree plot of eigenvalues.

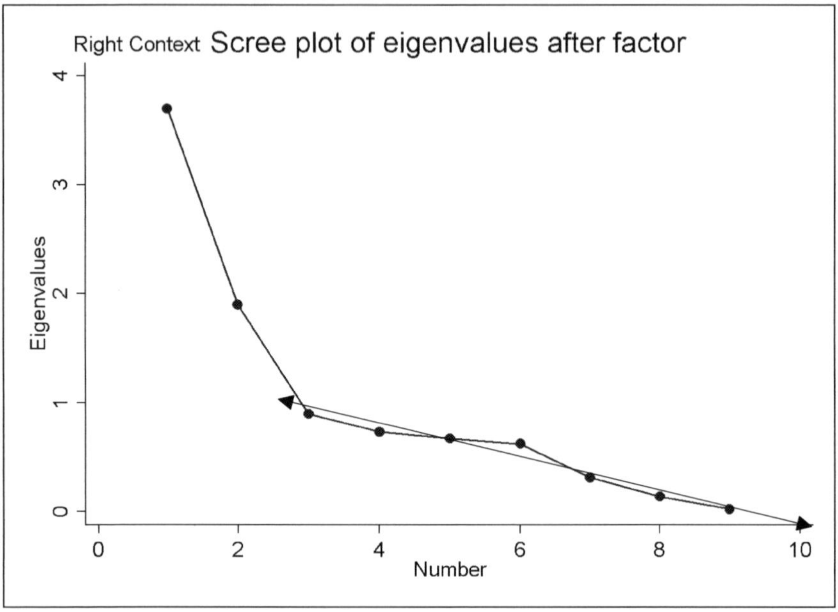

TABLE F-3. Stata: Right context—rotated factor loadings.

• rotate, factor (2)

Rotated factor loadings (pattern matrix) and unique variances

Variable	Factor1	Factor2	Uniqueness
sRC_HS_fb	**0.8531**	-0.0424	0.2704
sRC_low_LS	**0.6564**	0.1908	0.5327
sRC_labpa_fb	0.1660	**0.7456**	0.4166
sRC_sm~a_gap	-0.1975	**0.9009**	0.1494
sRC_ExpRD	0.0733	-0.6393	0.5859
sRC_low_ec~g	**0.5443**	-0.3847	0.5557
sRC_low_ad~g	**0.8982**	-0.1669	0.1654
sRC_low_ba~r	**0.8994**	-0.0220	0.1906
sRC_low_EPL	**0.5728**	-0.3730	0.5328

As for the second factor, the rotated loadings indicate that Factor 2 is composed of the following variables: sRC_labpa_fb and sRC small_labpa_gap. Correspondingly, each of these variables has a loading of at least 0.5 on Factor 2 and a lower loading on Factor 1.

The variable sRC_ExpRD cannot be included with any of the factors because its loading on the second factor is negative, and the study is interested (from the theoretical point of view) only in the positive loadings of the right context variables. Usually, the factor loadings are considered by their absolute value. However, for the clarity of the theoretical argument, in relation to the right context only the positive loadings can be considered when allocating the variables between the factors.

I argue that the right context has an enabling, positive effect on the relationship between diversity and innovativeness. Thus, I am interested in analyzing whether the higher levels of the right context would lead to the strengthening of the positive relationship between diversity and innovativeness. For that reason, the factor loadings concerning the right context variables should be considered only by their positive value, and thus the sRC_ExpRD cannot be included with any of the factors. If I would consider the negative value of the loadings when allocating the variables, it would make the interpretation of the factor scales much more complex than desirable. Since I want the factor solution to have a clear interpretation, I have to disregard the negative loadings.

Even though the sRC_ExpRD cannot be part of the factor scales, it is considered for further analysis because it is an essential variable for the theoretical argument posed by this study. It is treated as a separate variable in the regression analysis, which tests its individual impact on the relationship between diversity and innovativeness.

Turning our attention back to the variables that have positive and significant loadings on the factors, the next step is to combine the two groups of variables created through the factor analysis into single factor scales. However, before I would be able to do that I would have to test if the factors meet the reliability requirement, which means that their alpha reliabilities have to meet the threshold of 0.8.

In case of the first factor, the alpha reliability score exceeds the required threshold, with the alpha reliability for Factor 1 being 0.83. It means that I can combine the variables constituting Factor 1 into single factor scales and use them in further analyses.

That is not the case with the second factor, where the alpha reliability is below the required threshold with the score of only 0.73. Therefore, I cannot create a single factor scale out of the variables that constitute Factor 2. Furthermore, there is a problem of too little variables loading on the second factor, which gives an extra argument for dropping Factor 2 and not using it in further analysis.

To conclude, based on the eigenvalues, scree chart, percent of variance explained, factor loadings, content validity, and alpha reliability, it appears that there could be one factor scale created as a result of the factor analysis conducted on the right context variables. The second

TABLE F-4. Stata: Right context—factor alpha reliability.

```
Factor 1
• alpha sRC_HS_fb sRC_low_LS sRC_low_econ_busreg sRC_low_adm_bus-
reg sRC_low_barr_entr sRC_low_EPL, std

Test scale = mean(standardized items)
Average interitem correlation:        0.4551
Number of items in the scale:              6
Scale reliability coefficient:        0.8336

Factor 2
• alpha RC_labpa_fb RC_small_labpa_gap, std;

Test scale = mean(standardized items)
Average interitem correlation:        0.5781
Number of items in the scale:              2
Scale reliability coefficient:        0.7326
```

factor has to be disregarded due to an insufficient alpha reliability score. Table F-5 shows the list of variables that constitute Factor 1.

Based on the content, I can name Factor 1 as a Growth-Focused Strategy Scale (Growth_Focus_Strat_Scale) and use it in the regression analysis as a separate variable that indicates the country's strategic focus on growth.

The factor analysis did not prescribe the R&D expenditure (RC_RDExp) to any of the factors. Unlike what I would have expected, the R&D expenditure—which has been categorized as an indicator of an innovation-focused strategy—did not form a common factor with the growth-focused strategy variables. This means that the R&D expenditure variable has a variation distinct from the growth-focused strategy variables. Therefore, I consider it as a separate measure that indicates a country's strategic focus on innovation. I call it an Innovation-Focused Strategy Measure (Innov_Focus_Strat) and use it in the regression analysis as a separate variable.

It is important to note that due to the missing data, low alpha reliability for the Factor 2, and the fact that some of the value in diversity variables show common variance patterns with the growth strategy variables, I was not able to create a scale for the value in diversity variables.[14] Due to the missing data, from the outright I had to drop four variables that were originally on the list of value in diversity variables. Those variables were measuring the naturalization and the unemployment rates among foreign-born people (RC_naturaliz, RC_fb_citiz, RC_low_unem_fb, and RC_small_unem_gap).

TABLE F-5. Stata: Right context—composition of Factor 1.

	Factor 1
1.	RC_HS_fb
2.	RC_low_LS
3.	RC_low_econ_busreg
4.	RC_low_adm_busreg
5	RC_low_barr_entr
6	RC_low_ELP

To conclude, in result of the factor analysis I have created two measures of the right context, which are used as separate regression variables in further analysis. One of those measures is a Growth-Focused Strategy Scale, and the other one is an Innovation-Focused Strategy Measure.

The Growth-Focused Strategy Scale was created by summing all the variables constituting Factor 1 for each country.[15] It is standardized (mean 0, standard deviation 1) in order to assure comparability with all the other scales. The Innovation-Focused Strategy Measure is just a standardized value of the R&D expenditure variable where the mean is 0 and the standard deviation is 1. I have normalized the Innovation-Focused Strategy Measure in order to acquire comparable data with the Growth-Focused Strategy Scale, and with all the other scales that were created through the factor analysis. When examining the scores on both measures, one has to remember that the scores below zero do not indicate a negative value on a given measure. They simply indicate that a country scores below the average.

Table F-6 presents the scores on both the Growth-Focused Strategy Scale and the Innovation-Focused Strategy Measure for all of the 30 OECD countries under investigation. The bolded entries indicate the lowest and the highest values on the scale. For the growth-focused strategy scale, the maximum value is 1.73 (Canada) and the minimum value is –1.91 (Poland). For the Innovation-Focused Strategy Measure, the maximum value is 2.31 (Sweden) and the minimum value is –1.52 (Mexico).

TABLE F-6. Stata: Right context—country scores.

	country	Growth_~e	Innov_F~t
1.	Australia	1.56633	-.2419183
2.	Austria	-.4036231	.3984538
3.	Belgium	-.4331998	.5051824
4.	Canada	**1.732346**	.0782677
5.	Czech Republic	-1.236366	-.5621045
6.	Denmark	.469489	.7186399
7.	Finland	-.0722408	1.785927
8.	France	-.8622049	.3984538
9.	Germany	-.5782581	.8253685
10.	Greece	-.7581918	-1.202477
11.	Hungary	-.450718	-.8822905
12.	Iceland	.368834	1.252283
13.	Ireland	1.473509	-.7755617
14.	Italy	-.3679283	-.6688331
15.	Japan	.1540423	1.465741
16.	Luxembourg	.3860897	-.1351896
17.	Mexico	-.3155684	**-1.522663**
18.	Netherlands	-.8283322	-.028461
19.	New Zealand	1.350289	-.6688331
20.	Norway	.8780782	-.028461
21.	Poland	**-1.91228**	-1.309205
22.	Portugal	-1.162859	-.9890192
23.	Slovak Republic	.4181251	-1.309205
24.	South Korea	.4200454	.8253685
25.	Spain	-.9264266	-.7755617
26.	Sweden	.5173472	**2.31957**
27.	Switzerland	-.3374236	.8253685
28.	Turkey	-1.807458	-1.202477
29.	United Kingdom	1.476068	.0782677
30.	United States	1.242483	.8253685

Appendix G

Correlations and Summary Statistics

Independent Variables:	
Diversity (old minorities)	Div
Immigration diversity	Imm
Dependent Variables:	
Traditional creativity	T_C
Creativity	C
Openness	O
Innovation	I
Right Context Conditioning Variables:	
Right context growth-focused strategy	RCg
Right context innovation-focused strategy	RCi

Table G-1. Correlations between independent, dependent, and intervening variables.

• corr Div Imm T_C C O I RCg RCi Inc

(obs = 29)

	Div	Imm	T_C	C	O	I	RCg	RCi	Inc
Div	1.0000								
Imm	0.4533	1.0000							
T_C	0.0813	0.0660	1.0000						
C	0.4340	0.5376	0.4643	1.0000					
O	0.4111	0.4441	0.5876	0.8254	1.0000				
I	0.4325	0.4994	0.5390	0.9497	0.9497	1.0000			
RCg	0.2836	0.3612	0.2061	0.3832	0.6121	0.5292	1.0000		
RCi	0.0422	0.1361	0.8436	0.6008	0.7210	0.6755	0.2851	1.0000	
Inc	0.2384	0.7020	0.4044	0.6941	0.6854	0.6898	0.5339	0.5117	1.000

TABLE G-2. Summary statistics for independent, dependent, and intervening variables.

. sum Div Imm T_C C O I RCg RCi Inc DivRCg ImmRCg DivRCi ImmRCi

Variable	Obs	Mean	Std. Dev.	Min	Max
Div	30	10	3	6.234351	17.59944
Imm	29	10	3	6.994776	21.14144
T_C	30	10	3	6.044306	16.16541
C	30	10	3	3.575416	16.33048
O	30	10	3	5.530383	17.19677
I	30	10	3	4.291743	17.3781
RCg	30	10	3	4.26316	15.19704
RCi	30	10	3	5.432012	16.95871
Inc	30	10	3	3.966486	18.12771
DivRCg	30	10	3	5.817247	19.48419
ImmRCg	29	10	3	5.807812	17.79524
DivRCi	30	10	3	5.805481	16.94432
ImmRCi	29	10	3	5.65595	17.29972

ENDNOTES

1. The principal factor components analysis for creativity used 20 observations, which corresponds to two thirds of the whole sample of 30 countries, and thus can be treated as representative for the whole sample. In order to retain at least 20 observations in the factor analysis, in four cases I had to replace the missing values with the OECD averages. The guiding principles of the replacement were as follows: (a) to do the replacement for as little countries and variables as possible and only to the point where the number of 20 observations was reached, and (b) to fill the missing values with the averages only for countries where there was only one value missing for the whole set of variables (so that there would be no more than one average used for one country). Guided by those principles, I replaced five missing values with the values of the OECD average: three for the technological balance (sC_techbal) in reference to the Netherlands, Greece, and Sweden (note that the OECD average for technological balance did not include Ireland because it was a very strong outlier), and two for the ICT contribution (sC_ICT_contrib) in reference to Norway and Korea. Since the replacement referred only to 4 data points, it did not have any significant impact on the results of the analysis. It allowed, however, increasing the number of observations used in the factor analysis to 20.
2. Even though there are two more eigenvalues that exceed the threshold of 1.0, the three- or four-factor solution does not seem plausible because adding an extra factor to a two-factor solution would increase the variance explained only by 11%, and adding an extra factor to a three-factor solution would increase the variance explained only by 9%. Both values are very low and indicate that the two additional factors do not individually account for a substantial amount of the variance.
3. The loading of the sC_serv_contrib variable on the second factor is above 0.4, and it does not have a higher loading on the other factor, which could suggest that it is on the borderline to be included with the second factor. However, when the sC_serv_contrib is included to the list of the variables constituting Factor 2, the alpha reliability score for that factor is 0.77—which is below the acceptable threshold of 0.8. Therefore, the sC_serv_contrib cannot be included with Factor 2 and has to be left out from further analyses.
4. The command used in the Stata program for summing the variables for the scales is *rmean*; the command sums the variables by taking an average.

5. The factor analysis was performed using 21 observations, which corresponds to slightly more than two thirds of the whole sample of 30 countries, and thus can be considered representative for the whole sample.
6. See endnote 4.
7. The principal factor components analysis for innovation used 20 observations which corresponds to two thirds of the whole sample of 30 countries, and thus can be treated as representative for the whole sample.
8. The variable sC_Inv_Soft loads highly on Factor 1 (0.76), but its loading on the second factor also slightly exceeds the 0.5 threshold. However, since the loading on the second factor is just slightly above the threshold level, and since the loading on the first factor is more than 0.2 higher than on the second one, I can include the variable sC_Inv_Soft with Factor 1 (its content and alpha reliability of Factor 1 also support that idea).
9. There is one variable, sC_serv_contrib (services contribution to productivity), which is not part of the modern creativity scale but is a part of Factor 1. The sC_serv_contrib variable was also on the list when I conducted the factor analysis distinctively for the creativity variables. However, then the loading on that variable was too low to include it with the factor, which was later transformed into the modern creativity scale. Now, when I conduct the analysis of both the creativity and openness variables together, the sC_serv_contrib loads 0.5 on the first factor, which is just enough to include it with Factor 1. Also the alpha reliability score supports this.
10. I will not create any scale out of Factor 2 because, apart from one variable, all the variables are the same as in the traditional creativity scale. Thus, creating a new scale would not add any explanatory value to the analysis.
11. There were 23 observations used for the factor analysis, which corresponds to more than two thirds of the whole sample of 30 countries, and thus can be considered as representative for the whole sample.
12. The variables A_ethnic and A_language have very high loadings on Factor 2, but their loadings on Factor 1 that refer to immigration are also considerably high. The reason for the high loadings on Factor 1 could be related to the period of time of data collection. The data for those variables was collected in the period of 1981–2001; therefore, they might include some impacts of the previous waves of immigration. The ELF variable, even though constructed to measure the same aspects of diversity as A_ethnic and A_language, is not highly loaded on Factor 1 because the data for ELF was collected before 1961, so it does not include the effects of more recent waves of immigration.
13. The command used in the Stata program for summing the variables for the scales is *rmean*, the command sums the variables by taking an average.

14. When I tried to use one of the variables associated with Factor 2 separately, I did not achieve any meaningful results. Having examined the variables associated with Factor 2, I have noticed that they are not a good measure of the integration of immigrants to labor markets because they do not correspond to the judgments concerning the integration of immigrants existing in the literature of the subject. According to the RC_labpa_fb, the top countries with the best integration practices for immigrants are Portugal, Switzerland, and Spain; and according to RC_small_labpa_gap, the top countries are Italy, Luxemburg, Greece, Spain, and Portugal. On the contrary, the literature of the subject does not regard those countries as being very integrative toward immigrants (Kymlicka, 2003; Zachary, 2000).
15. See endnote 13.

References

Acs, Z., Anselin, L., & Varga, A. (2002). Patents and innovation counts as measures of regional production of new knowledge. *Research Policy, 31*(7), 1069–1085.

Adler, N. A. (1986). *International dimensions of organizational behavior*. Boston: Kent Publishing Company.

Aldrich, H. E., & Auster, E. R. (1986). Even dwarfs started small liabilities of age and size and their strategic implications. In B. M. Staw & L. L. Cummings (Eds.), *Research in organizational behavior* (Vol. 8, pp. 165–198). Greenwich, CT: JAI Press.

Aldrich, H. E., & Waldinger, R. (1990). Ethnicity and entrepreneurship. *Annual Reviews in Sociology, 16*, 111–135.

Alesina, A., Easterly, W., Devleeschauwer, A., Kurlat, S., & Wacziarg, R. (2003a). Fractionalization. *Journal of Economic Growth, 8*(2), 155–194.

Alesina, A., & La Ferrara, E. (2004). *Ethnic diversity and economic performance* (NBER Working Paper No. 10313). Retrieved January 15, 2005, from http://www.nber.org/papers/w10313

Alesina, A., & Spolaore, E. (2003). *The size of nations*. Cambridge, MA: MIT Press.

Alesina, A., Spolaore, E., & Wacziarg, R. (2000). Participation in heterogeneous communities. *Quarterly Journal of Economics, 115*(3), 847–904.

Alesina, A., Spolaore, E., & Wacziarg, R. (2003b, January). *Trade, growth and the size of countries* (HIER Discussion Paper No. 1995). Retrieved February 13, 2004, from http://post.economics.harvard.edu/hier/2003papers/2003list.html

Arcand, J.-L., Guillaumont, P., & Guillaumont Jeanneney, S. (2000). How to make a tragedy: On the alleged effect of ethnicity on growth. *Journal of International Development, 12*, 925–938.

Bruk, S. I., & Apenchenko, V. S. *Atlas Narodov Mira*. (1964). Moscow: Miklukho-Maklai Ethnological Institute at the Department of Geodesy and Cartography of the State Geological Committee of the Soviet Union.

Bank of England. (1999). *The financing of ethnic minority firms in the United Kingdom: A special report*. London: Author.

Barney, J. B. (1991). Firm resources and sustained competitive advantage. *Journal of Management, 17*(1), 99–120.

Barney, J. B., & Wright, P. M. (1998). On becoming a strategic partner: The role of human resources in gaining competitive advantage. *Human Resource Management, 37*(1), 31–46.

Basu, A., & Altinay, E. (2000, November 13–17). *An exploratory study of Turkish Cypriot small businesses in London*. Paper presented at the Third International Congress on Cyprus Studies, Gazimagusa, CY.

Bion, W. R. (1961). *Experiences in groups*. London: Tavistock.

Bonacich, E. (1973). A theory of middleman minorities. *American Sociological Review, 38*(5), 583–594.

Borjas, G. J. (1986). The self-employment experience of immigrants. *The Journal of Human Resources, 21*(4), 487–506.

Cain, B., Citrin, J., & Wong, C. (2000). *Ethnic context, race relations, and California politics*. San Francisco: Public Policy Institute of California.

Canning, D., & Fay, M. (1993). *The effects of transportation networks on economic growth* (Working paper). New York: Columbia University.

Chatman, J., Polzer, J., Barsade, S., & Neale, M. (1998). Being different yet feeling similar: The influence of demographic composition and organizational culture on work processes and outcomes. *Administrative Science Quarterly, 43*, 749–780.

Colecchia, A., & Shreyer, P. (2002). The contribution of information and communication technologies to economic growth in nine OECD countries. *OECD Economic Studies, 34*, 2002/I.

Collier, P. (2001). Implications for ethnic diversity. *Economic Policy, 16*(32), 129–166.

Collier, P., & Hoeffler, A. (1998). On economic causes of civil war. *Oxford Economic Papers, 50*(4), 563–573.

Collier, P., & Hoeffler, A. (2000). *Greed and grievance in civil war* (Policy Research Working Paper No. 2355). Washington, DC: World Bank.

Cox, T. J. (1994). *Cultural diversity in organizations: Theory, research and practice*. San Francisco: Berrett-Koehler.

Cox, T. J. (2001). *Creating the multicultural organization: A strategy for capturing the power of diversity*. San Francisco: Jossey-Bass.

Cox, T. J., & Blake, S. (1991). Managing cultural diversity: Implications for organizational competitiveness. *Academy of Management Executive, 5*(3), 45–55.

Cox, T. J., Lobel, S. A., & McLeod, P. L. (1991). Effects of ethnic group cultural differences on cooperative and competitive behavior on a group task. *Academy of Management Journal, 34*(4), 827–847.

Crano, W. D., & Chen, X. (1998). The leniency contract and persistence of majority and minority influence. *Journal of Personality and Social Psychology, 74*(6), 1437–1450.

De Dreu, C. K. W., & Beersma, B. (2001). Minority dissent in organizations: Its origins, and consequences for learning and group performance. In C. K. W. De Dreu, & N. K. De Vries (Eds.), *Group consensus and minority influence: Implications for innovation* (pp. 258–283). Oxford, U.K.: Backwell.

Donaldson, L. (2001). *The contingency theory of organizations*. Thousand Oaks, CA: Sage.

Doran, C. F. (2001). *Why Canadian unity matters and why Americans care: Democratic pluralism at risk.* Toronto, Ontario, Canada: University of Toronto Press.

Dumont, J.-C., & Lemaître, G. (2005). *Counting immigrants and expatriates in OECD countries: A new perspective* (OECD Social Employment and Migration Working Paper No. 25). Paris: OECD Publishing.

Easterly, W. (2001). Can institutions resolve ethnic conflict? *Economic Development and Cultural Change, 49*(4), 687–706.

Easterly, W., & Levine, R. (1997). Africa's growth tragedy: Policies and ethnic divisions. *Quarterly Journal of Economics, 111*(4), 1203–1250.

Elsass, P. M., & Graves, L. M. (1997). Demographic diversity in decision-making groups: The experiences of women and people of color. *Academy of Management Review, 22*(4), 946–973.

Ely, R. J., & Thomas, D. A. (2001). Cultural diversity at work: The effects of diversity perspectives on work group processes and outcomes. *Administrative Science Quarterly, 46*(2), 229–273.

Florida, R. (2002a). Bohemia and economic geography. *Journal of Economic Geography, 2*(1), 55–71.

Florida, R. (2002b). The economic geography of talent. *Annals of the Association of American Geographers, 92*(4), 743–755.

Fukuyama, F. (2004a). Economic, political, and cultural consequences of changes in generational relations. In Mary Ann Glendon (Ed.), *Intergenerational solidarity, welfare and human ecology.* Vatican City: Proceedings of the Tenth Plenary Session of the Pontifical Academy of the Social Science.

Fukuyama, F. (2004b, December). Świat według Fukuyamy: Koniec unilateralizmu? [The world according to Fukuyama: The end of unilateralism? (interview with Francis Fukuyama by Agnieszka Aleksy)]. *Puls Świata, 10*, 34–39.

Fuller, R. B. (1981). *Critical path.* Washington, DC: St. Martin's Press/World Future Society.

Georgsdottir, A. S., & Getz, I. (2004). How flexibility facilitates innovation and ways to manage it in organizations. *Creativity and Innovation Management, 13*(3), 166–175.

Gick, M. L., & Holyoak, K. J. (1987). The cognitive basis of knowledge transfer. In S. M. Cormier & J. D. Hagman (Eds.), *Transfer of learning: Contemporary research and applications* (pp. 9–46). San Diego, CA: Academic Press.

Glaeser, E., Scheinkman, J., & Shleifer, A. (1995). Economic growth in a cross-section of cities. *Journal of Monetary Economics, 36*(1), 117–143.

Glazer, N. (1997). *We are all multiculturalists now.* Cambridge, MA: Harvard University Press.

Gordon, M. M. (1964). *Assimilation in American life.* New York: Oxford Press.

Guilford, J. P. (1950). Creativity. *American Psychologist, 5*(9), 444–454.

Hagen, E. E. (1958). How economic growth begins: a general theory applied to Japan. *Public Opinion Quarterly, 22*(3), 373–390.

Hagen, E. E. (1961). *How economic growth begins: A study in the theory of social change.* Cambridge, MA: MIT Press.

Hambrick, D. C., Davison, S. C., Snell, S. A., & Snow, C. C. (1993). *When groups consist of multiple nationalities: Toward a new understanding of the implications* (Working paper). Lexington, MA: International Consortium for Executive Development Research.

Hammarstedt, M. (2001). Immigrant self-employment in Sweden—Its variation and some possible determinants. *Entrepreneurship & Regional Development, 13*(2), 147–161.

Harles, J. C. (2004, summer). Immigrant integration in Canada and the United States. *The American Review of Canadian Studies*, 223–358.

Harrison, D. A., Price, K. H., & Bell, M. P. (1998). Beyond relational demography: Time and the effects of surface- and deep-level diversity on work group cohesion. *Academy of Management Journal, 41*(1), 96–107.

Hartenian, L. S., & Gudmundson, D. E. (2000). Cultural diversity in small business: Implications for firm performance. *Journal of Developmental Entrepreneurship, 5*(3), 209–219.

Hobsbawm, E. J. (1990). *Nations and nationalism since 1780: Program, myth, reality*. Cambridge, U.K.: Cambridge University Press.

Ignatieff, M. (1993). *Blood and belonging: Journeys into the new nationalism*. New York: Ferrar, Straus, and Giroux.

Iles, P., & Hayers, P. K. (1997). Managing diversity in transnational projects teams: A tentative model and case study. *Journal of Managerial Psychology, 12*(2), 95–117.

Immigrant entrepreneurs. (1997, January/February). *Research Perspectives on Migration, 1*(2), 1–15.

ITU Technical Notes. Retrieved December 24, 2005, from www.itu.int/ITU-D/ict

Jackson, S. E. (1992). Team composition in organizational settings: Issues in managing an increasingly diverse workforce. In S. Worchel, W. Wood, & J. A. Simpson (Eds.), *Group process and productivity* (pp. 138–176). Newbury Park, CA: Sage.

Janis, I. L. (1982). *Groupthink: Psychological studies of policy decisions and fiascoes*. Boston: Houghton Mifflin Company.

Janssens, M., & Steyaert, C. (2003). *Theories of diversity within organisation studies: Debates and future trajectories* (FEEM Working Paper No. 14.2003). Retrieved March 7, 2004, from http://www.feem.it/web/activ/_wp.html

Johnson, P. J. (2000). Ethnic differences in self-employment among Southeast Asian refugees in Canada. *Journal of Small Business Management, 38*(4), 78–86.

Johnston, W. B., & Parker, A. E. (1987). *Workforce 2000: Work and workers for the 21st century*. Washington, DC: U.S. Department of Labor.

Kahin, B. (2004). Through the lens of intangibles: What patents on software and services reveal about the system. In OECD (Eds.), *Patents, Innovation and Economic Performance: OECD Conference Proceedings* (pp. 209–226). Paris: OECD Publishing.

Kanter, R. M. (1968). Creating the creative environment. *Management Review, 75*, 11–12.

Kanter, R. M. (1983). *The change masters*. New York: Simon & Schuster.

Kim, J.-O., & Mueller, C. W. (1978). *Introduction to factor analysis: What it is and how to do it*. Newbury Park, London, and New Delhi: Sage.

Kurtzberg, T. R., & Amabile T. M. (2001). From Guilford to creative synergy: Opening the black box of team-level creativity. *Creativity Research Journal, 13*(3 & 4), 285–294.

Kymlicka, W. (2001a). *Politics in the vernacular: Nationalism, multiculturalism, and citizenship*. New York: Oxford University Press.

Kymlicka, W. (2001b). Western political theory and ethnic relations in Eastern Europe. In W. Kymlicka & M. Opalski (Eds.), *Can liberal pluralism be exported: Western political theory and ethnic relations in Eastern Europe* (pp. 13–105). New York: Oxford University Press.

La Porta, R., Lopez de Silanes, F., Shleifer, A., & Vishny, R. (1999). The quality of government. *Journal of Law, Economics and Organization, 15*(1), 222–279.

Lado, A. A., Boyd, N. G., & Wright, P. (1992). A competency-based model of sustainable competitive advantage: Toward a conceptual integration. *Journal of Management, 18*(1), 77–91.

Lambert, W. (1977). The effects of bilingualism on the individual: Cognitive and sociocultural consequences. In P. A. Hornby (Ed.), *Bilingualism: Psychological, social and educational implications* (pp. 15–27). New York: Academic Press.

Lazear, E. (1999a). Globalization and the market for team-mates. *Economic Journal, 109*, 15–40.

Lazear, E. (1999b). Culture and language. *Journal of Political Economy, 107*(Suppl. 6), S95–S126.

Levinson D. (1998). *Ethnic Groups Worldwide, A Ready Reference Handbook*. Phoenix: Oryx Press.

Lewin, K. (1952). *Field theory in social science*. London: Tavistock.

Light, I. (1972). *Ethnic enterprise in America*. Berkeley, CA: University of California Press.

Lijphart, A. (1977). *Democracy in plural societies: A comparative exploration*. New Haven: Yale University Press.

Lipshitz, R., & Waingortin, M. (1995). Getting out of ruts: A laboratory study of a cognitive model of reframing. *Journal of Creative Behavior, 29*(3), 151–171.

Madison, J. (1987). *The federalist papers, No. X*. In J. Madison, A. Hamilton, & J. Jay, *The Federalist Papers* (pp. 122–128). London: Penguin Books. (Original work published 1788)

Mauro, P. (1995). Corruption and growth. *Quarterly Journal of Economics, 110*(3), 681–712.

McLeod, P. L., & Lobel, S. A. (1992). The effects of ethnic diversity on idea generation in small groups. *Proceedings, Academy of Management Meeting*, Las Vegas, NV.

McLeod, P. L., Baron, R., Marti, M. W., & Yoon, K. (1997). The eyes have it: Minority influence in face-to-face and computer-mediated group discussions. *Journal of Applied Psychology, 82*, 706–718.

McLeod, P. L., Lobel, S. A., & Cox, T. H., Jr. (1996). Ethnic diversity and creativity in small groups. *Small Group Research, 27*(2), 246–264.

Mednick, S. A. (1962). The associative basis of the creative process. *Psychological Review, 69*, 220–232.

Miller, D. (1983). The correlates of entrepreneurship in three types of firms. *Management Science, 29*(7), 770–791.

Milliken, F. J., & Martins, L. L. (1996). Searching for common threads: Understanding the multiple effects of diversity in organizational groups. *Academy of Management Review, 21*(2), 402–433.

Moore, R. L. (1983). Employer discrimination: Evidence from self-employed workers. *The Review of Economics ad Statistics, 65*(3), 496–501.

Moscovici, S. (1980). Toward a theory of conversion behavior. In L. Berkowitz (Ed.), *Advances in experimental social psychology* (Vol. 13, pp. 209–239). New York: Academic Press.

Nemeth, C. J. (1986). Differential contributions of majority and minority influence processes. *Psychological Review, 93*, 10–20.

Nemeth, C. J., & Staw, B. M. (1989). The tradeoffs of social control and innovation in groups and organizations. In L. Berkowitz (Ed.), *Advances in experimental social psychology* (Vol. 22, pp. 175–210). New York: Academic Press.

Novick, L. R. (1988). Analogical transfer, problem similarity, and expertise. *Journal of Experimental Psychology: Learning, Memory, & Cognition, 14*(3), 510–520.

OECD. (1998). *Technology, productivity and job creation: Best policy practices*. Paris: Author.

OECD. (2000). *A new economy? The changing role of innovation and information technology in growth*. Paris: Author.

OECD. (2002). *Frascati manual: Proposed standard practice for surveys on research and experimental development*. Paris: Author.

OECD. (2003). *ICT and economic growth: Evidence from OECD countries, industries and firms*. Paris: Author.

OECD. (2004a). *Science and technology statistical compendium*. Paris: Author.

OECD. (2004b). *Trends in international migration: Annual report*. Paris: Author.

OECD. (2005a). *Communications outlook: Information and communications technologies*. Paris: Author.

OECD. (2005b, September). Comparability of business start-up rates. *The Statistics Newsletter, 29*, 4–5.

OECD. (2005c). *Growth in services: Fostering employment, productivity and innovation. Meeting of the OECD Council at Ministerial Level, 2005*. Paris: Author.

OECD. (2005d). *OECD factbook 2005: Economic, environmental, and social statistics*. Paris: Author.

OECD. (2005e). *Oslo manual: Guidelines for collecting and interpreting innovation data* (3rd ed.). Paris: Author.

OECD. (2005f). *Science, technology and industry scoreboard*. Paris: Author.

OECD. (2005g). *SME and entrepreneurship outlook*. Paris: Author.

OECD. (2006). *Going for growth*: *Economic policy reforms*. Paris: Author.

Office for National Statistics (ONS). (1999). *The ethnic minority populations of Great Britain—Latest estimates*. London: Author.

Office for National Statistics (ONS). (2001). *Labour Market Trends, 109*(1).

Ottaviano, G., & Peri, G. (2004). *The economic value of cultural diversity* (FEEM Working Papers, No. 34.2004). Retrieved February 13, 2005, from http://ssrn.com/abstract=499702

Pelled, L. H., Eisenhardt, K. M., & Xin, K. R. (1999). Exploring the black box: An analysis of work group diversity, conflict, and performance. *Administrative Science Quarterly, 44*, 1–28.

Pfaff, W. (1993). *The wrath of nations: Civilization and the furies of nationalism*. New York: Simon & Schuster.

Polzer, J. T., Milton, L. R., & Swann, W. B., Jr. (2002, June). Capitalizing on diversity: Interpersonal congruence in small work groups. *Administrative Science Quarterly, 47*(2), 296–324.

Posner, D. N. (1999). *Ethnic fractionalization in Africa: How should it be measured? What does it explain about economic growth?* Paper presented at the 1999 Annual Meeting of the American Political Science Association, Atlanta, GA.

Putnam, R. D. (2007). E pluribus unum: Diversity and community in the twenty-first century. The 2006 Johan Skytte Prize lecture. *Scandinavian Political Studies, 30*(2), 137–174.

Radaev, V. (1994, August). Ethnic entrepreneurship: World experience and Russia. *Problems of Economic Transition, 5*, 57–73.

Ram, M., & Deakins, D. (1996). African-Caribbean in business. *New Community, 22*, 67–84.

Ram, M., & Jones, T. (1998). *Ethnic minorities in business*. Milton Keynes, U.K.: Open University Press.

Resnick, P. (1994). Toward a multination federalism. In L. Seidle (Ed.), *Seeking a new Canadian partnership: Asymmetrical and confederal options* (pp. 71–90). Montreal, Quebec, Canada: Institute for Research on Public Policy.

Reynolds, P. D., Carter, N. M., Gartner, W. B., & Greene, P. G. (2002). *The entrepreneur next door: Characteristics of individuals starting companies in America. An executive summary of the panel study of entrepreneurial dynamics*. Kansas City, MO: Ewing Marion Kauffman Foundation.

Richard, O. (2000). Racial diversity, business strategy, and firm performance: A resource-based view. *Academy of Management Journal, 43*(2), 164–177.

Richard, O., McMillan, A., Chadwick, K., & Dwyer, S. (2003). Employing an innovation strategy in racially diverse workforces: Effects on firm performance. *Group & Organization Management, 28*(1), 107–126.

Riordan, C., & Shore, L. (1997). Demographic diversity and employee attitudes: Examination of relational demography within work units. *Journal of Applied Psychology, 82*, 342–358.

Sauser, W. I., Jr. (1988). Injecting contrast: A key to quality decisions. *Advanced Management Journal, 53*(4), 20–23.

Schumpeter, J. A. (1934). *The theory of economic development: An inquiry into profits, capital, interest, and the business cycle*. Cambridge, MA: Harvard University Press.

Schumpeter, J. A. (1939). *Business cycles: A theoretical, historical, and statistical analysis of the capitalist process*. New York: McGraw-Hill. 2 vols.

Shreyer, P. (2000). *The contribution of information and communication technology to output growth: A study of the G7 countries* (OECD Science, Technology and Industry Working Paper No. 2000/2). Paris: OECD Publishing.

Simon, J. L. (1987). *Effort, opportunity, and wealth*. Oxford, U.K.: Basil Blackwell.

Simon, J. L. (1989). *The economic consequences of immigration*. Ann Arbor, MI: The University of Michigan Press.

Sternberg, R. J., & Lubart, T. I. (1993). Investing in creativity. *Psychological Inquiry, 4*(3), 229–232.

Strahan, K .W., & Williams, A. J. (1988). *Immigrant Entrepreneurs in Australia: A Report to the Office of Multicultural Affairs*. Office of Multicultural Affairs, Canberra.

Swann, W. B. Jr., Polzer, J. T., Seyle, D. C., & Ko, S. J. (2004). Finding value in diversity: Verification of personal and social self-views in diverse groups. *Academy of Management Review, 29*(1), 9–27.

Tajfel, H. (1982). *Social identity and intergroup relations*. Cambridge, U.K.: Cambridge University Press.

Tamura S., Sheehan, J., Martinez, C., & Kergroach, S. (2005). Promoting innovation in services. In OECD (Ed.), *Enhancing the performance of the services sector* (pp. 133–177). Paris: OECD Publishing.

Taylor, C. (1994). *Multiculturalism: Examining the Politics of Recognition*. Princeton, NJ: Princeton University Press.

Taylor, C. L., & Hudson, M. C. (1972). *World handbook of political and social indicators*. Ann Arbor, MI: ICPSR.

Thomas, R. R. (1999). Cultural diversity and work group effectiveness. *Journal of Cross-Cultural Psychology, 30*(2), 242–263.

Tsui, A., Egan, T., & O'Reilly, C. (1992). Being different: Rational demography and organizational attachment. *Administrative Science Quarterly, 37*, 549–579.

Turner, J. C. (1985). Social categorization and the self-concept: A social cognitive theory of group behavior. In E. J. Lawler (Ed.), *Advances in group processes: Theory and research* (Vol. 2, pp. 77–121). Greenwich, CT: JAI Press.

U.S. Small Business Administration, Office of Advocacy. (2002). *Minorities in business, 2001*. Washington, DC. http://www.sba.gov/advo/stats/min01.pdf

Van Dyne, L., & Saaverda, R. (1996). A naturalistic minority influence experiment: Effects on divergent thinking, conflict, and originality in work-groups. *British Journal of Social Psychology, 35*, 151–168.

Walzer, M. (1983). *Spheres of justice*. New York: Basic Books.

Walzer, M. (1992a). *What it means to be an American*. New York: Marsilio.

Walzer, M. (1992b). Comment. In A. Gutmann (Ed.), *Multiculturalism: Examining the politics of recognition* (pp. 99–103). Princeton, NJ: Princeton University Press.

Watson, W. E., Kumar, K., & Michaelsen, L. K. (1993). Cultural diversity's impact on interaction process and performance: Comparing homogeneous and diverse task groups. *Academy of Management Journal, 36*(3), 590–602.

Williams, K., & O'Reilly, C.A., III (1998). Demography and diversity in organizations: A review of 40 years of research. In B. M. Staw & R. I. Sutton (Eds.), *Research in organizational behavior* (Vol. 20, pp. 77–140). Stamford, CT: JAI Press.

Wright, P. M., & McMahan, G. C. (1992). Theoretical perspectives for strategic human resource management. *Journal of Management, 18*(2), 295–320.

Zachary, G. P. (2000). *The global me: New cosmopolitans and the competitive edge, picking globalism's winners and losers*. New York: Public Affairs.

Further Reading

Balkan, L. (1970). *Les effets du bilinguisme francais-anglais sur les aptitudes intellectuelles* [The effects of the French-English bilingualism on the intellectual aptitudes]. Bruxelles, BE: Aimav.

Bantel, K., & Jackson, S. (1989). Top management and innovations in banking. *Strategic Management Journal, 10*(S1), 107–129.

Ben-Zeev, S. (1972). The influence of bilingualism on cognitive development and cognitive strategy. Unpublished doctoral dissertation, University of Chicago.

Carrell, M., Elbert, N., & Hatfield, R. (2000). *Human resource management: Strategies for managing a diverse and global workforce.* Orlando, FL: Dryden Press.

Cormack, J., & Niessen, J. (2002). Immigrant and minority businesses: Making the policy case. *European Journal of Migration and Law, 4*(3), 329–337.

Covin, J. G., & Slevin, D. P. (1989). Strategic management of small firms in hostile and benign environments. *Strategic Management Journal, 10*(1), 75–87.

Cummins, J., & Gulutsan, M. (1973). *Some effects of bilingualism on cognitive functioning* (Mimeo). Edmonton, Alberta, Canada: University of Alberta.

De Dreu, C. K. W., & De Vries, N. K. (1993). Numerical support, information processing and attitude change. *European Journal of Social Psychology, 23*(6), 647–662.

De Dreu, C. K. W., & West, M. A. (2001). Minority dissent and team innovation: The importance of participation in decision making. *Journal of Applied Psychology, 86*(6), 1191–1201.

Dooley, R. S., & Fryxell, G. E. (1999). Attaining decision quality and commitment from dissent: The moderating effects of loyalty and competence in strategic decision-making teams. *Academy of Management Journal, 42*(4), 389–402.

Drach-Zahavy, A., & Somech, A. (2002). Building innovative teams: The role of team heterogeneity and interaction processes in teams. In Serge B. P. Shokov (Ed.), *Advances in psychology research* (Vol. 17, pp. 131–147). Hauppauge, NY: Nova Science Publishers, Inc.

Drucker, P. F. (1986). *Innovation and entrepreneurship: Practice and principles*. New York: Perennial Library.

Gruenfeld, D. H., Thomas-Hunt, M. C., & Kim, P. H. (1998). Cognitive flexibility, communication strategy, and integrative complexity in groups: Public versus private reactions to majority and minority status. *Journal of Experimental Social Psychology, 34*(2), 202–226.

Guildford, J. P. (1956). The structure of intellect. *Psychological Bulletin, 53*(4), 267–293.

Ianco-Worrall, A. D. (1972). Bilingualism and cognitive development. *Child Development, 43*(4), 1390–1400.

Jackson, S. E. (1999). Research on work team diversity: Progress and promise. *Performance Improvement Quarterly, 12*(1), 200–203.

Janis, I. L. (1972). *Victims of groupthink*. Boston: Houghton Mifflin Company.

Kossek, E. E., Lobel, S. A., & Brown, J. (2004). Human resource strategies to manage work force diversity: Examining "the business case." In: A. M. Konrad, P. Prasad, & J. K. Pringle (Eds.), *Handbook of workplace diversity* (pp. 53–74). Thousand Oaks, CA: Sage.

KPMG. (n.d.) *Everyone is different at KPMG: Our success depends upon it*. Retrieved November 3, 2004, from the KPMG Web site: http://kpmgcareers.co.uk/WorkExperience/AboutKPMG/Diversity.html

Lambert, W. E., & Anisfeld, E. (1969). A note on the relationship of bilingualism and intelligence. *Canadian Journal of Behavioral Science, 1*, 123–128.

Lattimer, R. L. (1998). The case for diversity in global business, and the impact of diversity on team performance. *Competitiveness Review, 8*(2), 3–17.

McClelland, D. C. (1961). *The achieving society*. New York: The Free Press.

Morgan, G. (1989). Endangered species: New ideas. *Business Month, 133*(4), 75–77.

Moscovici, S. (1985). Innovation and minority influence. In S. Moscovici, G. Mugny, & E. Van Avermaet (Eds.), *Perspectives on minority influence* (pp. 19–59). Cambridge, U.K.: Cambridge University Press.

National Westminster Bank (NatWest). (2000). *Ethnic Minority Businesses*. London: Author.

Nemeth, C. J. (1992). Minority dissent as a stimulant to groups performance. In S. Worchel, W. Wood, & J. A. Simpson (Eds.), *Group process and productivity* (pp. 95–111). Newbury Park, CA: Sage.

Nemeth, C. J., & Kwan, J. (1985). Originality of word associations as a function of majority versus minority influence. *Social Psychology Quarterly, 48*(3), 277–282.

Peterson, R. S. (1997). A directive leadership style in group decision making can be both virtue and vice: Evidence from elite and experimental groups. *Journal of Personality and Social Psychology, 72*(5), 1107–1121.

Peterson, R. S., Owens, P. D., Tetlock, P. E., Fan, E. T., & Martorana, P. (1998). Group dynamics in top management teams, groupthink, vigilance, and alternative models of organizational failure and success. *Organizational Behavior and Human Decision Processes, 73*(2–3), 272–305.

Priem, R., Harrison, D., & Muir, N. (1995). Structured conflict and consensus outcomes in group decision making. *Journal of Management, 21*, 691–710.

Scott, S. (1973). *The relation of divergent thinking to bilingualism: Cause or effect.* Unpublished research report, McGill University, Montreal, Quebec, Canada.

Simon, J. L. (1999). *The economic consequences of immigration* (2nd ed.). Ann Arbor, MI: The University of Michigan Press.

Taylor, C. L., & Hudson, M. C. (1973). *World Handbook of Political and Social Indicators II: Cross-National Aggregate Data, 1950–1965.* Ann Arbor, MI: ICPSR.

Thomas, R. R. (1990, March/April). From affirmative action to affirming diversity. *Harvard Business Review, 68*(2), 107–117.

Torrance, E. P., Gowan, J. C., Wu, J. M., & Aliotti, N. C. (1970). Creative functioning of monolingual and bilingual children in Singapore. *Journal of Educational Psychology, 61*(1), 72–75.

Toynbee, A. J. (1947). *A study of history.* New York: Oxford University Press.

Tsui, A., & Gutek, B. (1999). *Demographic differences in organizations.* Lanham, MD: Lexington Books.

Walzer, M. (1997). *On toleration.* New Haven, CT: Yale University Press.

Webster's Third New International Dictionary. (1976). New York: G. & C. Merriam and Co.

Index

Made in the USA
Monee, IL
12 November 2026

154002e5-2642-4d5d-8158-1c931bda2de3R01